Lilith in a New Light

CRITICAL EXPLORATIONS IN SCIENCE FICTION AND FANTASY
(a series edited by Donald E. Palumbo and C.W. Sullivan III)

1. *Worlds Apart? Dualism and Transgression in Contemporary Female Dystopias* (Dunja M. Mohr, 2005)

2. *Tolkien and Shakespeare: Essays on Shared Themes and Language* (edited by Janet Brennan Croft, 2007)

3. *Culture, Identities and Technology in the* Star Wars *Films: Essays on the Two Trilogies* (edited by Carl Silvio and Tony M. Vinci, 2007)

4. *The Influence of* Star Trek *on Television, Film and Culture* (edited by Lincoln Geraghty, 2007)

5. *Hugo Gernsback and the Century of Science Fiction* (Gary Westfahl, 2007)

6. *One Earth, One People: The Mythopoeic Fantasy Series of Ursula K. Le Guin, Lloyd Alexander, Madeleine L'Engle and Orson Scott Card* (Marek Oziewicz, 2008)

7. *The Evolution of Tolkien's Mythology: A Study of the History of Middle-earth* (Elizabeth A. Whittingham, 2008)

8. *H. Beam Piper: A Biography* (John F. Carr, 2008)

9. *Dreams and Nightmares: Science and Technology in Myth and Fiction* (Mordecai Roshwald, 2008)

10. Lilith *in a New Light: Essays on the George MacDonald Fantasy Novel* (edited by Lucas H. Harriman, 2008)

11. *Feminist Narrative and the Supernatural: The Function of Fantastic Devices in Seven Recent Novels* (Katherine J. Weese, 2008)

LILITH IN A NEW LIGHT

Essays on the George MacDonald Fantasy Novel

Edited by Lucas H. Harriman

CRITICAL EXPLORATIONS IN
SCIENCE FICTION AND FANTASY, 10
Donald E. Palumbo *and* C.W. Sullivan III, *series editors*

McFarland & Company, Inc., Publishers
Jefferson, North Carolina, and London

LIBRARY OF CONGRESS CATALOGUING-IN-PUBLICATION DATA

Lilith in a new light : essays on the George MacDonald fantasy novel / edited by Lucas H. Harriman.
      p.   cm. — (Critical explorations in science fiction and fantasy ; 10)
   Includes bibliographical references and index.

   ISBN 978-0-7864-3810-5
   softcover : 50# alkaline paper ∞

   1. MacDonald, George, 1824–1905. Lilith.   I. Harriman, Lucas H.
   PR4969.L55   2008
   823'.8 — dc22   2008008036

British Library cataloguing data are available

©2008 Lucas H. Harriman. All rights reserved

No part of this book may be reproduced or transmitted in any form or by any means, electronic or mechanical, including photocopying or recording, or by any information storage and retrieval system, without permission in writing from the publisher.

Cover image ©2008 Shutterstock

Manufactured in the United States of America

McFarland & Company, Inc., Publishers
   Box 611, Jefferson, North Carolina 28640
   www.mcfarlandpub.com

Acknowledgments

I wish to thank Tom Martin for his continuous inspiration and help in the preparation of this collection of essays. He has been a faithful mentor and friend, and without him this project would not have come to light. I would also like to thank the International Association for the Fantastic in the Arts for providing a space for the serious consideration of this long-neglected field of study. Lastly, I want to thank Diane for her patient encouragement through the editorial process.

An earlier version of the article by Bonnie Garden appeared in *Studies in the Novel* 37.1, Spring 2005, copyright © 2005 by University of North Texas, and is reprinted with permission of the publisher. Jeanne Murray Walker's article first appeared in *The Scope of the Fantastic: Culture, Biography, Themes, Children's Literature*. Ed. Robert A. Collins and Howard D. Pearce. Copyright © 1985 by Thomas Burnett Swann and is reproduced with permission of Greenwood Publishing Group, Inc. Westport, CT.

Table of Contents

Introduction 1

1. Liminality in *Lilith* 7
   ROBERT A. COLLINS

2. Liminality and the Everyday in *Lilith* 15
   TOM SHIPPEY

3. *Lilith*, Textuality, and the Rhetoric of Romance 21
   MICHAEL MENDELSON

4. Myth, Mysticism, and Magic: Reading at the Close of *Lilith* . . . 39
   VERLYN FLIEGER

5. The Logic of Fantasy and the Crisis of Closure in *Lilith* 46
   COLIN MANLOVE

6. The Demoness and the Grail: Deciphering *Lilith* 59
   JEANNE MURRAY WALKER

7. A Fresh Look at *Lilith*'s Perplexing Dimensions 71
   ROLLAND HEIN

8. Collins Agonistes; or, Why Did I Bother To? 83
   ROGER C. SCHLOBIN

9. The Revelatory Potential of *Lilith*'s Immanent Eternity 85
   LUCAS H. HARRIMAN

10. Frustrated Interpretation in *Lilith* 93
    JOHN PENNINGTON

11. Liminality as Psychic Stage in *Lilith* 103
    RODERICK MCGILLIS

12. Cosmic and Psychological Redemption in *Lilith* 111
    BONNIE GAARDEN

13. *Lilith* as the Mystic's Magnum Opus 128
    ELIZABETH ROBINSON

14. Chiasmatic Christianity: *Lilith*'s Sense of an Ending 143
    KELLY SEARSMITH

15. The (As Yet) Endless Ending of *Lilith* 161
    DAVID M. MILLER

About the Contributors 177
Index 179

Introduction

We are already years past the centenary of George MacDonald's death in 1905, and there is yet to be a single book-length study on *Lilith*—his last, most ambitious, and certainly most enigmatic work. All the markers point to the need for such a study. We have W.H. Auden's 1954 statement that "*Lilith* is equal if not superior to the best of Poe," and yet in the half-century since, the MLA index records only four dissertations and fewer than a dozen articles treating the work. And then we have within the last several years the release of the *Variorum Lilith* (1997), which compares five "radically different" manuscripts MacDonald produced on the way to his final text, strong evidence that this was the great work on which he expected to base his reputation. Auden and C.S. Lewis both discerned the importance of *Lilith*, but whether or not the rest of the critical community has remained puzzled by MacDonald's experiment, it has been slow to respond. To redress this situation, and make use of new scholarly materials, we have gathered a group of distinguished fantasy scholars from the United States, Canada, England, and Scotland, all of whom bring their expertise to bear on MacDonald's last great work, a book of inestimable importance to the genre of fantasy literature.

The current assemblage of essays, arguments, and inquiries began with a series of conversations sparked by a paper presented at the 24th International Conference on the Fantastic in the Arts in 2003. In his paper, Robert A. Collins, the original founder of the ICFA, offered an attempt to explain *Lilith*'s troublesome cyclical form and enigmatic ending. Collins drew from the anthropological work of Victor Turner and Mihai Spariosu to posit the concept of "liminality" as a helpful key to understanding MacDonald's masterpiece, as well as other fantastic literature written in the same vein, but only after discussing *Lilith*'s complexity and the wide variety of ways readers have interpreted it. This was enough to inspire renewed interest in this early example of modern fantasy, and scholars were quick to respond to Collins's provocative and challenging claims.

In addition to providing some important background scholarship on *Lilith*, our desire has been to present a veritable record of the scholarly exchange that ensued from that seminal set of conversations some years back. Therefore, to varying degrees, the selections that follow are in working dialogue with one another, sometimes presenting different facets of a single argument, and other times offering sharply contrasting viewpoints. But always (or nearly always) the writer is driven by the wonderful text of *Lilith* itself, a story filled with what C.S. Lewis referred to as "the quality of the real universe, the divine, magical, terrifying and ecstatic reality in which we all live."*

The collection begins with Collins's paper on liminality, in which he delineates the difficulties presented in *Lilith*'s penultimate chapter as Vane is thrust back into his own world rather than being received into heaven. His essay is followed by four reconsiderations of the problems the ending poses, attacking the issue from various critical stances. Eminent Tolkien scholar Tom Shippey considers especially the relationship of *Lilith* to "*le monde morne et mundain*: the sad world of everyday." Shippey argues that, in addition to being one of the first liminal fantasies, providing a model that is perennially revived in the genre, *Lilith* is a "medial" fantasy in that it acts as a mediatory myth to reconcile apparently unacceptable contradictions within MacDonald's (and presumably his Victorian readers') worldview. Coming at the project from a different angle, Michael Mendelson provides an important example of the purpose of this anthology as he returns to an argument he made in 1985 in which he posited *Lilith* as a "romance of ascent" and revaluates it in light of Collins's comments and his own twenty years of scholarship. While Mendelson continues to argue for a reading of the fantasy as a prose romance, he brings a fresh discussion of MacDonald's rhetorical strategy to his argument as he underscores the importance of *Lilith* for the development of modern fantasy.

Perhaps none of our contributors addresses Collins's argument more directly than Verlyn Flieger, who claims that MacDonald's effort to sustain a level of dissonance is crucial to the work's mythopoeic nature, instead of a deficiency to be resolved. While she admires the attention paid to the story's complexity, Flieger deems any attempt to imprint a classificatory stamp on

---

*The quotation is from Lewis's introduction to the 1981 Wm. B. Eerdmans edition of *Lilith*, xii. All quotations from *Lilith* in the present collection are taken from this edition as it is readily available to our readers.

Lilith inherently flawed since the impact of the story on the reader is more crucial than any artificially imposed coherence. Colin Manlove also finds fault with Collins's desire to ascribe a univocal meaning to the "Endless Ending" of *Lilith*. Instead, he sees the book itself suggesting a range of explanations, even to the point of including two discordant endings: one privileging faith and the other doubt, both so crucial to MacDonald's theology.

The next few readings offer overarching commentary on the book, providing important context for the more focused readings that follow. Jeanne Murray Walker's discussion of *Lilith* as a blending of the Western grail legend and the Near Eastern myth of the demoness provides an excellent commentary on the sources of MacDonald's final fantasy. Though originally presented at an earlier ICFA, Walker's argument gives further credence to *Lilith*'s depth and the plenitude of interpretive schemas with which one can approach it. One such schema is represented by Rolland Hein, the editor of *Lilith: A Variorum Edition*, as he brings his intimate familiarity with the *Lilith* manuscripts to bear on his reading. Hein relies on careful textual evidence to posit Dante's four layers of meaning as an important structural tool for MacDonald as he continually returned to his final work, revising it into his masterpiece. His claim that the book ends on the anagogical level is suggestive as we continue to contemplate the significance of *Lilith*'s final chapters. Of course, after spending so much time with the book, Hein shows a deep appreciation for its ambiguities and intricacies. Roger C. Schlobin, on the other hand, is not as impressed. He provides us with the sole dissenting voice in the collection as he sees the perpetual frustration of readers' expectations as merely that—frustration. Schlobin's brief comments provide an important counterpoint to the many attempts made here to attribute unified, worthwhile signification to the often infuriating plot of *Lilith*.

As we begin to move toward more focused discussions of interpretation, the next two selections treat *Lilith* on a metafictional level. Lucas H. Harriman gives a somewhat different perspective on the book's ending since he chooses to view *Lilith* primarily as a story about the process of reading fantasy. Harriman argues that the effect of an authentic encounter with fantastic literature is a central theme of *Lilith*, suggesting a way of reading fantasy that will prove more socially responsible than the alternative theorization of fantasy as escapist literature. As Vane comes to appreciate the fantastic world that lies within his own world, readers of fantasy ideally return to their own temporal moment more awake to the marvelous nature of reality. John Pennington likewise sees reading and interpretation as thematically central to MacDonald's fantasy. He claims that the reader's frustrated desire for closure is crucial to any reading of the text since it mirrors the indeterminacy of our actual experience. Positing *Lilith* as what Barthes calls a "writerly" text, Pennington claims MacDonald's refusal to satisfy Vane, Lilith, or his reader is productive rather than merely frustrating.

Many attempts to interpret MacDonald's work have been constructed on the theoretical scaffolding of psychoanalysis. The next two readings engage this mode of interpretation in order to move toward a more effective deciphering of *Lilith*. Roderick McGillis relies primarily on Freud and Lacan for his interpretation while Bonnie Gaarden presents a more strictly Jungian reading. McGillis offers a highly perceptive depiction of Vane's journey as an enactment of the passage from one state of psychic development to another. He uses Collins's evocation of liminality as the basis of the reading, suggesting the fertility of liminality for any discussion of psychological maturation. Gaarden, on the other hand, draws correspondences between MacDonald's universalist philosophy and Jungian psychology in order to explicate *Lilith* as a tale of hard-won spiritual maturity. She offers an important contribution to the study of *Lilith* as she uses Jung as a means of explaining possibly the most controversial aspect of MacDonald's theology: his belief that all would eventually be led to repentance.

From psychoanalysis, we move to a quite different reading of *Lilith* by Elizabeth Robinson, who uses her research on MacDonald as a mystic to inform her reading of his most influential and definitive statement. Contrasting this final work with what she sees as the mystic's earlier visionary fantasy, *Phantastes*, Robinson demonstrates that Vane's acceptance at the end of *Lilith* presents what St. John of the Cross called the "Night of the Spirit" to *Phantastes*'s "Night of the Senses." Her well-informed study of MacDonald's mystical side causes Robinson's unique argument to resonate with many of the perspectives already presented in this anthology. For Kelly Searsmith, however, the important influences working on the author of *Lilith* are not mystical—they are societal. Searsmith discusses the fantasy as a depiction of "managerial-class identity formation," along the same lines as those created by Dickens, Eliot, Trollope, and others, though the fantasy offers a new symbolic economy in which the reformation of the protagonist can take place. Well acquainted with Victorian society and mores, Searsmith gives us a view of Vane's ultimate expulsion from fairyland that has the potential to transform the self-centered protagonist into a more socially productive individual.

The collection concludes with a reading—or perhaps two readings—from David M. Miller in which he considers the present inquiry in light of the postmodern condition of indeterminacy. Miller returns to Collins's essay with an appreciation for his daring to ask *Lilith*, "What do you mean?" He then attempts, more intentionally than most of the contributors, to discern the answer. Miller offers a reading from a Christian worldview, but he is perpetually interrupted by a perspective he refers to as "Caliban," a sort of personified postmodernity, intent on frustrating any attempt at univocal significance. Ultimately, he uses this technique to discover in the final chapter the answers to the problems Collins detects in the penultimate one. His schizoid dialogue demonstrates the complexity of reading this text in the twenty-first century, a time when questions of textual meaning and significance are fraught with uncertainty.

The readings compiled here are intended to compel the reader back into this enigmatic story with a new appreciation for both its haunting ambiguity and its unquestionable influence. At a time when fantastic literature is increasingly being appreciated for its unique relationship to lived reality, MacDonald's masterpiece warrants careful reconsideration as an early liminal text. The varied perspectives represented by our fifteen contributors demonstrate the multifaceted nature of *Lilith*, and they suggest the innumerable possibilities that await any reader prepared to encounter MacDonald's masterpiece with one foot on solid ground and the other across the threshold, in the world of the fantastic.

CHAPTER 1

Liminality in *Lilith*
Robert A. Collins

At the close of the novel, Vane and Lona are climbing the throne of the Ancient of Days atop Mount Paradiso:

> My heart beating with hope and desire, I held fast the hand of my Lona, and we began to climb, but soon we let each other go, to use hands as well as feet in the toilsome ascent of the huge stones. At length we drew near the cloud which hung down the steps like the borders of a garment, passed through the fringe and entered the deep folds. A hand, warm and strong, laid hold of mine, and drew me to a little door with a golden lock. The door opened, the hand let mine go, and pushed me gently through. I turned quickly and saw the board of a large book in the act of closing behind me. I stood alone in my library [250].

Thus ends the penultimate chapter of *Lilith*, the last of MacDonald's adult fantasies, and according to most critics who have commented on it, his masterpiece. For at least a dozen years now, I have been attempting to explicate it for my seminar in fantastic literature, but with decreasing confidence. Of course I have consulted the various critical *apparati* for aid: MacDonald's fascination with old libraries confirms the relevance of biography, since it clearly stems from his seminal experience cataloguing an ancient estate library in the north of Scotland during his college years. Similarly, his pervasive didacticism is, by his own admission, the result of his frustration in being denied a pulpit by Calvinist parishioners. MacDonald's "heretical" religion, with its concept of a "spiritual evolution," inevitable for all men, draws upon the Victorian fascination with Darwin and the idea of progress, as well as German Romanticism, and fixes him firmly in that era's intellectual context, while his apparent use of a compartmented psyche anticipated the apparatus of Freud, though Freud's emphasis on Oedipal fixations was way wide of the mark in MacDonald's case, as C.S. Lewis has observed (v). More relevantly, MacDonald's archetypal figures anticipated those of Jung, particularly the Shadow persona which often appears in MacDonald's works. However, whether we view the work as a quest fantasy or as pure mythopoesis, as Lewis insists, the anti-climactic "return" of the ending demands explanation. Rolland Hein, MacDonald's biographer and editor of the *Lilith* Variorum, cites narrative plausibility as the essential reason: the return completes the narrative frame, so that the person telling the story is the same one who witnessed the events firsthand. But that pragmatic consideration strikes me as somehow incommensurate with what Lewis describes as mythopoesis, "the real universe, the divine, magical, terrifying and ecstatic reality in which we all live" (xii)—it does not explain the mythic import of Vane's return, any more than Campbell's pattern of the hero's journey does, though the Campbellian pattern is certainly present. If we consider Mr. Vane as hero, his sojourn in the alternate world and his epiphany there would certainly require a return to his fellows to communicate his enlightenment, but what does that enlightenment consist of—what message does the hero carry back to us? If the story is either mythopoesis or a heroic journey, it seems somehow to fail in the final phase of its mission.

In an attempt to understand MacDonald's pilgrimage through an alternate world, I have turned to the concept of liminality, that moment of "pure potentiality when everything ... trembles in the balance" (Turner 44), a term derived from the Latin word *limen*, a threshold, portal, or door, through which a protagonist passes from one context to another. The concept is basic to anthropological studies of rites of passage, and my definitions are drawn from works by anthropologist Victor Turner and Mihai Spariosu. In liminal spaces, protagonists lose their customary orientation, because the past is "momentarily negated, suspended, or abrogated, and the future has not yet begun" (Turner 44). The phrase seems to describe accurately the confusion and insecurity felt by Mr. Vane, the protagonist in *Lilith*, after he first blunders through the magical mirror/portal into Mr. Raven's world. It also describes, of course, key moments in the archetypal hero's journey, particularly the hero's separation from his cultural matrix at the outset of his quest. In fact, *Lilith* can indeed be parsed as a quest story up to a point, an exercise which my seminar students were encouraged to do. The general Campbellian structural pattern—separation, initiation, and return—is certainly there. But the pattern is inexplicably repeated, at least three times, and the journey appears unproductively circular. The point of origin, Mr. Vane's country estate, is too routinely the point of return. Most important, though, is the emotional context of the hero's return, which fits none of the categories in *The Hero with a Thousand Faces*. Unlike the archetypal hero, who brings back a great prize, a magical talisman or an epiphany of great value to himself and his fellows, Mr. Vane perceives all of his more or less involuntary returns to his "dreary old house" as misfortunes, interrupting his quest for divine perfection. As a quest story, then, the narrative fails.

Despite the relative ubiquity of magical doors in *Lilith* (the mirror in the attic, the library closet, the fountain on the lawn, the kitchen courtyard, ultimately even the various books on the library shelves, one of which closes behind him as he is pushed back from the throne of the Ancient of Days), MacDonald's fantasy does not fit Farah Mendlesohn's description of "portal fantasies" either. These, she insists, must be one-way passages in that "individuals may cross both ways [but] the magic does not" (173). However, the intimate relationship between parallel worlds in *Lilith* ensures that Mr. Vane's library is several times the scene of alternate world "magic," as Mr. Raven plucks forth, whole, the mutilated "half book" stuck to the masked door of the closet, and reads from it to the bedraggled cat that is Lilith, before her several transformations into leopardess and woman there in the library. Her ancient manuscript, we are told, half resides in the alternate universe until such time as Mr. Raven plucks it forth, either into Mr. Vane's space or Mr. Raven's alternate world.

"Liminal worlds are indeterminate ontological landscapes ... located in between alternate worlds," Spariosu tells us (68). MacDonald's parallel world may be a liminal space, since it does seem in many ways ontologically indeterminate. Moreover, Mr. Vane's "reality" and Mr. Raven's appear to be "incommensurate" (in Spariosu's terms) although they are said to occupy the same space. For example, in the "world of seven dimensions," Mr. Vane goes with Mr. Raven on a very long journey through a forest to the sexton's chapel, yet when Vane flees Mr. Raven's cemetery a few minutes later, he comes out the door to his own library closet. "Could both be real," he asks himself, "interpenetrating yet unmingling?" (37). Distances in these spaces are not parallel, though locations impinge: "That tree stands on the hearth of your kitchen, and grows nearly straight up its chimney," Mr. Raven assures Vane (22). Yet Lilith, in the alternate world, tricks Vane into pulling her through to his "primary" world from a location in the courtyard of her palace in Bulika: a tall palm there ends in a fountain on the lawn of Vane's estate (139). Lilith wants passage through Vane's three-dimensional world so she can get to the other side of an enchanted stream, which she cannot cross in her own world. (Her aim, it appears, is to destroy the children in the dry forest, located on the opposite side of the stream.) Although distances between these points in the alternate world are relatively vast, all impinge upon points mere yards apart on Vane's estate.

Such incommensurability results, Spariosu says, when the "weighting principles or frames of reference" of alternate worlds are not only incompatible but "untranslatable in terms of each other" (60). A sense of their incompatibility is Vane's first realization after he enters Mr. Raven's world. His own frames of reference are challenged by the Raven's behavior, and he lectures him about it. As the Raven pulls a worm from the turf and flings it into the air, where it spreads great wings and flies off, Vane cries, "Tut, tut, you mistake Mr. Raven, worms are not the larvae of butterflies! ... Would you have the air full of worms?" (20). He continues to remonstrate as prayers literally become pigeons or flowers. Finally, Mr. Raven's transformations from man to bird and back prompt Vane to recognize him as the old librarian of his estate, and he apologizes. "Why do you beg my pardon?" Raven says. "'Because I took you for a Raven,' I said—seeing him before me as plainly a raven as bird or man could look" (15). "Every one ... has a beast-self—and a bird-self, and a stupid fish-self, ay and a creeping serpent-self too," Mr. Raven tells him (30). But the most critical incompatibility Vane discovers concerns language: word meanings are not the same in this alternate world. "Are they not dead?" Vane asks of the sleepers in Raven's mausoleum. "I cannot answer you. I almost forget what they mean by *dead* in the old world. If I said a person was dead my wife would understand one thing and you would imagine another," Raven replies (34). And later, "You and I use the same words with different meanings. We are often unable to tell people what they *need* to know, because they *want* to know something else, and would therefore only misunderstand what we said" (45).

In his introduction, Mr. Vane tells us that he has been a student of the physical sciences; thus his frame of reference, at least at the outset, is that of the materialist. "Two objects cannot exist in the same space at the same time," he tells Mr. Raven, who scoffs, "No man of the universe, only a man of the world could have said so." In several of Mr. Raven's "guided tours" of this alternate world, it becomes clear that many objects in Vane's material world have direct reflections in the alternate one. Vane's housekeeper's niece is playing the piano, Raven says, and "those great long heads of wild hyacinth are inside the piano, among the strings of it, and give that peculiar sweetness to her playing." And again, "There, I smell Grieg's Wedding March in the quiver of those rose petals" (23). When Vane questions the prayer-pigeons, Raven says, "It must puzzle you! It cannot fail to do so!" Vane objects that a prayer is "a thought, a thing spiritual," and Raven agrees, adding that "when a heart is really alive, then it is able to think live things.... All live things were thoughts to begin with..." (25–26). Spiritual and physical laws seem somehow interchangeable here.

If the novel is truly mythopoetic, as Lewis suggests, the "frame of reference" of its incommensurate alternate world must somewhere reveal itself. As Spariosu demonstrates, the world of the "physicist," the materialist, is inevitably weighted toward power. So one might guess from the nature of the correspondences we have noticed that the frame of the alternate world will be metaphysical, weighted toward spirit. Vane's brief account of his studies in Chapter I tells us "I was constantly seeing, and on the outlook to see, strange analogies ... between physical hypotheses and suggestions glimmering out of the metaphysical dreams into which I was in the habit of falling" (5). This observation, according to my colleague, Tom Martin, "sets up the rest of the book," since the things of our physical world do seem to have counterparts in a metaphysical frame of reference. "The story," Tom says, "is primarily about ... awakening our spiritual sense of that other world."

But this observation, though probably true, does not bring us to an understanding of the circular plot, of the sudden anti-climactic reversal of expectations experienced by the protagonist. In pursuit of an understanding of this, I return to liminality, to doors and their functions. Vane is pushed back from the throne of the Ancient of Days to his own library through a door with a golden lock which appears, from his changed vantage-point, to have been the "board of a large book" in his library. But doors are ubiquitous in the novel, as I have remarked before. The door to Mr. Raven's mausoleum is in the shape of a coffin lid, and Mr. Vane's terrified exit from it at the end of Chapter VII places him in the closet of his library, just behind the masked door, from which he then emerges to throw himself upon a couch (37). It has long been clear to the reader that, for MacDonald, books are also graves of a kind, little tombs enclosing the worldly essence of their authors (cf. Donne 278–79). In a memorable moment, Mr. Raven, whose job as sexton is "to ring the resurrection bell," pulls from the earth and flings into the air a "bird-butterfly" which comes to Vane "pulsing like a fire-fly," and for some time guides him through the night. But then a great longing to possess it overtakes Vane. "The moment I had it," he reports, "its light went out ... a dead book with boards outspread lay cold and heavy in my hand. I threw it in the air — only to hear it fall among the heather. Burying my face in my hands, I sat in motionless misery" (47). Mr. Raven has, apparently, plucked a radiant soul forth from the grave; Vane's selfish act has re-buried it.

But if books are graves, graves are also doors. The irony that no one truly wakes who has not died into life is the *overt* lesson of the text, reiterated constantly by Mr. Raven and his wife (who are actually, as Vane discovers, Adam and Eve). The "sleepers" in their cemetery rise when they are "ripe" and go forth into new life. Eventually, as he comes to understand this, Vane agrees to "sleep the sleep." But in "the dreams that come" to him, having been told by Adam that he is dreaming, he finds himself wandering among the seven channels on the heath. Dreaming that he is weary, he lies down beside "a pit in the rock, whose mouth was like that of a grave" (235–36). As a dreaming child, he remembers, he could wake himself by jumping off a high place, and so he throws himself into the pit, only to find himself back in his garret. He is devastated, believing he has lost his chance to wake with Lona in Paradise, but after four sleepless days and nights of despair, during which he tries futilely to find a physical portal back into Mr. Raven's world, he falls asleep at last in his old house and awakens with the sure knowledge that he is back in his grave next to Lona in Adam's house of death. This time he really awakes, or believes he does, together with Lona on Resurrection Day, and they proceed hand in hand on a "glorious resurrection morning" toward the Holy City, where they are welcomed by angels and climb the steps of the heavenly throne. Yet, although the antepenultimate chapter is called "The Journey Home," the journey ends ironically as we have seen in the epigraph with an apparent reversal of expectations, another sudden, involuntary exile into the library of Vane's estate.

Why, as the novel comes to a close, do we have such a negative pattern of reversal twice repeated within relatively few pages? And why do the negative patterns enwrap his joyful account of "resurrection morning"? We have assumed in the course of the novel, that by trial and error, several times refusing the Raven's advice, going off on his own for silly, selfish, egotistical reasons, all of which end in disastrous returns, Vane has indeed learned, made spiritual progress, as all souls are supposed to do. If the novel is mythopoeic, how are these final incidents to be understood? Does the ending reflect a pilgrim's progress, or perhaps a pilgrim's regress? Or is it presciently postmodern, reflecting an apparently meaningless circuit, a cynical return to square one which negates the idea of progress altogether (cf. Cabell)?

Of course, if libraries and cemeteries are analogs, if books and graves are alike, and both are portals, Vane has merely been grave hopping across world-boundaries. At one point in the narrative, Mr. Raven has told him "home is the only place where you can go out and into ... the one place, if you do but find it, where you may go out and in both, is home" (15). We assume the library, or the physical reality it represents, is not Vane's home — indeed, Raven has told him as much, saying, "You thought you were at home where I found you: if *that* had been your home you could not have left it" (45). By Mr. Raven's maxims, then, he should be able again to leave this world which is not his home, but he accepts the implied judgment of "the hand" that sent him back, saying he has not sought the mirror, and will never again go out by that door. Does he, then, indeed have a home? Can he be at home in the metaphysical world of the seven dimensions? His rejection at the foot of the throne of the Ancient of Days seems to say no.

Various possible interpretations of that rejection occur to Vane, and he passionately reviews them in the final chapter, entitled "The Endless Ending." He voices the most obvious possibility, and perhaps the most plausible, first: "Can it be that that last waking also was in the dream? That I am still in the chamber of death, asleep and dreaming, not yet ripe enough to wake?" If this solution is accepted, of course, the apparent pragmatic function of the return, providing for the validation of the narrative frame, is moot. But the idea that he is at fault, that the rejection signifies failure of some sort, also soon occurs to MacDonald's protagonist: "Or can it be that I did not go to sleep outright and heartily, and so have come awake too soon?" (251).

The final chapter, with its aphorisms, its hysterical dialogue with "Hope," shows most intensely the influence of the German Romantic, Novalis, whose *Hymns to the Night* MacDonald translated. And in fact the book ends, famously, with a line from Novalis: "Our life is no dream, but it should and will perhaps become one" (252). As Joseph Campbell says, "Dream is the personalized myth; myth the depersonalized dream." Novalis's line suggests the process of mythmaking, and perhaps supports C.S. Lewis's claim that the novel is pure mythopoesis.

But Novalis also says, "We are near awakening when we dream that we dream." Within the symbolic structures of the book, the saying would seem hopeful. But finally, the personal nature of dream also suggests that the distress of the protagonist is MacDonald's, and thus his dream escapes the realm of myth altogether.

Liminality, with its alternate world structures and its definitions of incommensurate frames of reference within them, offers some small ground for speculation about MacDonald's world-building, and perhaps some insight into his obsession with doors. But it fails to solve ultimately the mythopoeic problem: what is the mythic significance of the "endless ending"? This ending does not seem to most serious readers to mirror what they already know of MacDonald's religious beliefs. In fact, it communicates an air of didactic failure on some level, though the failure is perhaps as likely to be that of its readers as of its author. I would welcome readings by others addressing this problem. Most readings to date blithely dismiss rather than address it.

Works Cited

Cabell, James Branch. *Jurgen: A Comedy of Justice*. New York: Robert M. McBride, 1919.

Campbell, Joseph. *The Hero with a Thousand Faces*. Princeton: Princeton University Press, 1968.

Donne, John. "From a Sermon Preached at the Funerals of Sir William Cokayne Knight, Alderman of London, December 12, 1626." *John Donne: Selected Prose,*

Chosen by Evelyn Simpson. Ed. Helen Gardner and Timothy Healy. Oxford: Oxford University Press, 1967. 277–88.

Lewis, C.S. Introduction to *Lilith*, by George MacDonald. Grand Rapids: Eerdmans, 1981. v–xii.

Mendlesohn, Farah. "Toward a Taxonomy of Fantasy." *Journal of the Fantastic in the Arts* 13.2 (2002): 169–83.

Spariosu, Mihai I. *The Wreath of Wild Olive: Play, Liminality, and the Study of Literature*. New York: State University of New York, 1997.

Turner, Victor. *From Ritual to Theatre: The Human Seriousness of Play*. New York: Performing Arts Journal Press, 1982.

CHAPTER 2

Liminality and the Everyday in *Lilith*

Tom Shippey

Robert Collins's piece on "Liminality in *Lilith*" (chapter 1) raises questions which seem, indeed, unanswerable within the ordinary constraints of narrative convention. Why is Vane returned to the library from Mount Paradiso? Surely, as Collins argues, this is not simply and literal-mindedly to explain how the story comes to be told. And why are magical events located both in the other world and in the mundane one? Is that because the library itself is neither "other" nor "mundane" but "liminal?" One attraction of this latter suggestion is that it fits well with other, later fantasies, such as Ursula LeGuin's suggestively titled *The Beginning Place* (with its almost equally suggestive alternative title, *Threshold*), or Robert Westall's *The Wind Eye* (or "window"). However, these two very clear cases of what Farah Mendlesohn has called "portal" fantasies stick to the rule that Mendlesohn has formulated and Collins repeats: "individuals may cross both ways, [but] the magic does not" (173). Why does *Lilith* not stick to the same rule? Collins notes that it fails to repeat another familiar pattern, part of the Campbellian monomyth, in that the hero brings back no magic talisman or epiphany, so that "as a quest story, then, the narrative fails."

I would begin to address some of these issues by noting that all monomyths or structural patterns are bound to fit some narratives better than others, and indeed, in some narratives, are bound to be challenged. The most prominent fantasy of modern times, Tolkien's *Lord of the Rings*, is not a quest story but an anti-quest story: it is not about retrieving a magic talisman but about throwing one away. Its ending too involves something like a return from Mount Paradiso. As one character, Frodo, sails off to the Undying Lands, his companion, Sam, returns to Middle-earth, to the land of mortality. The last words of the narrative, "'Well I'm back,' he said," have been described as the saddest ending in modern literature by another prominent writer of fantasy, Michael Swanwick, and one might well say, rightly so. Sam's words are characteristic of hobbits in being completely obvious on the literal plane — so obvious as to be hardly worth saying (of course he's back, if he were not back he would not be there to say so) — but at the same time, through the characteristic Anglo-hobbitic device of understatement, intensely powerful metaphorically. Sam is saying to his wife and family, in effect, "I gave up immortality for you. Like Arwen, I chose you and death rather than not-you and life." Though at the same time as choosing Middle-earth and death, he is choosing Middle-earth and life: for as Frodo points out to him, he has still a long and honorable life in front of him, with wife, children, grandchildren, gardens to grow, and work to do. Still, a word often repeated in the last couple of pages of Tolkien's work is "grey": Grey Havens, grey horse, grey firth, grey rain, grey sea, grey road. These are set against the "yellow light" of Sam's home and the welcome in it, but there is still a sense of something having gone out of the world, of the character being returned to what has been called by scholars of romance, *le monde morne et mundain*: the sad world of everyday.

Who would choose to return to this, given a choice? Most hero(in)es of fantasy are not given the choice, and this may say something about a further intractable problem, largely ignored by conventional scholarship: that of the purpose and appeal of, indeed the human need, for fantasy. Farah Mendlesohn's argument casts some light here, for while it is true that in portal fantasies the magic cannot come back across the borderline between worlds, something else can, and this may well be a solution. In both LeGuin's story already mentioned and William Mayne's *A Game of Dark*, young adults from this world go into another world in order to kill a dragon. It is, however, obvious to all readers that the dragon they kill there has something to do with, is perhaps a metaphorical projection of, a problem in the real world, in the life of the young protagonists. In killing their dragon, LeGuin's male and female pair learn, respectively, how to get away from the smothering possessiveness of his mother and the incestuous desire of her stepfather. Mayne's young hero learns similarly how to escape from his crippled father, his loveless mother. The teenage protagonists cannot deal with these real-world problems by magic, but the magic they have seen teaches them to act, to break the spells of convention and habit. They learn at least an attitude.

These stories furthermore end, fairly conventionally, with success, or at least the potential for success. It should be noted that fantasy may also instruct one on coping with failure. *The Lord of the Rings* does not exactly end with failure, though many of its characters see their life as a "long defeat," but one might note the ending of Tolkien's short and semi-autobiographical fantasy, "Leaf by Niggle." Both the story's central characters, Niggle and his neighbor Parish, die in the course of it, in Niggle's case rather early on. They go through Purgatory and end with something very like a vision of Paradise, but that is in the other world. The story makes clear that in this world, *le monde mundain*, the end for Niggle is defeat, contempt, final oblivion. In the story's penultimate scene a group of men are talking about him: one says that he was totally useless, another, that his paintings had some value. The third — and these are the last words said by anyone about him in direct speech — says dismissively, "Oh, poor little Niggle! Never knew he painted" (111). So much for Niggle's hopes and aspirations; and the point is rubbed in by the story's omniscient narrator, who confirms that one small fragment of Niggle's painting is preserved, anonymously, for a while, in a museum, but is then destroyed so that nothing whatsoever remains, in achievement or in memory. This wholly and determinedly negative scene is set, of course, against the final vision of Niggle and Parish the other side of Purgatory, laughing uproariously like Chaucer's Troilus looking down from his pagan heaven. But Tolkien makes it perfectly clear that whatever may or may not happen the other side of the grave, failing and being forgotten is the normal fate of almost all human beings.

Does this have a bearing on the return of Vane? Why is he sent back from the edge of Paradise? Because that is the normal fate of humanity. We would all like to have a shortcut to eternal life, or an escape from death, but that is neither possible nor (many moralists would say) desirable. "Men must endure / Their going hence even as their coming hither," as Shakespeare has Edgar say in King Lear (5.2.9–10), or as the Pearl-maiden puts it in the Middle English poem (she is dead, and speaking to her living father from the other side of the Water he may not cross), "Thy corse in clot mot calder keve.... Er over thys dam hym Dryghtyn deme" (Your body must sink colder in earth before the Lord allows it over this water [lines 320–24]). But like the teenagers of LeGuin's, Mayne's, and Westall's stories, what Vane now has is not a talisman, but an awareness, an assurance, an attitude which will enable him to face better what has to be faced anyway. And it is this, of course, that the author wishes to convey to the reader through his story — who, of course, can never leave *le monde mundain* except through fantasy.

A further suggestion I would make is that *Lilith* is not only a "liminal" story but also a "medial" or "mediating" one. It has been argued that the purpose of myth is to mediate what are seen as unacceptable contradictions within a world-view: so that, for instance, the Christian story of the Fall and the coming of Original Sin provides an explanation for the presence of evil in a world created by an omnipotent and benevolent God; the Tolkienian mythology of Middle-earth reconciles native pre–Christian belief in non-human species with the imported Christian cosmology; and so on. Looked at from this point of view, *Lilith* could be seen as an attempt to reconcile MacDonald's own strongly Calvinist background with a personal belief in goodness. The former doctrine insists that "there is none righteous, no not one ... none that doeth good" (Rom. 3.10,12), and that even the newborn baby has sin in its heart; the latter doctrine, strongly supported by Victorian sentimentality on the subject of children, insists that every Little Nell, Tiny Tim, or crossing-sweeper Jo is assured of salvation. One way of mediating these beliefs is, in a way, to suggest that original sin takes effect at puberty, and this is at least hinted at in *Lilith*, through the suggestion that the forever-threatened Little Ones have it in them to grow up to become Bags, blundering and malevolent giants. Meanwhile the opposing figures of the maternal Eve and the demonically child-hunting Lilith, a pair held together by their shared husband Adam, dramatize human beings' alternative potentials through the hint of double ancestry. Fantasy is a form, one may say, well adapted to having one's cake and eating it too. Characters can be presented in split form, as good-double and bad-double: perhaps the most obvious example being Cinderella's wicked stepmother and fairy godmother, representing the different aspects of the real mother. They may also be presented as both alive and dead, as in "Leaf by Niggle" already mentioned, or as in C.S. Lewis's last "Narnia" novel, *The Last Battle*, where we learn at the end that in fact (in fact?) all the child-characters were killed at the start of the novel and exist only within the world of the book, which is also the world of Plato, or of Aslan, or of (Lewis's view of) the Christian heaven. The device of splitting can be taken further, to present not only alternative characters but also alternative fates, alternative realities.

Something like this is true of *Lilith*, with its final words from Novalis, "Our life is no dream, but it should and will perhaps become one" (252). The implication is that we will one day wake up to reality, when what we presently accept as reality will fade to the status of dream. Very much the same thing is said in muted form by Tolkien's Frodo, returning to the *monde mundain* of the Shire. At the very end of the chapter "Homeward Bound," and just before the chapter "The Scouring of the Shire," Merry says to the three other hobbits, speaking of all the adventures that have gone before, "It seems almost like a dream that has slowly faded." "Not to me," replies Frodo. "To me it feels more like falling asleep again" (1034). In either world, then—

the world of Middle-earth/the world of the Shire, the world of Mr. Raven/the world of Mr. Vane — the other appears to be a dream. Neither has priority, or assured superior status. But of course the reader has to be persuaded of this equality, which is contradicted by all everyday experience, and the author has to keep a thumb firmly in the balance even to make it temporarily plausible. Yet the author would not trouble to do this if it were not for a quality that is hard to deal with in purely literary terms: namely, the quality of belief.

It is hard not to recognize that LeGuin, and Tolkien, and Lewis, and MacDonald, are all in their different ways (if I would suggest in an ascending order of degrees of commitment) trying to express something in which they firmly believe: with the latter three, belief in traditional, if sometimes unorthodox, Christianity. Essential parts of this traditional belief system are the conviction that this present world, *le monde mundain*, is relatively unimportant *sub specie aeternitatis*; and yet it is in a sense vitally important in that behavior here determines one's fate on the far greater stage of eternity; and that true success on that greater stage depends on an ability to close one's eyes to the apparently obvious rewards offered and punishments threatened in this one. And one has to take all this on faith.

It seems to me that we have here an adequate explanation of Vane's return and the strongly negative "pattern of reversal" in the last pages of *Lilith* noted by Robert Collins. That is because, to MacDonald as to Lewis, that is what life is like. Lewis indeed made the rather striking comparison of life-experience with his own childhood experience of alternation between a comfortable home with a loving father, in the school holidays, and life in a school run by an insanely sadistic headmaster, during term. Even wrapped in the comforts of home, he wrote, he knew it would end and he would be back in "Belsen." Similarly, even in life, he knew death was as inevitable as term-time; but that death too, like term-time, would have an end. This, surely, is one of the things that *Lilith* is saying. For human beings, there is no easy way or shortcut to Mount Paradiso, and even if one approaches that point in dream or vision, the hand will come and push him through the door to this-world reality. All one can hope for is that, just as the dream fades into reality, so one day reality will fade into the dream. But the two visions, the two worlds, can be held in balance only when one is on the *limen*, the threshold between the two, in the author's carefully-crafted liminal space, whether it be library or book or wardrobe.

Lilith remains a challenging, even an irritating work, if only from its author's love of paradox, often paradoxical banality: "No one who will not sleep can ever wake.... Nobody ever was or ever will be at home without having gone there.... A man can do nothing he is not fit to do.... No one can die who does not long to live" (and so on). One of the weak points of fantasy, as

Tolkien pointed out with reference to the urge to create fantasy-land languages, is that the imagination is unconstrained; the author can do anything. One often feels that MacDonald too did not resist the urge to create surprise through paradox, to throw in a striking scene or image (the other-world hyacinths sweetening the notes of the this-world piano) without caring too much about consistency. Nevertheless, he does, I think, keep his sights firmly trained on one thing, which is to have a moralizing impact on his reader. There can be no doubt that MacDonald, in a quite literal sense, is a preacher *manqué*. Probably one of the problems our age has with him is that he is preaching to rather specific Victorian concerns: Faith in a Darwinist age, femininity in a repressive society, parental love threatened by both child mortality and the boarding school. What Lewis took from him above all, one can see, is his doctrine of Hell: it exists, but its existence can be reconciled with the notion of the loving and forgiving Father through the insistence that people condemn themselves to it, that the gates of Hell are bolted only on the inside. Lewis would expand on this in *The Great Divorce* (in which MacDonald becomes a central character), but the idea is clear enough in the presentation of Lilith herself, who literally will not let go, cannot open her hand to the love of God. Like other fantasies, *Lilith* seems to draw its energy from doubt and contradiction. In the final chapter, Vane represents what MacDonald takes to be the true state of all human beings: they are led on by glimpses of something they can now grasp only fitfully and uncertainly, surrounded by a "solid mass" of reality which will be revealed in the end as illusion. In the MacDonald worldview, it is this world that is liminal: it is a doorstep, on the other side of which lies the great ascent.

Works Cited

LeGuin, Ursula. *The Beginning Place*. New York: Harper and Row, 1980.
Lewis, C.S. "My First School." In *Present Concerns*. Ed. Walter Hooper. London: Fount, 1986. 23–26.
Mayne, William. *A Game of Dark*. Boston: Dutton, 1971.
Mendlesohn, Farah. "Toward a Taxonomy of Fantasy." *Journal of the Fantastic in the Arts* 13.2 (2002): 169–83.
Shakespeare, William. *The Complete Works*: 2nd ed. Ed. Stanley Wells and Gary Taylor. Oxford: Oxford University Press, 2005.
Tolkien, J.R.R. *The Lord of the Rings*. Boston: Houghton Mifflin, 1991.
———. "Leaf by Niggle." *Tree and Leaf*. London: George Allen and Unwin, 1964. 85–112.
Vantuono, William, trans., *Pearl: An Edition with Verse Translation*. Notre Dame: University of Notre Dame, 1995.
Westall, Robert. *The Wind Eye*. New York: William Morrow, 1977.

CHAPTER 3

Lilith, Textuality, and the Rhetoric of Romance

Michael Mendelson

When I first wrote about George MacDonald's *Lilith* in 1985, I argued that readers could best address the symbolic richness of the text, along with its attendant thematic complexities, by considering MacDonald's innovative approach to the conventions of prose romance.[1] In particular, I claimed *Lilith* as a romance of ascent, a mythic journey with metaphysical intentions, a narrative in the tradition of Dante and Bunyan, a theodicy in which the hero must first exit the world of appearances and enter a *selva oscura* of doubt, before ultimately achieving a redemptive vision of spiritual identity and humanity's divine origins.

On the one hand, the present essay is an effort to reconfirm this critical perspective. While acknowledging the never-to-be-exhausted quality of MacDonald's imagery in particular and the indeterminate nature of mythopoetic narrative in general, I nevertheless hope to show that conventions of prose romance continue to operate as a useful heuristic for negotiating the hermeneutical complexities of this conspicuously ambiguous text (cf. Zimmer 4). On the other hand, scholarly commentary has raised important questions about both the artistic integrity and the thematic continuity of MacDonald's fantasy. Specifically, criticism of *Lilith* has tended to concentrate on links between the real world of the hero's actual residence and the imaginative world of his psycho-spiritual adventures.[2] This critical concern is focused productively in Chapter 1 of this collection by Robert A. Collins, who draws our attention not simply to the thematic continuity between one world and the other, but more specifically to potential incongruities in the means for crossing the border between the two worlds, the hero's unexplained oscillations across this border, and the seemingly unsatisfactory resolution of Mr. Vane's visionary quest. These critical reflections invite a reappraisal of my own argument for *Lilith* as an innovative extension of the conventions of quest romance. In addition, Professor Collins and this volume provide a welcome opportunity to reconsider *Lilith*'s contribution to the rhetoric of modern fantasy.

To begin, let me clarify what I mean by the rhetoric of romance. Put briefly, prose romance is a narrative language for the invention of arguments on the nature, scope, and mystery of human experience. The mystery is pivotal; for unlike the novel, romance is not bound to imitate actions that correspond with principles of verisimilitude (Aristotle 1447a–b; 2316–17). Rather, romance typically involves adventure into a purely fictional domain, an "otherworld" where mimesis is a matter of representing human desire in persuasive fashion rather than natural order in recognizable form (see Patch; Fry; Rose). Until the late nineteenth century, the otherworld journey was called *romance*; consequently, the many forms of modern *fantasy* constitute a revival of romance by virtue of their shared excursion beyond reality. Regardless of its name or the nature of its setting, otherworld romance carries a distinguished pedigree based principally on its time-honored ability to provide an imaginative vision its readers recognize as both creative and meaningful.

With *Lilith*, as with any successful romance, vision entails restraints if writers are to persuade their readers to suspend disbelief in what is obviously unreal and to adopt an alternative perspective that is imaginatively plausible. Romance becomes a rhetorical art — an art of epistemic proportions rather than an exercise in ingenuity only — when its strategies or *topoi* convince its readers that the semblance of things imagined in fiction reveal the substance of something meaningful in life. The present criticism of *Lilith* raises questions about MacDonald's rhetoric, questions I will try to address by concentrating on certain *topoi* I believe make this work an important contribution to the history of modern fantasy.

MacDonald himself discusses the rhetoric of romance in his essay "The Fantastic Imagination," in which he asserts that writers may "invent a little world of [their] own, with its own laws; for there is that in [them] which delights in calling up new forms" (*Orts* 313). Tolkien echoes MacDonald's concept when, in his own essay "On Fairy Stories," he writes about the Primary and the Secondary Worlds, terms that aptly describe the distinction between the actual world of routine experience and the imaginative world of fantastic fiction. Tolkien goes on to say that in order to cultivate belief in the "secondary" world of the writer's invention, the constituent features of the fictive world must operate with the binding authority of law (37). MacDonald's essay makes the same point in its distinction between works of Fancy, which may be delightful, and the products of Imagination, in which "law has been diligently at work." Indeed, the most important feature of the imaginative world is that there should be

> harmony between the laws by which the new world has begun to exist; and in the process of his creation, the inventor must hold by these laws. The moment he forgets one of them, he makes the story, by its own postulates, incredible.... A man's inventions may be stupid or clever, but if he does not hold by the laws of them, or if he makes one law jar with another, he contradicts himself as an inventor, he is no artist [314–15].

The problem with inharmonious inventions is not that individual acts of invention are not delightful, but that the narrative as a whole lacks the continuity necessary to present a credible analogue for the inner-nature of human experience. The rhetoric of romance revolves around this ability to shape the *topoi* of the secondary world in ways that are delightful in their originality yet cohesive in themselves and compatible enough with a shared vision of human desire to win the approbation of the reader.[3]

Critics of *Lilith* tend to focus on the narrative and thematic continuity of the primary and secondary worlds. Professor Collins raises the especially interesting question of the "textual" borders that frame this romance — its opening in a library and its ending with the closing of a book. How are these bibliographic figures related to the various mirrors, doors, and dreams that also operate as portals between the two worlds? My own position is that the textual frame is a unique rhetorical *topos* that establishes a persuasive framework for the structural and thematic order of the text and, in the process, extends the boundaries and potential of prose romance. To make this case, I will first address those conventions of the genre that structure what Wordsworth would call the "high argument" of MacDonald's *Lilith*.

1. *Lilith* is an invented myth based on Christian allegory. The story is biblical not only in its theology but also in the paradoxical cycle of its narrative from expulsion, descent, and alienation to an eventual ascent toward reunion with one's creator. This ritualized pattern of expulsion, wandering, and return had been part of pre–Christian literature since Homer and Virgil, as well as in the Greek romances of Xenophon, Heliodorus, and Apollonius Rhodius. But the theological valence of the circuitous adventure is given special emphasis by Christian writers for whom the epic of human experience is dominated by a desire to "return" to a place that is higher and more refined than one's terrestrial home, as in Augustine's *De Civitate Dei*. Odysseus returns home; Dante aspires to paradise. Spatially, the relation between the eternal world of infinite being from which we come (and for which we long) and the manifest world of changing form in which we are mired (and from which we must earn our redemption) is a vertical one; temporally, the relation between the two is represented by analogy with a journey that begins with decline and moves upwards. "The way down is the way up," writes Eliot; and in Christian literature, this paradoxical movement is given paradigmatic, though varied form by Dante, Spenser, Milton, Bunyan, and Blake, all of whom recount the ritual of history as a tragedy of descent followed by prolonged wanderings amidst demons of selfhood, evil, and death, culminating in the *peripeteia* of return to a place beyond and above. The process of wandering in the otherworld not only releases us from the constraints of the primary world, but it also reveals conditions of that world too often obscured by convention and familiarity. The transformative journey into the marvelous is thus removed from and related to our experience of the mundane, a foray into what seems foreign because it is also suspiciously familiar.

In 1584, Sidney described the content of the secondary world as limited only by "the zodiack" of the poet's wit (241). And yet, if the inventions of romance are to resonate with the reader, its constellations must seem to reside in the same sky we all see, though perhaps in a galaxy farther away than ones we have imagined. In romance, the need to identify the recognizable amidst the fantastic is routinely satisfied by a highly conventional narrative structure or *mythos*. This *mythos* is most familiar through the plotline of fairy tale, where the trajectory of abandonment, wandering, and eventual return home (or to a place better than home) organizes the majority of the Grimms' tales. Quest romance from Chrétien and "Sir Gawain" through Ariosto and Spenser follows this nuclear story, with the circuitous return as the most conventional ending. MacDonald follows this *mythos* closely in *The Princess and the Goblin*, "The Light Princess," and many, though not all his tales for children (see *Gifts of the Child Christ*).

MacDonald's stories also show the influence of *Kunstmärchen*, the artistic fairy tales developed in nineteenth-century Germany, first by Goethe (in 1795), then by writers like Tiecke (*Phantasus* 1812–16) and la Motte-Fouqué (*Undine* 1811). *Kunstmärchen* typically involve the romance quest; and it was, of course, the quests of Novalis and E.T.A. Hoffman that influenced MacDonald most directly. We know from Greville MacDonald that his father catalogued the neglected library of a Scottish mansion (*MacDonald and His Wife* 73), which MacDonald *père* describes as "a nest of German Classics ... which I found a mine inexhaustible" (*The Portent* 45). We also know from Greville's biography that his father was reading Hoffmann's *The Golden Pot* with great admiration at the time he was composing *Phantastes* (1857). Hoffman's tale is built around the hero's dilemma between the love for a burgher's daughter and for the fairy Serpentina, a typically Romantic contrast between the real and the ideal. Having the soul of an artist, Hoffman's hero ultimately chooses "the glorious kingdom [that] lies much closer at hand than we were wont to suppose" (41). A similar theme is at work in Novalis's major work, *Heinrich von Ofterdingen* (1799), an unfinished romance about the growth of the poet's mind as he searches for the "blue flower" of poetic inspiration. At a crucial moment in his development, Heinrich hears an elaborate *Märchen* that inspires him to remark that "in fable's teaching, the life of the higher world is variously presented ... the Bible and the precepts of fable are constellations with one and the same orbit" (167). Novalis is ultimately an apostle for spiritual insight as articulated through the rhetoric of romance; and yet, his hero, like Hoffman's and Shelley's Alastor, never achieves the divine vision that is his goal. This defeat in the final phase of the romance journey suggests that while the narrative quest was alive and thriving in the nineteenth century, fulfillment had become harder to imagine.

Before turning directly to *Lilith*, I would like to attend briefly to related events in the opening of MacDonald's earlier work, *Phantastes*. Subtitled "A Faerie Romance," this book begins with a long quotation from Novalis on *Märchen* as "a dream-vision without coherence" (14). The description recalls Schiller's essay "On Naïve and Sentimental Poetry," with "sentimental" defined as the self-conscious reworking of earlier, "naïve" forms of expression in a more controlled, modern style (see Wimsatt and Brooks 368). *Phantastes* is relatively "naïve" in its episodic exhibition of "Fancy," but it is nonetheless "sentimental" in its effort to build a more ambitious form of fantasy out of the conventions of quest romance. *Phantastes* opens on the twenty-first birthday of the hero, Anados, the day he comes into his inheritance. My *Greek-English Lexicon* translates "anados" as either "impassable" or "a way back"; but James Murray's 1888 Clarendon *New English Dictionary* translates "anados" (under "anodic," an upward force) as "the way up." I am myself inclined to think the hero's name is MacDonald's own compound of "ana" (upward) and "odos" (a path or way). This etymology is important because in the first chapter of *Lilith*, Mr. Vane, its hero, is told about his ancestor, Sir Upward, whose portrait is the only one in the massive library that is his inheritance (8). Anados is, thus, a possible ancestor of Vane, which would establish a family history of travel to the otherworld.

The two books are also linked in the means by which they access the otherworld. Anados is invested with the keys to a cabinet that holds his father's private papers, a desk that

> lay shrouded in mystery whose deepest folds were gathered around the dark oak cabinet which I now approached with a strange mingling of reverence and curiosity. Perhaps, like a geologist, I was about to turn-up to the light some buried strata of the human world, with its fossil remains charred by passion and petrified by tears [15–16].

The metaphor of geological excavation hints at the internalized direction of the hero's impending journey, a direction characteristic of the spiritualized romance of the English Romantic poets (cf. Bloom). Northrop Frye notes the continuity in romance between genealogical investigations and geological descent, both of which involve digging into the past (122). Anados is about to enter a world that is unknown but deeply personal, a world he must "excavate" in a journey that invokes the paradoxical trajectory of quest romance, of going down to get up. If Anados is indeed Sir Upward, he must earn his name through this journey.

Even more provocative than these genealogical speculations is the role of *text* in the entry to the otherworld of this early romance. As noted, Anados uncovers the secondary world of his own spiritual adventure by first exploring the desk of his father. This is not Narnia's wardrobe, filled with clothes, but a textual space, stuffed with written records, packed into "little drawers and slides and pigeon-holes," with one small cupboard that "attracted my interest as if there lay the secret of this long-hidden world" (16). In this *sanctum sanctorum*, Anados discovers a "small packet of papers" and it is from this packet that a tiny fairy appears who will guide him to fairyland. The rest of *Phantastes* is beyond the scope of this essay; but as a precedent for *Lilith*, it is interesting to note that the *topos* of entry into the otherworld is specifically a discursive space, that digging into papers has transformative potential, and that Anados, like Vane, undertakes what we can call a bibliographic excursion.

As with Anados, the story of Mr. Vane begins with an inheritance:

> I had just finished my studies at Oxford, and was taking a brief holiday from work before assuming definitely the management of the estate.... I had made little acquaintance with the history of my ancestors. Almost the only thing I knew concerning them was, that a notable number of them had been given to study [5].

The situation is a familiar one in nineteenth-century romance: John Melmoth, Edward Waverley, and Davie Balfour of *Kidnapped* all begin their adventures by returning to the ancestral seat, and in all cases the return initiates a rite of passage in which youth seeks to explore the obscurities of its heritage. Vane is both solitary and an intellectual. Beyond these rudimentary characteristics, we know nothing about his appearance, his acquaintance, or those quirks of manner that round out a character. What we do know is that he and his ancestors are bookish to an extraordinary degree. It makes sense, then, that MacDonald would take pains to tell us the details of his family's most distinctive possession: its library, "whose growth began before the invention of printing, and had continued to my own time, greatly influenced of course, by changes of taste and pursuit." One wonders how this library remained up-to-date, since Vane's parents died when he was "yet a child" and he appears not to know the house himself. And yet, despite recent neglect, this library appears to have a life of its own:

> like an encroaching state, [it] absorbed one room after another until it occupied the greater part of the ground floor. Its chief room was large and the walls of it were covered with books almost to the ceiling; the rooms into which it overflowed were of various sizes and shapes, and communicated in modes as various — by doors, by open arches, by short passages, by steps up and steps down [5–6].

This labyrinth of knowledge proves an irresistible attraction, and Vane spends all his time there. As in *Phantastes*, succeeding to "an ancient property" (6) has surprising consequences. The Latin root for "property" is *proprius*, or one's own, as in *in propria persona*. Locke writes that when he uses the term he implies "that property which men have in their persons as well as goods," and N.O. Brown comments that Locke is referring to "the psychological root of private property" (145). Such reasoning suggests that the library is a synecdoche for Vane, his family, and perhaps the "moving panorama" of human consciousness (6). How are we to read this rhetorical figure? Is Vane like the library in his multiplicity, in his potential for randomness and order, in the element of interiority only hinted at on the surface of his life? Or, more abstractly, is the self like a text, which accrues substance only through careful attention, which requires interpretation to be understood?

In *Lilith*, the first crossing from the primary to secondary world takes place in the library. It also happens under the auspices of Sir Upward and with the help of his mysterious librarian, Mr. Raven. Vane is reading on "a gloomy day" when an unexpected ray of sun comes into the library and illuminates the portrait of one of his ancestors nestled amidst the books. We learn shortly that this ancestor is indeed Sir Upward and that a Mr. Raven was his librarian (8). At just the moment the sun strikes Sir Upward's portrait, Vane imagines that it nods at him, and, even more mysteriously, Mr. Raven enters the library to take a book that Vane himself will soon seek out. Perhaps the librarian is already guiding Vane's development. In any case, Vane's attention is attracted later to a bookshelf that "masks" the door to a small closet. The books on this shelf are artificial, represented only by their spines, a "harmless trick" that Vane particularly enjoys. One book rests on its side wedged between the shelves of this bookcase-door. When Vane notices this volume missing, he becomes uncharacteristically angry. Moments later, the apparition of Mr. Raven replaces this book and disappears through the faux bookshelf into the mysterious closet (7–8).

Mr. Raven is soon revealed not only as the family librarian, but also as a bird, as a sexton of souls waiting to be reborn, and as the primal Adam.

These multiple identities are characteristic of the density of MacDonald's semiotics and set a pattern for the polysemous implications of the characters, settings, and events to follow. In this instance, the Raven operates as a mystagogue, one who prepares initiates for entry into a new order. The *topos* of entry is particularly important because it defines the relation between the two worlds of romance and, in the process, sets the context for the adventures that follow. MacDonald's approach to this first entry is considerably more innovative than a journey "into the woods" and merits particular scrutiny. The library, of course, exists in the primary world, though it allows access to the secondary one. In the portal door, there are books that may coexist in both places; or maybe their cover exists in the primary world while their content is located on the other side. A collection of good books has similar properties: they can exist in more than one place at a time, they persist longer than almost any other human product, their significance changes according to context, and their practical value is independent of their physical stature. And yet, substantial as the influence of books may be, they remain artificial constructs that depend for their status solely on their readers. They are also, at least potentially, liminal, an opening to another side, a portal the Raven knows how to use and Vane is only beginning to suspect.

A week after the Raven's disappearance through the bibliographic door, Vane remains fascinated by the manuscript that is wedged between the shelves and repeatedly tries ("in vain") to release it from its place. When he sees the Raven returning through the door of books, Vane follows him as they ascend a winding stairway to an expansive garret that Vane describes as "the brooding brain of the building" (16). This ascent to the top of the building does not have the allegorical exactness of Spenser's Castle of Alma; and yet, the image is one of a cluster that connects the garret with the hero's own mind and signifies something about the impending journey. MacDonald remarked to his son that winding stairs had always fascinated him as an analogy to "our own 'secret stair' leading up to the wider vision" (*MacDonald and His Wife* 489; cf. 530). Assuming that expanded vision is the eventual goal of this quest, the hero begins his journey by following a magical bird, who is also a bibliophile, up a secret stair into a territory that lies, he imagines, "at the heart of my brain" (16). We need only gloss these events to realize that the passage into the otherworld is somehow cerebral, though I think "mental" is probably a more accurate term because Vane's sojourn will turn out to be filled with pent-up emotions, imaginative apparitions, and spiritual longings. For now, it is enough to know that the general direction of the journey is "farther in and higher up." On her birthday, Sleeping Beauty wanders into an unknown garret of her own castle and meets her own agent of transformation. In the *Princess and the Goblin*, there is a similar fairy godmother who inhabits the upper rooms of a palace and whose space is bathed in light. Vane, the student of metaphysics, is following a librarian/sexton, bird/man upward into a space similarly illuminated and about to make his own way across the border.

Once in the garret, Vane notes "with mingled awe and pleasure [that] this wide expanse was my own, and unexplored!" (10). He immediately sees a tall mirror with an ebony frame "on top of which stood a black eagle with outstretched wings, in his beak a golden chain, from which end hung a black ball" (11). This mirror proves to be the specific point of entry into the otherworld, and mirrors in general have been an analogue for the self at least since the reflecting pool of Narcissus (see Frye 108–09). In MacDonald's hands, however, conventional symbols receive unconventional embellishments: in this case, the black eagle and the golden chain present provocative references to both Dante and Milton (cf. McGillis 6). Dante dreams that he is transported upwards out of Purgatory by an eagle (*Purgatorio*, Canto 9), while the "pendant world" on the golden chain is Milton's vision of earth seen from afar (*Paradise Lost* 2.1052). These allusions attend a hero named Vane, who ascends upward from his library to a region that is the architectural equivalent of his own undiscovered consciousness, where he steps across a mirror that is also a door and into the enduring province of romance.

The "elevated" nature of this entry resists comparison to the Romantic convention of an initial descent into the subconscious, though Vane's adventures, especially with Lilith herself, have the libidinal force and primal power routinely connected to personal nightmare. However, in comparison with *The Princess and the Goblin* or "The Light Princess," with their subterranean threats, the "upward" thrust of this quest seems clear. And, as events unfold, the progress of this romance will ultimately prove a form of history *sub species aeternitatis*, an ascent towards vision.

2. MacDonald's first substantial literary work was a long poem, "Within and Without" (1855). The title serves as a motto for the pattern of Vane's adventures in the otherworld, which he will soon enter, then exit, then reenter and exit regularly throughout the romance. Vane himself is what Wayne Booth calls an "unreliable narrator," a guide the reader cannot depend upon to clarify much about the mysteries of the otherworld (159). Once across the mirror boundary, Vane has considerable trouble explaining both what he sees and what he thinks things mean. His principal difficulty is that in the otherworld "a single thing would sometimes seem to be and mean many things, with an uncertain identity at the heart of them, which kept constantly altering their look" (46). Part of the problem is linguistic, finding language for secondary-world events that correspond with primary-world phenomena or experience.[4] But the challenge is also one of perspective, since the otherworld is a place where mirrors are doors, where we die to live, where worms become birds, pigeons become prayers, and where, as the Raven puts it, the truth itself is a riddle (20–21, 26). And yet, if the hero's perceptions are uncertain, and the Raven is cryptic, the author remains very much at work, structuring the *topoi* of the otherworld, orchestrating the rhetoric of his romance to make the laws of the "little world" harmonious and meaningful. As Booth puts it, the author "cannot choose to disappear," and MacDonald — the ex-minister and author of 29 novels of spiritual education — remains deeply didactic, even in his fantasies (20). However, his mythology is larger and more mysterious than his doctrine; and to develop the unique rhetoric of this romance, he depends upon the *topoi* that surround the boundary moments.[5]

We can begin to get a sense for the relation between the two worlds and the implications of Vane's oscillations between them by reference to the long quotation from Thoreau's "Walking" that operates as an epilogue to *Lilith*. The passage deals with Thoreau's ambles through the woods of Concord where he senses the life of a family, the Spauldings, who had once resided there but have now vanished. And yet, "after a long and serious effort to recollect my best thoughts," Thoreau comments that he has become "again aware of their cohabitancy," their continued presence in the wood he now frequents (2–3). For Vane, his dual existence in two worlds suggests something of the same idea. After he returns home following one of his five visits to the otherworld, Vane wonders if two places can cohabit the same space, if they are "interpenetrating, yet unmingling?" (37). The Raven seems to corroborate this view when he says to Vane that, while it may seem as if they are walking in a pine forest (like that of the Spauldings), these woods actually inhabit the same space as Vane's own home. In fact, there is a tree in the secondary world that grows in the same space as Vane's kitchen chimney (23).

The original manuscript of *Lilith* was subtitled: "A Tale of the Seventh Dimension," a reference to the esoteric spiritualism of Jacob Boehme. For Boehme, there is no distinction between body and spirit, the physical and the divine, the latter inhabiting the same space as the former. In the first edition of *Lilith*, few references to multiple dimensions remain (21), but the concept of overlapping domains remains part of *Lilith*'s geography and metaphysics.[6] In his own effort to grasp the relation between the two worlds, Vane remarks, "I was in a world, or call it a state of things, an economy of conditions, an idea of existence, so little correspondent with the ways and modes of this world [i.e., the primary one], that the best choice I can make of word or phrase is but an adumbration of what I would convey" (12). In large part, his journey *is* the effort to understand the cohabitation of two worlds. A Platonic view would separate and organize the two hierarchically, with the primary world as a changeable and obscure "adumbration" of what is permanent and absolute in the abstract world of universal concepts. For Descartes, the division is between things inside the mind and those without, *res cogitans* and *res extensa*, the cognitive and the material dimensions of the world; and in his *Second Meditation*, he insists that the two are strictly separate. Cohabitation, on the other hand, assumes a very different frame of reference.

When Vane returns to the primary world for a second time, he enters his library through the bibliographic door. Moments later, at sunrise, the sun shines on the door and, like Anados, he discovers within it "a nest of drawers in a dark corner" filled with his father's papers (37). He carries these manuscripts into the library and reads his father's account of a meeting with Mr. Raven, the librarian, who tells Vane's father "of a certain relation of modes" between the worlds (38). Somewhat later, the Raven reappears through the magical door, and he and Vane's father venture together into the attic where there is a door "one step through which carries me into a world very much another than this," a world which is not better, per se, but which observes "mental laws different from those of this world" (40). The Raven gives Vane's father the same lecture on the paradox of "doors out" being "doors in" that he will give his son (cf. 13 and 40); he also adds that, like a library, there are "more worlds, and more doors" than one can possibly imagine (41). The point of transporting one's self from one world to the next is to experience an "economy of conditions" where the actual and the imaginative "intermingle," and, in the process, to liberate experience from routine assumptions by exposure to the marvelous. "If you understand any world besides your own," says the Raven, "you understand your own much better" (25). The fact that the two worlds are, according to Boehme and Thoreau, essentially the same, that the spiritual comprehends the local, that the secondary world is an anagogic vision of the primary one, this cohabitation allows the hero to learn through experience what books alone have been unable to teach.

Several paragraphs before the passage cited in the epilogue, Thoreau notes, "I live a sort of border life, on the confines of a world into which I make occasional and transient forays only" (627). Vane too is a regular traveler across the border. These routine excursions are very different from the itinerary of Anados, who enters the otherworld, then wakes up from it three weeks later. Nor are such crisscrossings conventional to prose romance, though there are precedents, like Hoffman's *Golden Pot* or the serial adventures of Gulliver. The hero of MacDonald's *At the Back of the North Wind* (1871) makes an early visit to the otherworld, to which he sadly returns in the end. But Vane crosses the border five times, in various ways, sometimes by choice, sometimes not. MacDonald is clearly tampering with convention; and while the visits may seem to begin and end at random, the regularity of these passages is a rhetorical strategy, a trope that says something about our relation to the otherworld.

In a word, the passage between the two worlds is routine because the boundaries between the two worlds, like the borders between states, are fundamentally artificial. The distinction between the self and the spirit, body and mind, inside and outside, intellect and imagination — these dualisms are constructs, something we invent. In *Lilith*'s geography, dualisms cohabit the same space, so Vane can cross over into the otherworld using various means because the boundary between the two is imaginary (as opposed to imaginative). Indeed, the burden of romance is to breach the boundary, to get the hero on the other side, where something out of the ordinary might happen that makes a difference in the primary world. In the first edition of *Lilith*, MacDonald subtitles the story simply "A Romance." The progress of conventional romance transports the hero into an imaginary space where he or she is exempt from the customary restraint of the real world and can learn something that can be brought back when the adventures are over. If the boundary is a construct, then we can routinely pass into an imaginative state that allows us to see differently, to extend our vision, even perhaps unify our allegiances. The boundaries may be artificial, the Raven may be able to transport himself at will, but Vane has yet to learn how to make best use of his access to enchantment. The first time he enters the otherworld, he flees because it is confusing, the second time because he is frightened. So, while Vane may know how to go back and forth, he does not know how to overcome the artificiality of the borders and forge a relationship between the two places, places that remain "interpenetrating, yet unmingling."

Indeed, Vane will never fully unify his vision; never break down the barriers between the imaginative and the actual. Like the heroes of more conventional romance, however, he does begin to sense that the otherworld journey has its benefits, as I will try to show shortly. But even in the end, the relationship between the two worlds is not a union; Vane will always return. And yet, the rhetoric of this romance is ultimately addressed to its readers, for whom it is possible to contemplate the relation between the diverse "laws" that govern the two worlds. The alternative to dualism is dialogue; thus I will now concentrate on the backend of the textual frame and consider, in particular, the dialogical potential of MacDonald's rhetoric and its implications for the development of prose romance.[7]

3. The last five chapters of *Lilith* constitute a reworking of the "mystic cycle of ascent," with its typological origin in the stories of Adam, Israel, and the Gospels (see *SSL* 210). This section culminates in a Pisgah vision, the equivalent of Moses's panoramic view of paradise seen from afar (Deut. 34.1–2). The reasons for stopping short of apotheosis are intimately connected with the textuality of the narrative frame; so to comprehend the close, we need to rehearse the main events briefly, then examine the *topoi* of the ending with care. In Chapter XLIII, "The Dreams that Come," Vane has begun the sleep that precedes the final awakening, though he is fully conscious and still fears the outcome of "dying into life." So, with considerable effort, he purposefully wakes himself, only to finds himself back in his garret, separated from those he has come to love and now desperate to return to the otherworld. Though he tries, the old portal mechanisms no longer work, but sleep eventually does; soon he wakes again in the secondary world, the "dark night of the soul" having given way to the sunrise of resurrection.

With Lona and the Little Ones, Vane begins to climb toward a "great city," perched on rocks, guarded by an angel. Having already risen a considerable distance, he arrives in sight of his goal and is prepared for the ultimate ascent, which each must undertake alone (247–50). As he struggles upward, these often cited, but still surprising events take place: "A hand, warm and strong, laid hold of mine and drew me to a little door with a golden lock. The door opened; the hand let mine go, and pushed me gently through. I turned quickly and saw the board of a large book in the act of closing behind me. I stood alone in my library" (250). I have already rehearsed the homology of books and doors, but to prepare for MacDonald's peroration, there is a bit more to say on the *topoi* of textuality.

As noted, the Raven explains the dialogical nature of doors twice, once to Vane (13) and years before to his father (40–41). With Vane he claims that doors are passages *into* a new world because they offer a way *out of* the confines of the self. The metaphoric identity of books with doors consequently argues that books too are dialogical, their discourse goes both ways. At the outset of his adventures, Vane had been unaware of the dialogics of reading. To extend the metaphors one step further, books had become only a mirror, a reflection of the reader's own image. Or worse, the library had become a catacomb of "dead bodies" because reading itself had become a form of vanity (30). In contrast, the Raven's metaphors are more hopeful in his conversation with Vane's father. He recalls having learned from Sir Upward about the passage through the library, up to the garret, where there is a door with a large lock and a small key (39). This is a door out, a door that is also a book, an open book into another world which a good reader can enter. Moreover, according to the "laws" of this "little world," the more you go out, the further you get in, the more doors you try, the wider your experience becomes. With these *topoi* in mind, we can turn to the question of keys.

Golden keys were hardly new additions to the rhetoric of the otherworld. MacDonald and his family had read *Alice's Adventures Underground* in manuscript and knew of its golden key into Wonderland. Two years later,

MacDonald's own characters, Mossy and Tangle, use "a golden key" to enter a rainbow that takes them to heaven. In "Comus" (1634), Milton mentions those who "by due steps aspire / To lay their hands on the Golden Key / That opes the Palace of Eternity" (ll.12–14). So golden keys open doors to coveted locations. Most interesting, however, is a reference attached to Blake's illustrations of Robert Blair's "The Grave" (1743), which MacDonald kept on the wall of his study (*MacDonald and His Wife* 554). In the verses that accompany these illustrations (referred to as "To the Queen"), Blake writes that

> The Door of Death is made of Gold,
> That mortal eyes cannot behold;
> And when the mortal eyes are closed,
> The soul awakes, and wond'ring sees
> In her mild hand the Golden Keys [471].

This time, the golden keys are intended to lock the door, because Blake, like MacDonald, believes that the gates of heaven are only open to those who have passed the "Door of Death." In the last chapters of *Lilith*, among the host who make the final ascent on the heavenly city, only Vane comes from the primary world, and only Vane has avoided the sleep of death. It comes as no surprise, then, that a golden key would lock the door on Vane. This holy portal is the door to a place from which there is no exit, nor any desire to leave. Indeed, the laws of this otherworld would not allow a living man to enter. Nor would Vane choose to do so if he could, as he has repeatedly shown. The Raven expounds at length on the statutes that govern these matters, but MacDonald relies principally on the rhetoric of prose romance — and on the unique *topoi* of textuality in particular — to articulate the imaginative implications of these closing events.

Vane clearly understands what has happened and why. He is not depressed by his rejection, nor does he seek the mirror or the magic door again. He feels confident that he has "not been the sport of a false vision!" (251). When he does question his own vision, Hope responds to him, just as Hopeful comforts Bunyan's Christian. Hope argues that dreams are divine in origin, that the brain is a violin made and played by God. MacDonald addresses the same issue in his essay "The Imagination: Its Function and Culture" (1867), in which he writes that the "imagination of man is made in the image of the imagination of God" and that "God sits in that chamber of our being in which the candle of our consciousness goes out in darkness, and sends forth from thence wonderful gifts into the light of that understanding which is His candle (*Orts* 3, 25)." If so, then Vane's adventures are indeed inspired; but assuming that they are the vision of "mortal eyes," there are limits to what even a visionary can see.

This discussion of dreaming contextualizes the famous quote from Novalis that concludes *Lilith*. But the last page of *Lilith* also includes a quotation from Job: "All the days of my appointed time will I wait till my change comes" (Job 14.14). In fact, Job prefaces this commitment to patience with his own reference to death; i.e., "If a man die, shall he live again? All the days of my appointed time will I wait...." By invoking Job, Vane expresses his own faith in the eventual arrival of the "endless ending" (cf. Hawkes).

But if Vane is content to wait, can we really say that *Lilith* fulfills the conventions of ascent? If he is separated from his loved ones and back in the primary world, can we reasonably call this quest a success? I think so. He has gone through the conventional cycle of departure, wandering, and return, like Odysseus, Dante, Sir Gawain, Christian, and Bilbo. He has been "farther in and higher up" than he ever imagined, and he has come home with a purposeful vision of life's journey. This is not resurrection; which is reserved for the dead. But he has been to Pisgah, and his ongoing life will be informed by that vision. Indeed, there are vestiges of this vision clearly at play in the primary world.

"Now and then [says Vane], when I look round on my books, they seem to waver as if a wind rippled their solid mass, and another world were about to break through" (251). Much earlier, as he is trying to decipher the copy in the mysterious book in the bookshelf door, he comments that "mere words" had the power to wake in him "spiritual sensations" and "great longing" (17). As we know, there are many doors to the otherworld, but books and words constitute special currency in the economy of *Lilith*. Like Sir Anados before him, it is discourse, *human discourse*, which allows Vane access to romance, vision, and transformation. Greville MacDonald calls books "doors ... into spiritual possibilities" (Introduction xix). Prior to the initiation of his own adventures, Vane treats books as inert objects, and the Raven describes such objects as a collection of corpses. What is it that makes the difference? What gives the library, its books and papers, their transcendental potential? Roland Barthes writes that the goal of literature is to turn the reader from a consumer into a producer of text, from an idle spectator into a coauthor, someone who inhabits the text like Thoreau and the Spauldings cohabit the Concord woods (4–5). By framing the quest romance as a bibliographic adventure, MacDonald makes the case for romance as an agent of transformation. When the reader is able to approach books as doors into another world, as dialogical opportunities to converse in a new key or rhythm, the possibility opens that he will understand his own world better. The goal of romance has always been to reimagine the world in such a way that it wakes readers up, prompts them to respond with engagement and sympathy, to interact with adventure as though it were their own. *De te fabula*.

For a long time, I have thought of *Lilith* as a *passage intérieur*: the story that structures the text is Vane's story, with the dominant portal as the mirror. We enter a world of reflected fears and desires, and we exit when the hero's refashioned identity is stable enough to survive. I have also thought about *Lilith* as MacDonald's story: the product of the ex-preacher whose persuasive strategies modify the conventions of the otherworld to proselytize his mystical ideology, a door into doctrine. But I also believe *Lilith* is a romance of textuality: an adventure into the process of scripting the limits of our desires in an idiom of ancient conventions. We do this because we cannot view the Celestial City directly; so we employ rhetoric's network of signs and strategies, tropes and figures as building blocks to shape a world in the image of our own imaging. In most cases, the story is the same: an epic journey up out of vanity and into vision, but we retell the story to ourselves in new ways commensurate with changing views of what we believe makes sense. *Lilith* adopts the time-honored rhetoric of the great quest, but it also acknowledges that the story is a book the reader enters, exits, and influences. In so doing, *Lilith* not only incorporates the linguistic turn of modern epistemology into the framework of romance, but also opens the interpretation of romance to the poetics of pluralism. MacDonald writes, "A genuine work of art must mean many things; the truer the art, the more things it will mean" (*Orts* 317). By imaging the quest as book, *Lilith* makes an historic contribution to the "progress of romance."[8]

Notes

1. Michael Mendelson, "George MacDonald's *Lilith*: The Conventions of Ascent." *Studies in Scottish Literature* 20 (1985). 197–218, hereafter *SSL*.

2. See Wolff 332, 369. Reis wonders if Vane is "running in circles" (131). Tolkien, who generally admires MacDonald's fantasies, refers to *Lilith* as a "partial failure" (26). Even Greville MacDonald expresses concern that the "intellectual drift [of *Lilith*] looks obscure" in his Introduction to the 1924 edition of *Lilith* (ix).

3. *Topoi* literally means "places"; *topos* is the singular. For rhetoric, *topoi* are strategies for the invention of content that will persuade readers to credit arguments.

4. See pages 14, 46–47, 65, 136–38, and 191. Given the complications of language in the otherworld, it seems appropriate that *Lilith* is also filled with riddles.

5. For a convenient synopsis of MacDonald's realistic fiction, see Reis, Ch. 6.

6. Boehme's cosmology posits an overlay of physical, psychological, and metaphysical principles that correspond with one another, point by point, so that the spiritual represents an anagogic interpretation of the material. Put another way, the universal comprehends the local reality (Edwards vol. 1, 328).

7. In my previous essay, I attempted to provide a comprehensive reading of the epic struggles that fill out Vane's journey and the contribution made by various episodes to the overall cycle of ascent (see *SSL* 202–13). To that account, I here add two brief notes about these middle episodes. First, Vane's adventures are dominated

by his contact with women. That is, in the course of the romance, Vane transfers his attention from a male-oriented obsession with *logos*, or formal logic, to pathetic or emotional knowledge, a development for which he is indebted almost entirely to Mara, Eve, Lona, even Lilith. Second, when we first meet Vane, he is not simply solitary, he is passive. When he asks the Raven how he should comport himself in the otherworld, his is told directly to do something (14). The structure of romance is in large part a pretext for adventure, a chance to prove one's self through action. In Vane's case, romance has the power to break the spell of solitary speculation and encourage him to operate as the agent of his own fate rather than simply an observer. Both female and pragmatic influences have a bearing on the closing events.

8. Clara Reeve's *Progress of Romance* (1785) was perhaps the first sustained critical appraisal of the genre in English.

Works Cited

Aristotle. "Poetics." *The Complete Works of Aristotle: Revised Oxford Translation*. Vol. 2. Ed. Jonathan Barnes. Princeton: Bollingen, 1984. 2316–40.
Barthes, Roland. *S/Z*. Trans. Richard Miller. New York: Hill and Wang, 1974.
Blake, William. *The Poetry and Prose of William Blake*. Ed. David V. Erdman. New York: Doubleday, 1965.
Bloom, Harold. "The Internalization of Quest Romance." In *Romanticism and Consciousness*. Ed. Harold Bloom. New York: Norton, 1970. 3–23.
Booth, Wayne. *The Rhetoric of Fiction*. Chicago: University of Chicago, 1961.
Brown, Norman O. *Love's Body*. New York: Random House, 1966.
Edwards, Paul. *Encyclopedia of Philosophy*. Vols. 1–2. New York: MacMillan, 1967.
Frye, Northrop. *The Secular Scripture*. Cambridge: Harvard University Press, 1976.
Hoffmann, E.T.A. *Tales from Hoffmann*. Ed. J. M. Cohen. London: Hazel, Watson, and Viney, 1950.
Liddell and Scott's Greek-English Lexicon. Rev. ed. Oxford: Oxford University Press, 1940.
MacDonald, George. *Dish of Orts*. London: Sampson, Low, and Martin, 1894.
⎯⎯⎯. *The Gifts of the Child Christ*. Vols. 1 and 2. Ed. Glenn Edward Sadler. Grand Rapids: Eerdmans, 1973.
⎯⎯⎯. *Phantastes and Lilith*. Ed. C.S. Lewis. Grand Rapids: Eerdmans, 1964.
⎯⎯⎯. *The Portent*. San Francisco: Harper and Row, 1974.
MacDonald, Greville. Introduction to *Lilith: A Romance*. London: Allen and Unwin, 1924. ix–xx.
⎯⎯⎯. *George MacDonald and His Wife*. London: Allen and Unwin, 1924.
McGillis, Roderick. "George MacDonald and the Lilith Legend in the XIXth Century." *Mythlore* 19 (1979): 3–11.
Mendelson, Michael. "George MacDonald's *Lilith*: The Conventions of Ascent." *Studies in Scottish Literature* 20 (1985): 197–218.
Murray, James. *New English Dictionary*. Oxford: Clarendon, 1988.
Novalis. *Heinrich von Ofterdingen*. Trans. Palmer Hilton. New York: Fredrick Ungar, 1964.
Patch, Howard. *The Other World: According to Descriptions in Medieval Literature*. New York: Octagon, 1950.

Reeve, Clara. The Progress of Romance. London: W. Keymer, Colchester. 1785.
Reis, Richard A. *George MacDonald*. New York: Twayne, 1972.
Rose, Christina Brooke. *The Rhetoric of the Unreal*. Cambridge: Cambridge University Press, 1981.
Sidney, Sir Philip. "An Apology for Poetry" in *Major Elizabethan Poetry and Prose*. Ed. James E. Ruoff, 235–81. New York: Thomas Crowell, 1972.
Thoreau, Henry David. *Walden and Other Writing*. New York: Modern Library, 1950.
Tolkien, J.R.R. "On Fairy Stories" in *The Tolkien Reader*, 3–86. New York: Ballantine, 1966.
Wimsatt, William K. and Cleanth Brooks. *Literary Criticism: A Short History*. New York: Knopf, 1969.
Wolff, Robert Lee. *The Golden Key: A Study of the Fiction of George MacDonald*. New Haven: Yale University Press, 1961.
Zimmer, Heinrich. *The King and the Corpse: Tales of the Soul's Conquest of Evil*. Princeton: Bollingen, 1948.

CHAPTER 4

Myth, Mysticism, and Magic: Reading at the Close of *Lilith*

Verlyn Flieger

It is an honor as well as a pleasure to be invited to respond to Robert A. Collins' essay (chapter 1), but it is something of a challenge as well, and I venture into the deep water with considerable hesitation. Bob is a fine MacDonald scholar, while I am not one at all. Consequently, I found his essay on liminality not just an education but a rather daunting one. My reading of it left me in a state of scholarly discouragement and with an alarming sensation of being in over my head. I hadn't read *Lilith* in years, I didn't know the criticism, and Bob's unpacking of the principles underlying Vane's return in terms of liminal theory was revelatory. I realized that elements in the novel I had not only accepted but indeed enjoyed and found most moving in their stubborn resistance to rational explication — in their very *mystery*— were precisely the things that Bob was engaging with most deeply. I realized further that if I were to respond, I must address precisely those areas where Bob and I most differ, in the ultimate impact of the reading experience.

So here goes.

The core of Bob's essay I take to be his statement that "whether we view the work as a quest fantasy or as pure mythopoesis, as Lewis insists, the anticlimactic 'return' of the ending demands explanation." I wonder. Quest fantasy is not incompatible with "pure mythopoesis," even in Lewisian terms, but however viewed, the "demand" of the ending for explanation coupled with the book's failure to provide this, may in fact be not just MacDonald's strategy, but his ultimate point. Bob is entirely right in engaging with the problem, for any serious and committed reading of the book will have to come to grips with Vane's return and its implications. But his engagement may be self-defeating in its attempt to answer a demand which could finally be rather a provocation, and which may be in place deliberately to encourage, or even to force a more intuitive, less rational response.

Of all the mysteries in *Lilith*, none is more of a mystery in the literal sense (that is, in dictionary terms as something that "arouses curiosity because it is unexplained, inexplicable, or secret") than the return of Mr. Vane to his library in the penultimate chapter. As a punch-line, it is bound to be a disappointment to readers who, carried rather high with the impetus of MacDonald's at once soaring and deeply mythic imagination, come back to earth, or more particularly to Vane's library, with a thud. The failure to sustain the tension produces neither bang nor whimper, but an almost physical let-down, an apparent fizzle, a damp squib. As an ending, it demands, as Bob declares, an explanation, yet by its inconclusiveness it frustrates the very need it arouses.

But mysteries, when they are explained, cease at once to be mysteries and become mere solved puzzles, and it is well to remember that this never happens with *Lilith*. It may puzzle, tease, frustrate, even infuriate, but it does not devolve. The magic remains; the aura is not dispelled. Rolland Hein's suggestion of "narrative plausibility," in which "the return completes the narrative frame," is practical but simply avoids the whole question by addressing structure instead of meaning, and Bob quite rightly finds this inadequate. The external relevancies to MacDonald's creative life that Bob cites and also dismisses — the fascination with old libraries, heretical religion and spiritual evolution, the mix of Darwinian progress with German Romanticism with Freud and compartmented psyche, not to mention Jung and archetypes — offer little further help in getting to the heart of the puzzle.

Nor do the more myth-oriented paradigms that he offers but also finds wanting, among them Campbell's admittedly circular hero journey, and Farah Mendlesohn's portal fantasies. These may explicate, but they fail to illuminate. Parsing *Lilith* as a quest story and/or hero journey in Campbellian terms, if only "up to a point" will work as analysis, for the pattern is more than plain to see. It is, as Bob points out, "inexplicably repeated at least three times, and the journey appears unproductively circular." The hero is supposed to come back with something more than he had when he started, and Bob's point that unlike the archetypal hero, Mr. Vane perceives his returns as misfortunes, seems to rule that one out. But finally, the "point" is passed, and the journey concept proves less than satisfactory, leading Bob to conclude that, "as a quest story, then, the narrative fails."

But success or failure in conforming to a paradigm, even so universal a one as Campbell's hero path, may not be the only applicable criterion by which to judge. Moreover, it is worth remembering that the path of the hero exists in all its variants, not in any conformity to a pre-determined road map. And among the variants, as Campbell himself points out, are included the hero's failure in any one of several areas. He can (1) return without a boon, or (2) not return at all, or (3) return but be unable to fit in. Frodo Baggins is the best-known illustration of these in modern mythopoeic literature. Moreover, such attempts to fit art to an external standard address themselves, perforce, to the visible structure rather than to the underlying meaning. They are less useful in penetrating what is, after all, a mystery, something unexplained or inexplicable.

So much for Campbell. But Mendlesohn's description of "portal fantasies" does not fully account for *Lilith* either. If, as she maintains, portal fantasies are two-way passages in that individuals can cross back and forth, but one-way in that the magic does not, then *Lilith* escapes this paradigm as well. As Bob points out, its magic can — and does — pass the door in either direction. Indeed, words such as "return" and "portal" may be themselves problematic terms, since in *Lilith* the experiences can occur on both sides of the door. The half book glued to the sham bookshelf on the closet door is whole when Raven takes it out.

Of all the theoretical approaches offered, Bob's choice of liminality, using the anthropologically derived definitions and terms of Turner and Spariosu, seems to save the appearances most economically. Liminality locates the experience of passage in the middle, in the no place and no time poised between the worlds — a threshold occurrence of, "pure potentiality, when everything trembles in the balance." According to Spariosu, liminal worlds are indeterminate ontological landscapes located in between alternate worlds that are, in Spariosu's term, "incommensurate." This occurs, says Spariosu, when the reference frames of alternate worlds are not translatable in each other's terms.

The apparent contradiction, where the discrepancy is in the eye of the beholder, not in the appearances themselves, is the essence of the experience. Mr. Raven's world and Vane's world are "incommensurate" in Vane's eyes, although for Raven they occupy the same space at the same time. The pine tree in the forest in Mr. Raven's world "stands on the hearth of [Vane's] kitchen and grows nearly straight up its chimney" (22), and the tall palm in the courtyard of Lilith's palace in Bulika ends in a fountain on the lawn of Vane's estate (139). Is there a threshold between these worlds, a moment of pure potentiality when everything trembles in the balance? Not necessarily.

We might turn for analogy to any of those visual puzzles that tease the viewer with their ability to be two things at once but not to be seen simultaneously as both. One example is the well-known line drawing of a roundish shape with a narrowly elliptical protuberance. Facing one way, the outline looks like a duck with a projecting bill. Facing the opposite way, it becomes a rabbit with long ears. Is it a duck or a rabbit? It is at once both and either. But not, in the gaze of the viewer, both at the same time. The puzzle resides in the viewer's inability to process, not the drawing's ability to be. The threshold, if there is one, is within the viewer, not between the worlds.

At this point it would be well to remember that MacDonald was, in the words of William Raeper, "first and foremost a Scot, and more than that, a Highlander and a Celt" (15). That last word is a reminder that an imaginative legacy to MacDonald from generations of Celtic forebears might well have been the capacity to acknowledge mutually contradictory realities without trying to decide between them. This capacity accepts, as in the case of the duck and the rabbit, the possibility of "both and" instead of insisting on "either or." For it is the very nature of the Celtic myths and the Celts who made them that they prefer paradox to contradiction, that they can hold in tension things mutually incompatible and deal matter-of-factly with mystery, embracing without needing to explain that which is inexplicable.

Keeping in mind MacDonald's Celtic heritage, it is not impossible to imagine that in this vision, the apparently "incommensurate" double reality of the tree in the forest and in the chimney, intended to be an unsolved mystery both to Vane and (surely intentionally) to the reader, MacDonald was invoking earlier, equally Celtic expressions of a similar nature, expressions in which such a double reality would have been precisely the point. This sublime disregard for apparent reality, the recognition of contradiction as paradox to be accepted rather than interrogated, is a hallmark of much of the early Celtic mythic literature.

An example is the Irish poem, *Voyage of Bran*, in which Manannán, lord of the otherworld, addresses the voyager Bran in words that, according to Proinsias MacCana, "express vividly the inversion of reality which characterizes the otherworld vision" (72). Here is a representative passage:

> It seems to Bran a wondrous beauty
> in his curragh on a clear sea;
> while to me in my chariot from afar
> it is a flowery plain on which I ride.
>
> What is a clear sea
> for the prowed craft in which Bran is,
> is a Plain of Delights with profusion of flowers
> for me in my two-wheeled chariot.

Bran sees

> A host of waves breaking across the clear sea;
> I myself see in Magh Mon
> red-tipped flowers without blemish.

> Speckled salmon leap from the womb
> of the white sea on which you look;
> they are calves, they are bright-coloured lambs,
> at peace without mutual hostility

And particularly apposite to the tree in Vane's chimney, the following double vision of Bran's boat on the sea yet sailing across the top of a wood:

> It is along the top of a wood
> that your tiny craft has sailed across the ridges,
> a beautiful wood with its harvest of fruit
> under the prow of your little boat.
> A wood with blossom and fruit
> and on it the true fragrance of the vine;
> a wood without decay or death,
> with leaves the colour of gold [MacCana 72].

The images in the poem are not parallel but incompatible realities with a door between them, but overlapping, co-existing, and uncompeting perceptions occupying the same space and the same time. So it is with the sea and the wood, and so it is with the tree and Vane's chimney.

Might it not be possible that the apparent failure of Vane's return to match up to the mythopoesis (in Lewis's use of that term as "the real universe, the divine, magical, terrifying and ecstatic reality in which we all live") of the rest of the novel and thus to accommodate critical explication, is more a function of the theories applied to it than of the work itself? It is worth remembering that in literature as in life, theory arises out of practice, not the other way round. Freud, Jung, Lewis, Campbell, Mendlesohn, even Turner and Spariosu, construct their theories from the observable phenomena, whether related dreams, or written texts, or observed or reported tribal rites of passage. These authorities are describing, not prescribing, and the felt experience of the phenomena will — indeed must if they are to be effective — transcend the description. If MacDonald's work doesn't conform when measured against their descriptions, it may be the descriptions themselves that are wanting, and not MacDonald's work.

William Raeper, a MacDonald biographer (but not the one cited by Bob, Rolland Hein), said no more than the simple truth when he commented that *Lilith* "is not an easy book to read" (364). This puts it in good company. A survey of some of the great works of spiritual fantasy — Dante's *Comedia*, David Lindsay's *A Voyage to Arcturus*, Chrétien de Troyes' *Perceval*— will show that none of them is an easy book to read. Each in its own way demands that the reader yield completely to the power of the story, entering it and experiencing it rather than remaining outside it and thus critical and analytical.

Each in its own way is compelling precisely because it eludes analysis and defies vivisection. These works are mysteries in the truest sense of the word, and their power lies in their ability to engage the reader at the feeling rather than the intellectual level. So it is with *Lilith*.

Raeper's take on the "return" motif is that the book, which begins, in his words, with "MacDonald's [NB not Vane's] very last visit to a library," explores Vane's "journey to self-knowledge." His comment that "MacDonald expects his readers to identify themselves with Vane and so become heroes of their own tale" would seem to suggest that we all wind up where we started, in the library. And that this is no accident, nor is it unfitting: "Back with his books, it appears that Vane has come full circle, but not quite — for now he is not sure whether his experience in the other world was a dream or whether he is still asleep in the House of Death and the library is but a dream: 'Now and then, when I look round on my books, they seem to waver as if a wind rippled their solid mass, and another world were about to break through'" (Raeper 328).

Finally, and in this context, we might inquire if Mr. Vane's own perception of his returns as misfortunes is a trustworthy one. He doesn't seem to be very bright (though in his defense, he has not read *Lilith*), and he responds to Mr. Raven with more indignation than understanding. Is Vane a reliable narrator? Raeper's answer would seem to be "no." Vane is not the best judge of his own experience. He is still not fully awake. He is still in process, still on the journey, and we are left with Bob's conclusion that even liminality "fails to solve the mythopoeic problem," to answer the question, "what is the mythic significance of the 'endless ending'? This ending does not seem to most serious readers to mirror what they already know of MacDonald's religious beliefs. In fact, it communicates an air of didactic failure on some level, though the failure is perhaps as likely to be that of its readers as of its author." What I am arguing here is that there are two assumptions which are at least open to question. The first assumption is that there is a mythopoeic problem that needs to be solved. The more myth is addressed as problem, as something not just open to but requiring a solution, the less mythopoeic it becomes. Thus to solve the apparent problem may be to undermine its intended effect. The second assumption is that what "serious readers" already know of MacDonald's religious beliefs is all there is to know, and that if the ending doesn't match what is "known," it is the ending that must be at fault and not the extent of the knowledge.

In this context, the "didactic failure" is only a failure if you are expecting didacticism, and Bob's observation that the failure is "as likely to be that of its readers as of its author" is his final and best comment on the whole issue. MacDonald's theology, as Raeper points out, was "tinged with both mysticism and magic" (257), and his work is strongest when these supersede didacticism to imply rather than state. *The Princess and the Goblin* is a far more powerful and evocative work than its sequel, *The Princess and Curdie*, precisely because, in the former, the message is implied rather than stated. The enchantment is not broken through by didacticism. *The Princess and Curdie*, in contrast, is all message; consequently, there is no enchantment to be broken through. Raeper's final understanding of the ending of *Lilith*, an understanding with which I am in complete sympathy, is that,

> Vane is left to wake into that greater reality which will be his Home. The title of the final chapter of the book, "The Endless Ending," shows how this process of change and appropriation must be a constant one. Vane finally occupies two places at once—the couch in the House of Death and the library. He is always arriving, always waiting, always learning—just as the reader must go on pondering [NB not solving] the meaning of the myth and absorb it into his psyche [382].

The essence of myth is to be inexplicable in rational terms. The less it yields itself to analysis, the more mythopoeic it is, and the more effective and compelling it becomes.

WORKS CITED

MacCana, Proinsias. *Celtic Mythology*. London: The Hamlyn Publishing Group Limited, 1970.
MacDonald. George. *The Visionary Novels of George MacDonald*. Ed. Anne Fremantle. New York: The Noonday Press, 1954.
Raeper, William. *George MacDonald*. Tring: Lion Publishing, 1987.

CHAPTER 5

The Logic of Fantasy and the Crisis of Closure in *Lilith*

Colin Manlove

Robert A. Collins is not the first to find (chapter 1) the ending of *Lilith* something of a jolt; but he is unusual in finding no explanation for it. Robert Lee Wolff for instance felt that Mr. Vane was "cruelly frustrated.... MacDonald has turned him back at the throne of the Lord Himself" (370), and concluded that this showed how for MacDonald "something had gone wrong with Christianity" (371). For Richard Reis, however, "perhaps the most striking attribute of *Lilith* is the fact that, at the end, its narrator has *not* attained ultimate transcendence"; but, in reply to Wolff, he says, "It is clear that MacDonald is advocating acceptance of *both* life and death, the latter as the God-given if bitter way to enlightenment and salvation" (102). Following Roderick McGillis, William Raeper takes a more "postmodernist" view, seeing the divine nature as being such that the narrative of *Lilith* cannot conclude, cannot arrive at an infinite objective, and must be a continual "becoming," an "Endless Ending" as MacDonald terms the last chapter of the book: "Vane fully occupies two places at once — the couch in the House of Death and the library. He is always arriving, always waiting, always learning — just as the reader must go on pondering the meaning of the myth and absorb it into his psyche" (382). David Robb by contrast sees MacDonald as sending Vane back because he is unable adequately to imagine the state of death (106–08).

This generally acknowledged jolt at the end of *Lilith* cannot be dismissed as a blunder of MacDonald's, for it is present as the conclusion to the story right from *Lilith A* onwards: other things he revised, but not this. And if he meant his conclusion, he also meant the shock it gives; and therefore he meant us to think about what it might portend. Quite *what* we think depends on us, as these very different readings show. As MacDonald says, "Everyone ... who feels the story, will read its meaning after his own nature and development: one man will read one meaning in it, another will read another" ("The Fantastic Imagination" 316). This is not just pure subjectivity, for each is seeing something that the work gives him or her: "A genuine work of art must mean many things; the truer its art, the more things it will mean" (317). By a "genuine work of art" MacDonald means one that directly or indirectly draws on the divine nature, and hence must be as infinite in capacity as its source. Here it is relevant that MacDonald is said to have believed that his writing of *Lilith* had been "a mandate direct from God" (Greville MacDonald 548).

Unlike the other commentators, Bob Collins does not find any answer to his sense of disturbance at *Lilith*'s conclusion. He looks to Joseph Campbell's pattern of the mythic quest and finds only disagreement; he feels that *Lilith* does not fit Farah Mendlesohn's concept of "portal fantasies"; and even his adoption of Mihai Spariosu's notion of "liminal space" to describe the ontology of the Region of the Seven Dimensions quite fails to overcome his sense of disjunction at Vane's exclusion from heaven. If we have been made to see Vane as "improving" during the narrative, he feels, how can we not feel it discordant that he is refused his reward along with others such as Lilith?

The problem with Bob Collins's approach is that he is continually looking to some external pattern into which to fit *Lilith*. He wants to see its peculiarities as being underwritten by some general anthropological or literary schema to which it belongs. But he does not direct his attention sufficiently to *Lilith* itself, and how its own inherent nature may determine its ending. Further, he is looking for fixity of explanation, whereas *Lilith* is essentially hostile to fixity, both as a sign of selfishness and as a false picture of a fluid divine universe.

What I want to do here is show how a whole range of explanations for its ending, not always consistent with each other, is suggested by *Lilith* itself. And the first point to remember about *Lilith* is that it is a dream and a vision, from which at the end the hero Vane awakes. Vane, whose bookish mind is already detached from the world, and who has told us of "the metaphysical dreams into which I was in the habit of falling," begins his journey from the library of his house in the evening, after a day spent reading. In short, he is to be seen as being asleep and dreaming; that is, he has entered his imagination. He is in his own imagination throughout, while at the same time being in the imagination of God; and his journey marks a deepening penetration of this inner territory. He sees a long-dead librarian pass, and follows him up to the attics of the house, symbol for MacDonald of the unconscious (as with the attics of the "Curdie" books). There he finds a huge mirror which, rather than obeying the physical laws of this world and reflecting back the material surroundings about it, instead portrays another country, which is an image of Vane's soul. His passage through the mirror marks his entrance into his inner territory.

Vane can then be seen as traversing a series of symbols of his inner life — self-giving in the shape of Mr. Raven (whom he refuses), infantile urges in the form of the Little Ones, boorish materialism in the gross forms of the Bags, distorted values in the warring armies of the Evil Wood, and then the all-devouring self-love of Lilith, before which he is passive. After this educational tour through his merely human and often bestial unconscious, Vane is increasingly alert to the spiritual promptings that he at first ignored, symbolized in Mr. Raven and his wife, and in Mara, the Lady of Sorrows. He sets out a second time on the same journey, and this time he opposes the more "secular" urges of his mind by helping to overthrow the Bags, who before captured him, and securing the capture of Lilith. Later he drowns the monsters of his own evil imagination in the Bad Burrow by releasing the long-hidden waters of his soul.[1]

This journey of Vane through his own spirit ends when he yields up his resistant self altogether by at last accepting the injunction of Mr. Raven that he lay himself down to sleep in the underground house of the dead. Dying and becoming unconscious are metaphors for one another, and when Vane is fully dead, he will have reached the deepest levels of his unconscious mind, where God makes His home in man, "in the very roots of his own being" (*Life Essential* 24).[2] He will have come to the end of the dream: he will be fully awake. Then he can approach heaven; but because he is mortal, his waking must for the time be in his own world. He returns in a Platonic descent back again from mental to material existence.

That is one way of looking at the inner dynamic of *Lilith* and its conclusion. By its light, if we feel a jolt when Vane is sent back to this world, that is because we are seeing the region of the seven dimensions as a real other world like Narnia or Middle-earth, and not as the world in Vane's mind. In a sense we will find ourselves judged as materialists in the same way that Vane is by Mr. Raven at the outset of his story. For those who read aright, MacDonald says in his 1893 essay on "The Fantastic Imagination" (and they are mostly the child-like), the true other country is both material and spiritual, inner and outer, at once. Vane wakes from what is both dream and truth.

However, it is just as possible to read the end of *Lilith* in opposite, non-evolutionary terms. For instance, when Vane is journeying towards his heaven, his description can seem curiously inept compared to the vividness with which he has earlier described Lilith or Bulika or the Bad Burrow or the underground dormitory. MacDonald says that all pictures of heaven and God are by definition inadequate (*Unspoken Sermons* 441, 451), but inadequacy is not the same thing as ineptitude. Vane falls to quotations from Dante, becomes linguistically frenzied, allows the most dreadful indecorums to Christ ("'Ou's all mine's, 'ickle ones: come along" [248]), and at length describes God as sitting somewhere on a mountain in the midst of a damp cloud. The last is so poor an account of heaven, making it a small-seeming part of the geography of the region of the seven dimensions, that even the most benighted of readers can realize that we are not seeing heaven itself so much as Vane's weak picture of it. And that picture is so inadequate, because as a man not yet dead Vane cannot grasp it, and therefore cannot yet enter it — and even then would not, as creature rather than creator, be able fully so to do (*Life Essential* 56). Or, in more empirical terms, on the verge of a consummation he is unable to imagine or dream, Vane wakes up.

But in MacDonald's view, it is not just Vane who does the dreaming. Vane himself is also dreamt by God. Or as one of his characters once put it, "I do not dream dreams: the dreams dream me" (*David Elginbrod* 3: 194). This is what is suggested to Vane at the end by Hope: "When a man dreams his own dream, he is the sport of his dream; when Another gives it him, that Other is able to fulfil it" (251). In this sense his dream is not only a dream, but a granted vision. Man, for MacDonald, is a thought in the mind of God, an imagining, like the whole world itself, out of His grand imagining: "man is rather *being thought* than *thinking*, when a new thought arises in his mind" ("The Imagination" 5). In this sense God is presenting Vane with an analysis of his soul and a spiritual route map for his salvation. Once Vane approaches the goal of his spiritual journey, he has been shown enough, and the vision can be ended. Here of course it will be significant that it is not Vane who ends his dream, but rather a hand which leads him through the cloudy skirts of heaven and puts him back through a door into his own world.

A similarly more objective pattern can be seen when we consider the region of the seven dimensions as what it also is, a landscape through which all dead souls must move, a vision of purgatory itself. The Queen of Hell, Lilith, is here not just a part of Vane's soul only, but of all men and women, who if they would find salvation must open their own grasping hands to be rid of her. The underground dormitory which is the focus of the book's spiritual direction is filled with people who have been there for differing lengths of time dependant on their spiritual conditions. When they are spiritually "ripe," they wake. In this context Vane is effectively an observer, and when he has seen all that is necessary to his mortal benefit, he can be returned to describe it. And this description will be like the half-book that in the world of the seven dimensions is found to be whole: it will help to take us from this world to a larger one, and from a text half-understood to one that will reveal the truth.

There remain more formal possible explanations of the ending. One is that, as Vane himself thinks, he may not actually have returned home at all, but simply be dreaming that he has, while still asleep on his purgatorial couch in the underground dormitory in the strange land. After all, he has already returned home twice during his dream-adventure: first, when Lilith uses him to draw her into his own world (138–39), and later, more significantly, when he is asleep on the dormitory couch itself (236). But were this argument true about Vane dreaming his return, we would also have to suppose that he dreamt himself writing this book, and every one of his readers down to the present day perusing it.[3]

It can also be argued that MacDonald's use of two worlds, however bilocal he makes them, makes it necessary for Vane to return to his own. For if he goes to heaven from the region of seven dimensions, we are left out of it — and relating Vane's adventures to human experience is one of MacDonald's prime aims as a Christian. This does not happen with "The Golden Key," where much of the landscape through which the children move is "this world," which then with their deaths simply continues as the next world. A similar situation obtains with one of MacDonald's favorites, *Pilgrim's Progress*, where the strange country that Christian journeys through figures this life, and we can readily translate his experience into what should be our own. Seen thus, Vane has to come back, not merely to relate his story, but to relate to us as people living a life without the kind of spiritual certainty and unambiguous holy promise that permeates the world beyond the mirror.

More widely, it can be argued that in putting Vane back in the library from which he started his adventures, *Lilith* is doing no more than what many fantasies do — coming full circle (Manlove, *Impulse* ch. 5; cf. Mendelson 214). Thus, in other fantasies, Alice finds herself out of Wonderland and back on the bank with her sister, Frodo and Sam come back to the Shire, and C.S. Lewis's Ransom is returned to earth after his cosmic adventures. Such fantasies are not without their own disappointment at resumed mortality: the magic is past and Frodo must leave for the Undying Lands; the children return to school from Narnia, Christopher Robin must bid farewell and grow up. But it is still different with *Lilith*, for in other books the hero has the reward of his victory, whether now or to come, whereas in *Lilith* the reward is at once proffered and abruptly removed. There is no closure before we are returned to the beginning and to our own reality. MacDonald in *Lilith* gives us two incomplete endings: Vane is denied bliss at the moment he thought to have it, and back on earth he can only wait and hope for a future now veiled from him.

Lilith may also be seen as an example of the class of subversive fantasies, which undermine beliefs, vanities, bigotries, and all complacencies of the human mind (Manlove, *Scottish Fantasy* 4–5, 245–56; *The Fantasy Literature of England* ch. 7). We can see this in the way that Vane's assumptions about the world are undercut by Mr. Raven's riddles, by the mixture of love and disdain with which Lilith treats him, by his not knowing throughout whether his experiences are real or a dream, and in his continual movement from one mental place and people to another. But such subversiveness would not seem appropriate to someone on the verge of reaching his heavenly reward. This, however begs the question: was he?

To answer this, let us first look at the ways in which Vane might seem to have deserted heaven. The ending of *Lilith* is most problematic for Bob Collins because of his sense that Vane does not deserve it, that he has so progressed that he should be rewarded like the others, not thrust back down into our world. It is he after all who helps destroy the threat of the Bags, leads the Little Ones out of their narrow home and with their help overcomes and captures Lilith; he too, who at the end journeys to restore water to the wasted land. He is not like Dante, or the narrator of the Middle-English *Pearl*, or like C.S. Lewis's narrator in *The Great Divorce*, a mere onlooker in the Christian hereafter: he actually participates in this society and changes it (even if what he is changing is in one sense all himself). He is indeed permitted to be a kind of savior. And at the end he at last obeys Adam and lies down to sleep the purgatorial sleep with the others. Here it can feel rather like landing on the long chute down at number 98 on the *Chutes and Ladders* board just when one is poised to reach 100.

Continuing this picture of Vane getting better and better, there is a pattern in the narrative that seems to move from subversiveness to assurance, and from an enclosed to an opened mind. Vane follows Mr. Raven from the closed library up to the house attics which, via the mirror, open on a new and wide world, a wilderness compared to the ordered civility of the library. Once there, he finds that he has lost his sense of self, and even the knowledge of his own name (13–14). He is faced by a whole series of spiritual paradoxes uttered by Mr. Raven which confound his mind and effectively overthrow his intellect. Further, his narrow conceptions of time and space are blown away by his being told that he is in a world of seven, not three, dimensions, that time there moves at a different speed from his own, and that this strange world is coincident with his own. Mr. Raven also removes Vane's categories of "matter" and "spirit" by showing him a prayer in the form of a dove. Faced by the flexible ontology of this world, Vane finds even the range of his language unable to express or contain it in the medium of fixed referents (45). By this point he has lost all his bearings, and like Lear wanders the madness of his own unconscious in the landscape of the strange world.

This deconstruction of Vane's old self can be seen as part of his moral development, taking him into a wider spiritual world. As this begins to happen, he learns Mr. Raven's true name, Adam, and also that of Lilith. Thereafter, this former dabbler in metaphysics begins to perceive the true metaphysical nature of the universe. At first the passive victim of all he sees, captured by the Bags, blood-sucked by a giant leech and enslaved by the Queen of Bulika, he later comes to deal with them, and follows the same journey a second time, this time with purpose, and with success. At first clinging to his old self and past values, he is drawn to the arch self-preserver Lilith, Adam's first wife. But later he aligns himself with Adam, here the New Adam, who lives by the future rather than the past, and by a continual dying out of self.[4] In the end Vane chooses to surrender choice, by pursuing the task assigned to him of restoring water to the parched land, and by lying down to sleep in the great dormitory of the dead — till he wakes to the boundlessness of God's love.

That is the sequence: and if this sequence were all there was, then one would have to see the ending as discrepant — an unfair thrusting back of this expanded soul into the narrow room and doubt-shrouded world from which he began. But in fact much of the business of Vane's self-improvement is deeply compromised by the fact that he was asked not to do it. He was supposed to lie down and let God look after his and others' improvement. In any case, Mr. Raven regarded him as being unfit to help others, and said, "you will do [the Little Ones] other than good if you go" (158). Vane could have saved himself his entire painful story if he had simply obeyed Mr. Raven in the first place: all his action, and indeed the entire plot of *Lilith* was from this point of view a waste of time.[5] (Curiously though, when Vane agrees to lie down in the house of the dead, he is told he must first go out and do something — bury Lilith's hand in the desert.) Of course, most readers will instinctively prefer Vane's adventures and eventually helpful actions to the notion of sleeping and dreaming one's way to betterment (Robb 105–06). And in that sense the book divides our sympathies: for in adventuring rather than "doing nothing" Vane is putting his own wishes before God's.

Nor do we as readers always feel as much spiritual change in Vane as might be imputed to him (Hein 111). Quite late in his journey, for instance, he tells us that he intends to make Lona Queen of Bulika with himself as consort; and that he is planning a trade in gems between the strange world and his own: here supposedly banished greed and materialism return. Even when he has arrived at an acute sense of his past sins in his sleep in Adam's dormitory, Vane thinks to repent for them by doing things rather than by asking and accepting forgiveness, and by an excessive prostration that can seem like evasion:

> I was the eager slave of all whom I had ... anyhow wronged. Countless services I devised to render them! For this one I would build such a house as had never grown from the ground! For that one I would train such horses as had never been seen in any world! For a third I would make such a garden as had never bloomed, haunted with still pools, and alive with running waters! [231].

There is little sense of the people he has sinned against as individuals, no awareness of what sin is being atoned, only of Vane accomplishing amazing feats of restitution (for which perhaps he will be celebrated). Earlier, when Vane claims to Adam that he must ride off to rescue the Little Ones before he can obey the injunction to sleep, he is similarly inaccurate, for he is really longing to have a gallop on the horse that Adam has let him bestride — a horse which, when he does ride off on it, becomes the symbol of his uncontrolled passions and eventually dies under him (155–59).

Another alien element is Vane's persistently sexual attitude towards women — natural no doubt in a young man, but we are beyond nature here. He first shows this proclivity in his enthrallment to the vamp Lilith — but later he is supposed to have put all that behind him. Yet he is clearly passionately in love with Lona as a woman; and it is she that he feels cut off from at the end as much as from heaven (where we are told all human love is transferred from one another to God [229]). Even as Vane is about to lie down in the holy dormitory, he is still prepared to flirt with Eve, when he tells her he will obey the trial she will ask of him "[b]ecause you require it" (220). For all that the pattern and implicit narrative of *Lilith* portend in terms of Vane's spiritual education, he himself does not always evince much sign of it.

And here one would mention too the way in which Vane continues to talk like a university graduate and an intellectual throughout — and this despite supposedly having had his intellect overthrown. His dominant note throughout is one of doubt, unlike Anodos in *Phantastes*, who hopes always. So while Vane is journeying into wilder and stranger regions of his own unconscious, he yet maintains the guise of a skeptical rationalist: "Surely reason was the same in every world, and what reason could there be in going to sleep with the dead, when the hour was calling the live man?" (154–55). We have little sense of a new man in the way that he thinks and speaks, still less of shame at his failures, or of love for others. He can sometimes talk like someone who has had development conferred upon him as much as undergoing it.

Most of all, there is little sense through all Vane's adventures that he has actually come to understand the true nature of the metaphysics with which he previously dabbled. Though at the end we find him propounding to an old man barred from Adam's dormitory the very sorts of riddles that previously baffled him — "no one can die who does not long to live"— the old man retorts: "It ill becomes your youth to mock a friendless old man. Pray, cease your riddles" (225). And indeed we are left wondering just how much Vane understands of what he says. A little later, when he doubts the reality of his dreams in the house of death, Adam tells him, "Thou doubtest because thou lovest the truth" (234). We do not feel he is altogether describing the Vane we know, and we may recall the very different opinion Adam had of the doubting Vane's earlier refusals to lie down in the house of death.

A crucial point is when Vane, having witnessed Lilith's transformation by Adam, Eve and Mara, suddenly announces his readiness to follow the same course (229). Little in Vane's feelings has prepared us for this. He may have done some of the right things, associating himself with Mara and returning to Adam and Eve's cottage, bringing Lilith to repentance; but from the time of his intense regret for his rash incursion into Lilith's throne room and her killing of Lona, our attention is for a long time directed at Lilith, and Vane and his spiritual life are forgotten. That is, unless we see Lilith's conversion as somehow including Vane's; but, given that we are made strongly aware of her as a particular subject with a special history and significance for the whole world of the seven dimensions, and given too that we are continually made no less aware of Vane and the others looking at her torments from outside, this is hard to do.

Thus, looked at from the point of view of Vane having developed towards spiritual insight and perfection of soul, the sending of him back to this world at the end of *Lilith* feels like an inconsistency; but considered from the standpoint of how Vane himself and his supposed development come over to us, it is more acceptable, the shutting out of someone not yet ready for heaven. The book does not leave us with one or the other, and effectively gives us two "un-endings": the one where Vane is on the point of entering heaven and meeting God, and the other where, back in this world, trapped again in his mortality, he must continually oscillate between doubt and hope.

Why is this? Is there anything in MacDonald himself that makes him do this? For the division cannot be explained simply in terms of *Lilith* itself— whether its characteristic multivalency, or its use of paradox, metamorphosis, and inversion. But there are two impulses that can be traced throughout MacDonald's thought and work, which can throw light on *Lilith*'s double ending. On the one hand a reading of his sermons or his *The Diary of an Old Soul* will show the great principle of his Christian life: getting into an ever-closer relation to God. A central theme of his sermons is "atonement," by which he means "at-one-ment" with God: "Because we are his children, we must become his sons and daughters. Nothing will satisfy him, or do for us, but to be one with the Father!" (*Unspoken Sermons* 284). Or again, "The true idea of the universe is the whole family in heaven and earth.... The life-germ at the root of the world — that by and for which it exists — is its relation to God the Father of men" (*Life Essential* 61). And the most perfect relation is the devotion of Christ to his Father, whereby God's own nature, separated from him through creation as man, loves his creator steadfastly through all trials, and enters back into perfect harmony with him. This devotion we must, with Christ's help, try to mirror in our own lives (*Unspoken Sermons* 454), for then we shall know

> that our existence is not the moonlight of a mere consciousness of being, but the sun-glory of a life justified by having become one with its origin, thinking and feeling with the primal Sun of life, from whom it was dropped away that it might know and bethink itself, and return to circle forever in exultant harmony around him. Then indeed we are; then indeed we have life; the life of Jesus has through light, become life in us; the glory of God in the face of Jesus, mirrored in our hearts, has made us alive; we are one with God for ever and ever [457].

But beside all this joyous certainty of the joy of union with God, there is an equally strong sense in MacDonald of being stuck in a world which separates him from Him and makes him often have to struggle to believe that He exists. At the beginning of "August" in *The Diary of an Old Soul*, MacDonald looks towards his entry to heaven and "liberty's divine expanse," but then shrinks back with "It will be so — ah, so it is not now!" and the cold awareness that "liberty is distant many a mile." He is in continual flux between hope and despair:

> Sometimes it seems pure natural to trust,
> And trust right largely, grandly, infinitely,
> Daring the splendour of the giver's part;
> At other times, the whole earth is but dust,
> The sky is dust, yea, dust the human heart;
> Then art thou nowhere, there is no room for thee
> In the great dust-heap of eternity [st. 27].

The whole of *The Diary of an Old Soul* is a continual oscillation between a longed-for heaven and the all-too earthly present, between hope and doubt, rapture and emptiness.

Both of these outlooks are mirrored in the fantasies. On the one hand there is a continual move towards unity through personal relationships. We have Diamond and North Wind, Irene and her grandmother, Curdie and Irene, Anodos and the white lady, Vane and Mr. Raven (whose names inversely share one another). In *Lilith* all the people who have slept the good sleep come together to the precincts of heaven. Developing personal relationships are at the center of many of the shorter fairy tales — the princes who woo the Light Princess and Little Daylight, the increasing depth of understanding between Ralph Rinkelman and the Shadows, Colin's symbolic courtship of Fairy in "The Carasoyn," the growing affection between Alice and Richard in "Cross Purposes," the coming together of the Day Boy and the Night Girl through their developing knowledge of moon and sun.

But at the same time there is another drive in MacDonald's fantasies: towards separation. Anodos seeks, but in the end has to yield up the White Lady to another; Agnes and Rosamond polarize morally in their reactions to the old woman's spiritual education; Irene in *The Princess and the Goblin* may come together with her mystic grandmother, but the more skeptical Curdie does not. And throughout his fantasy MacDonald shows a fascination with pairs of opposites — the Day Boy and the Night Girl, the goblins and the grandmother, the White Lady and the Alder Maiden, Lilith and Mara, the Little Ones and the giants. More general polarities also abound, such as death and life, sleeping and waking, dream and reality, mind and world, art and nature. And *Phantastes* and *Lilith*, written at the beginning and end of MacDonald's creative life, are at once similar in dream form and opposite in content, the one dealing with waking and living, the other with sleep and dying, the one with the First Things, the other with the Last.

Lilith is not the only one of MacDonald's fantasies with a dual end. At the end of *Phantastes*, when Anodos, like Vane, has "died" and is resurrected and on the point of new joy, he finds himself abruptly returned to his own world: "a writhing as of death convulsed me, and I became once again conscious of a more limited, even a bodily and earthly life." There is the ending looked to by the fantastic vision, and the ending painfully resigned to of "real life." *The Princess and the Goblin* ends without Irene and Curdie coming together, and when they are eventually united as future King and Queen of Gwyntystorm at the end of *The Princess and Curdie*, the narrator reveals the future when their line will die out with them, their subjects become once more so greedy for gold that their minings bring down the rock on which the city is built, and their realm reverts to a wilderness. In *At the Back of the North Wind*, instead of Diamond being whirled off finally by the mystic lady he has been with so often, we are left with him as a child dying in a London slum, and with only the benign faith of a doting narrator that he has gone to the country at the back of the North Wind. And *The Lost Princess* concludes with one of the morally-schooled children gone irretrievably bad. In his fantasy writing MacDonald often gives two endings, a potentially happy one, and then an often sadder one.

More broadly still, there is the extraordinary duality across MacDonald's writing as a whole, between his fantasy fiction on the one hand and his many novels of "real life" on the other, in both of which kinds he wrote with equal commitment throughout his forty-year literary career. The idea that he wrote novels simply because, as he was told by his publisher, "fiction pays," has been sufficiently discredited (Robb 27–29): the genre clearly gave him scope to give life to societies and to explore issues close to his heart, and produced some of his best work. Here, as has been said by Stephen Prickett in another context, is a writer who lives in two worlds. The fantasy world expresses MacDonald's lifelong yearning to be one with God beyond life. The novels portray his world of doubt and hard-won faith, harder as he grew older, in which he had to live before that would be possible. Between these two there could be no resolution, only the continued desire that the one would give way to the other, and the mingling of acceptance and resignation in their not yet doing so, yearned-for joy and lived doubt.

What is being suggested here is that MacDonald has given us two endings in *Lilith*: one that celebrates "atonement" and arrival at the joys of heaven and God, and the other that depicts MacDonald's own condition of separation in this life. For him, constituted as he was and living in the age that he did, the condition of doubt was as painfully real as that of faith, and separateness held sway over his imagination as much as unity. He could not, pulled as he was, more painfully pulled by his sufferings in old age, give the one side final reality: he had to give us two discordant endings, each as real as the other, in *Lilith* perhaps even more than in his other fantasies.

Notes

1. Cf. "The Imagination" 25: "If the dark portion of our own being were the origin of our imaginations, we might well fear the apparition of such monsters as would be generated in the sickness of a decay which could never feel — only declare — a slow return towards primeval chaos." In *Unspoken Sermons* 317, MacDonald speaks of a descent into atheism leading to "spiritual chaos with all its monsters."

2. Again, *Life Essential* 26: "The region in which the work [of banishing sin] has to be wrought lies in the very roots of [a man's] own being, where, knowing nothing of the secrets of his essential existence, he can immediately do nothing, where the maker of him alone is potent, alone is consciously present." "The Imagination" 25: "God sits in the chamber of our being in which the candle of our consciousness goes out in darkness." MacDonald reused this statement and the whole passage from which it comes in *Unspoken Sermons, Second Series* (1886): see *Unspoken Sermons* 255–56.

3. Not altogether dissimilar is the argument that Vane had to return in order to write *Lilith*.

4. Lilith seeks to destroy the future in the form of the children, the Little Ones, in contrast to those in purgatory, who are continually killing "their dead" (44). Her realm of Bulika is a selfish and sterile society. This selfishness is seen throughout the

region of the seven dimensions in the way that many of its inhabitants have their locality and do not communicate, or are separated, like the Bulika mothers from their children; and in the dryness of the landscape, which the fluidity of water would permeate and draw together. When the Little Ones travel out of their area to Bulika, something radically new is happening. However, the fact that Vane himself travels through numbers of the societies and areas in the strange land does not here reflect credit on him: it is partly a means of showing us the whole of the country through his eyes, and partly of reflecting different aspects of his own condition.

5. Hence the notion of "home," which is with you all the time. The house of the dead where Vane must go in the end is almost bi-local with his own house from which he started his adventures. Vane and Lilith are not to develop, but to find out what they are (207–08); true spiritual change lies in going back (229, 242). It is Lilith who believes in the idea of self-development: "the older we grow, the nearer we are to our perfection" (129).

Works Cited

Hein, Rolland. *George MacDonald: Victorian Mythmaker*. Whitethorn, Calif.: Johannesen, 1999.

MacDonald, George. *A Book of Strife, in the Form of the Diary of an Old Soul*. London: George Allen and Unwin, 1927.

_____. *David Elginbrod*, 3 vols. London: Hurst and Blackett, 1864.

_____. "The Fantastic Imagination" in *A Dish of Orts: Chiefly Papers on the Imagination, and on Shakespeare*. London: Sampson Low Marston, 1893.

_____. "The Imagination" in *A Dish of Orts*.

_____. *Life Essential: The Hope of the Gospel*. Wheaton, Ill.: Howard Shaw, 1974.

_____. *Unspoken Sermons, Series I, II, III*. Whitethorn, Calif.: Johannesen, 1997.

MacDonald, Greville. *George MacDonald and His Wife*. London: George Allen and Unwin, 1924.

Manlove, Colin. *The Fantasy Literature of England*. London: Macmillan, 1999.

_____. *The Impulse of Fantasy Literature*. London: Macmillan, 1983.

_____. *Scottish Fantasy: A Critical Survey*. Edinburgh: Canongate Academic, 1994.

McGillis, Roderick. "*Lilith*" in *Survey of Modern Fantasy Literature*. 5 vols. Ed. Frank N. Magill. Englewood Cliffs, N.J.: Salem, 1983.

Mendelson, Michael. "George MacDonald's *Lilith* and the Conventions of Ascent." *Studies in Scottish Literature* 20 (1985): 197–218.

Prickett, Stephen. "The Two Worlds of George MacDonald." *North Wind* 2 (1983): 14–23.

Raeper, William. *George MacDonald*. Tring, Herts.: Lion, 1987.

Reis, Richard. *George MacDonald's Fiction: A Twentieth-Century View*. Eureka, Calif.: Sunrise Books, 1989.

Robb, David S. *God's Fiction: Symbolism and Allegory in the Works of George MacDonald*. Eureka, Calif.: Sunrise Books, 1987.

Wolff, Robert Lee. *The Golden Key: A Study of the Fiction of George MacDonald*. New Haven: Yale University Press, 1961.

CHAPTER 6

The Demoness and the Grail: Deciphering *Lilith**

Jeanne Murray Walker

Since its publication in 1895 George MacDonald's *Lilith* has prompted outbursts of passionate response from its readers. These outbursts may be due, in part, to the unorthodox theology that lies at the heart of the romance, but it is the form of the book at which the outbursts usually are directed.¹ Although *Lilith* asserts the final redemption of all creation and emphasizes the role of individual choice in bringing about that redemption, the power of those statements is derived not so much from the unorthodoxy of the doctrine as from the dramatic force with which the fiction narrates this vision. Appearing at the close of the Victorian period, when realism was the conventional mode of expression, *Lilith*'s form seemed shocking, even grotesque.² To create this form MacDonald employed two major elements, each deeply rooted in Western tradition—the ancient, Near Eastern figure of Lilith, and the literary form of the grail quest.

Critical comments on *Lilith*'s form began with a storm of protest from its initial reviewers. One reviewer for *The Critic* admitted that he was disinclined to write precisely what he thought of the book. A devotee of MacDonald's

---

* Jeanne Murray-Walker, "The Demoness and the Grail: Deciphering *Lilith*," in *The Scope of the Fantastic—Culture, Biography, Themes, Children's Literature: Selected Essays from the First International Conference of the Fantastic in Literature and Film*. Ed. Robert A. Collins and Howard D. Pearce. Copyright © 1985 by The Thomas Burnett Swann Fund. Reproduced with permission of Greenwood Publishing Group, Inc., Westport, CT.

earlier work, he was puzzled by the new "erratic tale." It was, he protested, "a wild goose chase from the Here into the Nowhere" whose conclusion is "welcome." A reviewer for *The Athenaeum* was even more scathing: "To us who remember David Elginbrod, Sir Gibbie and many another stimulating and poetic creations of this accomplished author, it is not less than grievous to find the sweet bells jangled, and the imagination, once lofty and penetrating, declined to the incoherent and grotesque." To this critic *Lilith* seemed nothing but "shifting phases of nightmare," about which it is not worth thinking too long if a reader has "any regard for the preservation of sanity."

Yet *Lilith* not only survived those first angry reviews, it has been acclaimed more recently by critics as astute and diverse as W.H. Auden and C.S. Lewis. Again, in the views of these twentieth-century critics, it is the *form* of the work that draws comment. For both Auden and Lewis *Lilith* seemed "mythopoetic." Indeed, Lewis claimed that MacDonald was the "greatest genius" of the mythological that Lewis knew. He observed that *Lilith* "arouses in us sensations we have never had before, never anticipated having, as though we had broken out of our normal mode of consciousness," for it "shocks us more fully awake than we are for most of our lives" (x–xi).

From our perspective in the late twentieth century, we can see that both the indictments and the praise of *Lilith* comment less on its artistic quality than on its acceptability in two cultures whose assumptions and expectations about art differ. The book, whose puzzling form has occasioned both such rage and reverence, awaits more careful scrutiny.

1. The ancient Hebrew story of Lilith as Adam's first wife is the best-known version of MacDonald's demoness figure. The following excerpt recounts that story:

> Lilith ... is identified with the "first Eve," who was created from the earth at the same time as Adam, and who, unwilling to forgo her equality, disputed with him the manner of their intercourse. Pronouncing the Ineffable Name, she flew off into the air. On Adam's request, the Almighty sent after her the three angels Snwy, Snsnwy, and Smnglf; finding her in the Red Sea, the angels threatened that if she did not return, 100 of her sons would die every day. She refused, claiming that she was expressly created to harm newborn infants [*Encyclopedia Judaica*].[3]

MacDonald's figure of Lilith depends upon this version of the Lilith myth more than on any other version. In the novel she is, indeed, Adam's first wife, who remains egocentric and blasphemous, who causes her only child's death, and until the end of the novel is unable to repent, to turn — or, as the romance puts it, to "return." Water also bears a decisive part in MacDonald's story, but he has reversed the use of the symbol. Whereas in the original Hebrew myth Lilith resides in a place of "roaring waters," of too much water, a place where people are drowned, in MacDonald's romance Lilith makes her home in a place plagued by too little water, in a place of drought.

Although the Hebrew version of the Lilith myth reveals much of the origins of MacDonald's figure of Lilith, it does not go all of the way. What of the lady by the stream, whose life is restored by Vane? What of the cats? What of Lilith's vampirism? Her queenship? Why do Vane's meetings with her occur primarily at night? Who is the character "Samoil" on whom Lilith calls? Even more significantly, what of Lilith's power to dry up the waters, and what of her power to release them with her tears? A closer look at the tangled skein of other demoness myths from the Near East supplies sources to answer these questions beyond the information available in the Hebrew tradition.[4] From information commonly available in folklore dictionaries and well-known primary works, it is possible to trace in detail the complex background and characteristics of the Lilith figure and, pairing the names of goddesses and demons in Sumerian, Assyro-Babylonian, Greek, and Hebrew myths, to correlate them with the motifs that appear in *Lilith*.[5]

First, although Assyro-Babylonian, Sumerian, and Greek mythology represent the multiple characteristics of the demoness figure under a variety of names, the demonesses are generally equated by folklorists, and MacDonald has drawn on aspects of all to create his demoness Lilith.[6]

Second, MacDonald's figure of Lilith draws on the Greek, Sumerian, and Assyro-Babylonian role of fertility goddess, a role not present in Hebrew mythology. This aspect of MacDonald's demoness is essential to his myth, since it coincides with a basic identifying characteristic of the ruler in the grail-romance form. But it is complicated by the Hebrew, Greek, and Sumerian aspects of the demoness as a child slayer, as a *destroyer* of the products of fertility. That Lilith should be goddess both of fertility and of infanticide seems paradoxical. Yet it is precisely these paradoxical characteristics within the demoness figures that energize MacDonald's use of the grail-romance form. The plot of that form allows the demoness figure to act out both characteristics in a way that exploits their ancient resonances and creates new meaning.

Finally, although the cat motif is not connected directly to the ancient demoness figures, associative logic makes that form seem an appropriate one for MacDonald's demoness to take in her child-slaying sprees. Part of a Babylonian inscription describing the seven evil sprits of Sumeria reads, "The third is a grim leopard / that carrieth off children" (Thompson xliii).[7] Lilith's spotted evil cat attacks Mara's white cat Astarte, which is the name of a pagan fertility goddess. These clues suggest that the cat into which Lilith metamorphoses furthers the fertility/infanticide theme in MacDonald's *Lilith*.

2. The second major factor that shapes *Lilith* is the form that unites a group of works Jessie Weston grouped together as grail romances. Weston described this form at length in her influential book *From Ritual to Romance*.[8] In grail romances the recovery to health and goodness of the ruler depends upon the actions of the hero — the quester — and, in turn, the health and goodness of the ruler's people depend upon that of the ruler. Because the ruler has grown ill, aged, or evil in these romances, the land has become dry and infertile. The quester journeys to the land, arriving with the unique power to free the waters. Yet even after the arrival of the quester the land continues to be afflicted while the quester experiences confusion, mistaken identity, wandering, and fear. Eventually, the hero asks the right question or performs the right action, which restores the king, frees the waters, and causes the land to flourish. That MacDonald knew this form when he wrote *Lilith* is beyond question, for he wrote a work called *Origins of the Legend of the Holy Grail*.

In MacDonald's prose romance, the evil ruler is Lilith herself, queen of the afflicted land Bulika. Lilith's evil lies in her desire to remain young and beautiful, always to occupy center stage. To perpetuate her own immortality and to deny the necessity of her own death, Lilith prevents generation and kills children. "The birth of children is in her eyes the death of their parents," Adam explains, "and every new generation is the enemy of the last" (150). Her fear is focused in her hatred of her own daughter Lona, who, it has been prophesied, "will be the death of her" (115). In her effort to see that Lona does not escape alive, Lilith hunts for and kills all children. Therefore, her land is bereft of children.

As in the grail romances, in *Lilith* the ruler's affliction affects the land's vegetation. Because Lilith impounds all of the waters in an egg, her land, which was originally The Land of Waters, grows barren. In her selfishness she "gathered up in her lap what she could of the water over the whole country, closed it in an egg and carried it away" (75). Reversing the process of generation, in which an egg is hatched and its waters are broken out, Lilith rules over a grim and desolate people.

The quester whose task it is to free the land by freeing the ruler of her evil is the young Englishman Vane, who is very concerned with everyday matters of the material world. At first his call to perform this task is far from clear. In fact, Vane's task includes trying to comprehend the "world" in which his quest takes place, for "many of its mental laws are different" from those of everyday Victorian England (40). In fact, this world is one in which objects represent mental and emotional states instead of material objects in an everyday, "real" world. By the alien logic of this "world" — a world where death is life, where sleeping is waking, where the first father Adam (who fell from grace) represents grace and truth, where becoming a child is gaining wisdom — his task demands that he go back to Adam, that he become as a child, and eventually that he die. But he stubbornly balks at this task and therefore his quest becomes a *parody* of the grail-quest form. He discovers the demoness-ruler Lilith, emaciated and lifeless; he revives her; she regains her throne at Bulika and rules over a childless and evil kingdom. In short, he perpetuates evil instead of curing it as grail questers are supposed to do. His quest fails and Vane storms Bulika, captures Lilith, and carries her to Adam, who helps to free her of evil. Then the water flows and the land grows fecund.

The grail-quest pattern is used twice in *Lilith*, first, ironically, where the quester's actions further barrenness and, second, in its traditional form, where the quester's actions wake the land to fertility. As in traditional quest forms, Vane's discovery of his identity and his attempt to free the waters are combined in the same motion. So Vane's failure, at first, to free the waters implies his failure to understand the world in which he quests, his mistaken identity, and his moral confusion. His eventual success signals not merely the restoration to the ruler of her original, proper goodness and to the land of its native fertile condition but the restoration of Vane to himself in his most heroic form, tested and validated as a man by the forces that define good and evil in the world.

3. One can best discern the significance of *Lilith*'s form by asking what MacDonald achieved by combining the demoness figure with the grail-quest form that he could not have achieved with either alone. The grail quest is a linear form, a structure in which the meaning of images depends, at least in part, upon their sequence. But more than that it provides a magical correlation between quester, ruler, and land. MacDonald heightened the correlation between the ruler and the quester in *Lilith* by portraying the two as members of the opposite sex, linked by perverted love. He made the land's barrenness more clearly the fault of the ruler by portraying the ruler as a female who murders children. Finally, he decisively broadened the meaning of the quest beyond the social to the metaphysical by portraying the ruler not as a mere human being but as a demoness. MacDonald managed these three changes in the grail-quest form by adapting the characteristics of the Near Eastern figure, which we have already reviewed, to the traditional figure of ruler in the grail quest.

But to what end are these adaptations? In fact, two of them — the perverted love relationship of the quester and the ruler and the ruler's policy of infanticide — emphasize the burden of individual choice in the moral shape of the world. Infertility, the traditional evil in the grail-quest form, grows out of Lilith's egocentric decision to supersede and annul the next generation: that evil flourishes when the quester Vane misapprehends Lilith's nature and chooses, by saving her, to perpetuate her egocentrism. Because of Lilith's and Vane's conscious choices, the whole land lies in waste and drought.

Individual responsibility is one thrust of *Lilith*'s connection between the two forms; the return of all creation to its original goodness is the other. Since the ruler is a demoness, consort to Satan in traditional Near Eastern mythology as in MacDonald's romance, the evil she represents stands neither for mere social misrule nor for metaphysical evil that is limited by national boundaries. Lilith's evil permeates the cosmos; in MacDonald's romance it is the source of all human evil. Furthermore, this evil is the active, willing, efficacious desire of Lilith. Therefore, her rejuvenation, the traditional rejuvenation of the ruler in the romance quest, cannot be imaged simply as the return of the ruler to physical health, which is a condition beyond the capacity of the human will to choose. In fact, when Vane nurses Lilith back to physical strength, she uses that strength to go on willing moral ill, and Vane's quest ends in ironic reversal. Evil, the infertility of the land, cannot be cured until Lilith chooses moral health; therefore, her repentance is the only rejuvenation that can possibly bring about fertility. The ruler is eventually rejuvenated in *Lilith*; MacDonald played the grail romance form to its conclusion. But in doing so he dramatized the unorthodox notion that evil will finally and permanently come under the rule of good, that even the devil will be redeemed—but only by the devil's free choice.

MacDonald portrayed the role of the individual in bringing about this final conversion in three scenes: early, where Vane bathes Lilith in a stream; later, where he brings Lilith back to Adam; and near the end of the romance, where Vane buries Lilith's severed hand. All of these scenes emphasize the grail quest's dependence of the ruler on the individual quester: the first, ironically; the second two, straightforwardly.

In the first of these two scenes Vane brings Lilith to life, an act that Adam has prophesied represents "some evil that is good for you" (95). By a stream bed Vane discovers Lilith, cold as a corpse, emptied of strength. Lovingly, he restores her to life by bathing "the pitiful form" in water, which has restorative powers, because, as the reader discovers at the end of the work, it flows from the rock behind the throne of God (99–100). Vane's act revives the ruler, whose perverted will is the force of evil in the land. The quester in MacDonald's romance, therefore, has power not only to cure but to perpetuate infertility. "What you have made me is yours," Lilith tells Vane (131). This is literally true, since Lilith leeches Vane's blood at night, and he, who is seduced by her beautiful form, willingly feeds her with his own being. Their love, then, is an image of the reciprocity by which evil grows. Through Vane's vanity, Lilith returns to her original position of power, withholder of water from the land of Bulika.

After Vane attempts to take the city Bulika, and to free the water, a futile and egocentric attempt that causes the prophesied death of Lilith's one child Lona, Vane repents of his vanity, an act that initiates Lilith's repentance (187).

Vane turns back to Adam, the guide whom he has impulsively deserted. Without much psychological description, MacDonald described Vane's repentance as a literal, physical journey back. When he returns, Vane takes the captive Lilith to Adam, for as Vane recognizes, "I had no power to make her repent" (189). Yet ironically, it is Vane's very recognition of his own ineffectuality and his consequent return to Adam that guarantees Lilith's eventual repentance and *its* consequent freeing of the waters. In fact, then, Vane the quester initiates both the action that reinstates the bad ruler and also the action that brings the ruler back to goodness and that, in turn, makes fertile the barren land.

After the scene in which Lilith repents, MacDonald again focused on Vane's responsibility, the burden the quester bears, his role in freeing both the ruler and her people. Since Lilith has been unable to open her clenched hand, Adam has severed it with a sword. He gives it to Vane, who journeys deep into the desert and buries it. As a result, water springs up from the hidden streams and flows over all the barren land, making it fertile again. The freeing of water, with all its complex network of Christian associations, depends upon Vane, the quester. As he realizes near the end of the book: "my life was not all a failure! I had helped to set this river free!" (233). The lonely and beleaguered hero in the romance finally discovers his own meaning in the meaning of his quest; the redemption of the world ultimately rests in the hands of each individual who must choose between good and evil.

If individual choice seems pressing and catastrophically important in MacDonald's portrayal of the quester, it is also crucial in his portrayal of the ruler. Unlike the typical grail romances that describe helplessly impotent male rulers, MacDonald's romance portrays a female ruler who is fertile, who has borne a child but who actively seeks to destroy the product of her own womb and therefore, as in the tradition of Pharaoh and Herod, seeks to destroy all children. In *Lilith* infertility is imposed upon the land by a ruler who could choose otherwise, and thus individual choice is an issue even in MacDonald's portrayal of the ruler figure.

In fact, MacDonald both heightened the irony of the land's barrenness and portrayed its metaphysical cause in one image by using the Near Eastern female demoness figure as ruler in the grail-romance form. Since women and not men bear children, if a woman refuses to bear children she denies one of the unique functions of her being. By refusing motherhood Lilith refuses not merely to perpetuate life; she refuses to acknowledge the purpose for which she was created. This refusal to acknowledge her creation and definition by someone outside herself lies at the center of Lilith's evil, and Lilith's evil lies at the center of evil in the book.

The ruler's rejuvenation, the land's fertility, the freeing of the waters, the success of the quester — all depend upon this one thing: Lilith's willingness to acknowledge that her being depends upon her creator. Her repentance, or returning to her original, created state, is the act on which the romance structure of the book pivots. As we have seen, her repentance is possible only because Vane returns with her to Adam. Vane's return, his own repentance, which is precipitated by the prophesied death of Lona, occurs in a matter-of-fact scene, filled with details of landscape and external action. But MacDonald portrayed Lilith's repentance with vivid psychological realism. The description of Lilith's conversion makes repentance plausible in images already charged with meaning from use in previous chapters of the romance — light and shadow, the closed and opened hand, adulthood and childhood, death and life, freedom and slavery, drought and rain. But if Lilith's conversion serves as a convincing psychological model of individual repentance, it does more. It also presents an argument for the inevitable and final redemption of all creatures.

In fact, MacDonald's complex intertwining of Near Eastern mythology and the grail-romance form in *Lilith* ultimately serves his radical theological belief in the final reversion of *all* of the world to the state of goodness in which it existed at creation. The importance of this belief in *Lilith* is evidenced by the fact that it is revealed at precisely the juncture in the book where the quest is accomplished and where the Near Eastern figure changes from child slayer to fertility goddess. It is revealed as the knot of the plot is untied. Furthermore, it is dramatized in powerful, even violent psychological images.

MacDonald's argument for the controversial belief in the redemption of all created beings is fictionalized in the slow, step-by-step process of Lilith's conversion. According to imagery rooted deeply in MacDonald's portrayal of Lilith, her evil consists of her negation of good as a shadow consists in the blocking out of the sun. So Lilith is imaged as a spotted cat, and Mara is portrayed as a white cat; Lilith hides a spot in her side and sucks blood while the sun is down. These images imply that her evil is not substantive but that her "true" nature is merely perverted, that she has failed to acknowledge her own goodness. As Mara, the Lady of Sorrows, contends, "You are not the Self you imagine." Lilith responds: "So long as I feel myself what it pleases me to think myself, I care not. I am content to be to myself what I would be. What I choose to seem to myself makes me what I am. My own thought makes me me; my own thought of myself is me. Another shall not make me!" (199–200). In this response Lilith asserts that she is her own creator. But Mara argues that since Lilith cannot cause her own nonbeing, she cannot possibly have caused her own being; whoever has power to create being must have power to destroy it at will. Then Mara shows Lilith an image of herself in her original, created goodness. For several pages Lilith vacillates tortuously between that true image of herself and the false image of herself that she has created. Finally, choosing the false, self-created image, she ceases to know herself as a living being and becomes what Vane describes as a "consciously dead thing.... She had tried her hardest to unmake herself, and could not! She was a dead life! She could not cease! She must *be*!" (206). In the grip of horror at her inability to destroy her own being, which itself demonstrates the superiority of her creator, Lilith admits her "defeat" (207). She acknowledges her own *being*, which is good. In short, she understands that her existence and therefore her moral quality must be derived from her creator, who is good.

The argument implicit in Lilith's conversion is reminiscent of Origen, a second-century theologian from Alexandria. Origen posited that in the end God might reclaim all spirits, both human and supernatural; W.R. Inge summarizes Origen's eschatological position this way:

> Purgation must continue after death; "even Paul or Peter must come into that fire." But will any remain in torment for ever? Origen hopes and thinks not, but will not dogmatize; he remembers the guest who was cast into outer darkness, with no promise of pardon. There are passages in Origen which imply at least a *poena damni* never to be made good; but he would himself have disclaimed any certitude on the subject. Only he insists that promises like "love never faileth," "God shall be all in all," must somehow be fulfilled. Even the devil *might* find salvation, as a spirit made in the image of God, though, as devil, he would be destroyed (*in Rom.* v. 3). The final consummation is complete likeness to God: "God shall be all in all"; *i.e.* He will be all in each individual (*de Prino* v. 6). Then there will be no more diversity, when all shall have reached the highest degree of perfection [317].

Although Origen was never condemned by the church for this view, it has been considered from its beginning to be unorthodox. Origen of Alexandria, like MacDonald in Scotland, was relieved of his clerical duties for such radical theologizing.

To convey the force of his unorthodox argument, MacDonald reached for Lilith, a figure damned in centuries of well-known folk tales. If Lilith, the consort of Satan, can retrieve her form as a "spirit made in the image of God," logic dictates that all less evil spirits, ones whose evil depends on Lilith's power to corrupt, must surely be capable of a return to goodness. This theological argument asserts a cause and effect relationship between Lilith and the characters who surround her in Bulika — those led into evil by her.

The structure to embody this cause and effect was already available to MacDonald in the grail-romance form, where the goodness and fertility of the people are magically dependent upon the well-being of the ruler. When Lilith repents, as MacDonald's romance postulates, all creation is saved. As the narrator in *Lilith* puts it, "Now, the soul of everything I met came out to greet me and make friends with me, telling me we came from the same and meant the same" (245). We can gloss this with Inge's description of Origen's theology: "there will be no more diversity." The apocalyptic unity and goodness of all of the characters after the demoness-ruler's conversion follows the magical grail-romance formula of cause and effect, and it articulates an argument similar to the unorthodox one Origen made over seventeen centuries ago.

The water imagery of the final chapters, drawn from both the grail romance and the characterization of the Near Eastern demoness figure, presents an unashamed, full-blown, accomplished eschatological vision. In these chapters MacDonald portrayed not merely the contentment of fertile lands and satisfied harmonious human life on Earth; he moved beyond physical fulfillment.[9] The water freed when Vane buries Lilith's hand is finally shown to be not the copy or symbol of life but life itself:

> We went up though the city and passed out. There was no wall on the upper side, but a high pile of broken rocks, unsloping like the moraine of an eternal glacier; and through the openings between the rocks, the river came billowing out. On their top I could dimly discern what seemed three or four great steps of a stair, disappearing in a cloud white as snow; and above the steps I saw, but with my mind's eye only, as it were a grand old chair, the throne of the Ancient of Days. Over and under and between those steps issued, plenteously, unceasingly new-born, the river of the water of life [250].

In case anyone should mistake these archetypes, MacDonald ripped off their covers and showed them to be alive not merely with meaning but with the source of meaning: "in which I saw, not the intent alone, but the intender too; not the idea alone, but the imbodier present, the operant outsender; nothing in this kingdom was dead; nothing was mere; nothing only a thing" (250). In this radical, apocalyptic imagery MacDonald told his final vision, the vision that all creation will cooperate in goodness at the end of time.

Yet this ecstatic vision is modified by the crushing emphasis on individual choice, on its purgatorial aspects, which are never absent from human life on Earth. The torture that choice entails is portrayed most keenly in Lilith's conversion scene. The fact that conversion is insured does not reduce the element of painful choice. Rather, the intensity of the conversion scene grows out of its purgatorial qualities. Vane, the quester, watches Mara — an allegorical figure representing sorrow — convince Lilith to repent, and he records the action in images that overtly describe hell: "She is far away from us, afar in the hell of her self-consciousness," he writes. "She knows that she is herself the fire in which she is burning, but she does not know that the Light of Life is the heart of that fire" (201–02). As Inge remarked, Origen understood the figurative nature of eschatological statements in the Bible: "Can we suppose the damned will literally 'gnash their teeth'?" Purgatory is a process of psychological suffering that brings redemption, according to Origen, and in Lilith's conversion scene we witness that process as it occurs not in purgatory but in a created will.

Lilith's conclusion further dampens the euphoria of final, universal good. At the end of the work Vane, still an upper-class Victorian, who finds himself sitting again in his own library, cannot find his way back into the "other world" of the romance. He experiences moments of intense doubt and exclaims, "Mara is much with me" (250). The pressure of human consciousness, then, the weight of importance given to each human choice, however small, modifies MacDonald's vision of final, absolute good.

The theology of *Lilith* is embodied in the intertwined forms of the Near Eastern demoness and the grail romance. MacDonald's interweaving of these two forms resulted in a work castigated by Victorian reviewers and praised by twentieth-century critics. Whatever a reader's response may be to the form of *Lilith*, it seems beyond question that, complicated, even in some ways grotesque, the romance MacDonald produced is rooted deeply in the Western tradition. It draws on that tradition with brilliant economy to articulate MacDonald's specific, idiosyncratic vision of individual choice that must lead ultimately to universal good.

Notes

1. MacDonald was charged with heresy by the deacons of his parish. See Lewis vii.

2. Northrop Frye, among others, noted the nineteenth-century taste for what he called the "low mimetic" forms of fiction (33–67).

3. A figure remarkably similar to the Lamia-Lilith figure has a long history in Chinese folklore and is well known in China now. See Macomb.

4. Thompson asserts, on the basis of etymology, that the Sumerian demoness is the ancestress of Lilith (xxxvi). This connection has been challenged. See *The Jewish Encyclopedia*. On the relationship between the figure in Babylonian and Hebrew folklore, see also *Encyclopedia Judaica*.

5. See *The Jewish Encyclopedia*, *Encyclopedia Judaica*, Kravitz 259, and Sykes 126. For a detailed table showing correlations between the various myths and the motifs that appear in MacDonald's *Lilith*, see the original publication of this article in Greenwood's *The Scope of the Fantastic*, page 182.

6. Macomb emphasizes that in European literature that draws upon the Lamia figure, between Philostratus's *Life of Apollonius* and John Keats's *Lamia*, that figure increasingly comes to represent desirable but unavailable love rather than lust (158–70); Macomb traces the history of the lamia through Walter de Map and Robert Burton in *The Anatomy of Melancholy*.

7. See also Jer. 13.23: "Can the Ethiopian change his skin, or the leopard his spots? Then may ye also do good, that are accustomed to do evil."

8. My argument does not depend upon Weston's essential thesis that grail romance grew out of fertility rituals but only looks to Weston for a synopsis of the grail-romance forms. Whatever the case concerning the relationship of the grail-romance form to ritual, the concept that the ruler's health directly affects the well-being of his land is very old; it is present in Ugaritic myths and legends unearthed in the French excavations of Ras Shamra-Ugarit in the early 1930s. See Prichard 129–55.

9. See Rev. 22.1, where a clear "river of water of life" flows from the throne of God.

WORKS CITED

Frye, Northrop. *Anatomy of Criticism*. New York: Atheneum, 1969.

Inge, W. R. "Alexandrian Theology." *Encyclopedia of Religion and Ethics*. Vol. 1. Ed. James Hastings. New York: Scribner's, 1957, 317.

Lewis, C.S. Introduction to *Lilith: A Romance*. By George MacDonald. Grand Rapids: Eerdmans, 1981. v–xii.

"Lilith." *Encyclopedia Judaica*. 1971 ed.

"Lilith." *The Jewish Encyclopedia*. 1916 ed.

Macomb, Nai-tung. "The Holy Man and the Snake Woman." *Fabula* 8.3 (1966): 145–91.

Prichard, James B., ed. *Ancient Near Eastern Texts Relating to the Old Testament*. Princeton: Princeton University Press, 1950.

Review of *Lilith*, by George MacDonald. *The Athenaeum* 9 November 1895: 639.

Review of *Lilith*, by George MacDonald. *The Critic* 25 January 1896: 26.

Thompson, Reginald Campbell. *The Devils and Evil Spirits of Babylonia*. London: Luzac, 1903.

Weston, Jessie L. *From Ritual to Romance*. Garden City, N.Y.: Doubleday-Anchor, 1957.

CHAPTER 7

A Fresh Look at *Lilith*'s Perplexing Dimensions
Rolland Hein

The enigma of the "endless ending" to George MacDonald's *Lilith* that Robert A. Collins highlights in his close and probing reading (chapter 1) should be considered, it seems to me, in regard to the anagogical level of meaning in the work. Inasmuch as *Lilith* represents a relatively rare literary undertaking, that of imaginatively presenting a Christian view of Higher Reality, it would seem wise to consider it in the light of the most celebrated work that represents a similar undertaking, Dante's *The Divine Comedy*. Doing so sheds remarkable light upon its nature and meaning. MacDonald held Dante's work in very high esteem. That he had it in mind as he was composing *Lilith* can readily be demonstrated. One is tempted to speculate, on the basis of the evidence, that he endeavored to construct his myth in terms of the same four layers of meaning that Dante Aligheri infused into his work. *Lilith* closes on the fourth level, that of the anagogical.

As he aged, MacDonald became increasingly interested in Dante's art. To read the novels and sermons that he produced in his latter years is to be struck with the number of references to *The Divine Comedy*, the depth of his involvement with the text, and the high respect he had for Dante's achievement. A noted earlier expression of this interest appears in *At the Back of the North Wind*, in which Dante is referred to as the Italian poet "Durante" who has visited the "country at the back of the north wind," and whose "books will last as long as there are enough men in the world worthy of having them" (ch. 10). Apparently, the family's taking up residence in Italy in 1877 increased his interest in Dante's work, as his later publications contain many allusions to it.

In the three series of *Unspoken Sermons*, for instance, I find no direct references to Dante in the first two, published in 1867 and 1885 respectively, but in *Series Three*, published in 1889 (the year prior to his writing the first draft of *Lilith*), there are no fewer than eight. MacDonald was not given to extensive quoting from other authors, although his knowledge of not only British but also European literature was extensive. I note in *Series Three* only a passing reference to Milton, another to Wordsworth, and a third to Shakespeare. Further, each reference to Dante suggests a close involvement with the text. In the final sermon, which is entitled "The Inheritance" and is based on Colossians 1:12, he begins by quoting twenty-one lines from *Purgatorio*, offers his own translation of them, and then proceeds to build upon Dante's thought.[1]

The presence of Dante in the earlier manuscripts of *Lilith* is also striking. *Lilith* was composed and painstakingly revised over a four-year period. The initial manuscript is dated March 28, 1890, and the final version was published in 1895. During this time MacDonald agonized over his work, allowing it to evolve through a series of distinct phases, each an elaborate and fastidious revision of the former. In 1893 he remarked in a letter to his daughter Winifred, "I am a little tired, having been hard at work cutting and killing and re-embodying and shifting, and trying generally to restore order, and draw out hidden meanings from their holes" (Hein, *Victorian Mythmaker* 528). It is a severe understatement, for the extent of the emendations and deletions defies description. The exact number of revisions of the entire manuscript is uncertain, as evidence suggests not all are extant. Eight manuscripts were deposited in the British Museum by the surviving children before their deaths in mid-twentieth century. They are referred to by the letters A through H; F, G, and H are printer's copies which were corrected for various errors in transcription and contain but few final alterations. Manuscripts B through E, however, contain such extensive additions and deletions that the substance of the final version stands at an immense distance from A.[2]

As this narrative slowly evolves and develops through its successive phases, specific allusions to *The Divine Comedy* appear in steadily increasing numbers. Then, strikingly, in the published version there are but three. Several that regularly appeared in the earlier versions were omitted. I count two references in manuscript A, three each in B and C, six in D, and seven in E. Most of these allusions are sophisticated, referring to details in Dante's text that only a close reader would notice. They clearly reveal that MacDonald developed an intimate and astute knowledge of Dante's work. That all but three were deleted from the final version suggests he may not have wanted his readers to conclude his dependence on Dante was unduly large, detracting from the stature of his own work. The three that remain were carefully chosen and strategically positioned to enrich appreciably the meaning of the text.

Like Dante, MacDonald wanted to impress upon his readers that the anagogic or spiritual reality into which Vane enters is a truer and more momentous one than the empirically known reality of the world to which he returns. He designated it as The Region of Seven Dimensions. Why seven, four in addition to the three we commonly know? Why not just one above the normal three? In his many earlier attempts in this fantasy genre, such as, for instance, "The Golden Key," MacDonald uses the image of Fairyland as a metaphor for anagogic reality. It served him well there, and would no doubt have been less confusing to his contemporary readers. In an edition of *Lilith* that Greville MacDonald published on the centenary of his father's birth in 1924, he conjectured in a footnote that his father *may* have derived the idea from the writings of Jacob Boehme, a seventeenth-century German mystic. Perhaps so. But in his other writings MacDonald gives little if any indication of any debt he owed to Boehme.

In his biography of his father, Greville ventures an explanation for the seven which is perceptive in noting that the additional four are vitally interrelated:

> Like *Phantastes*, *Lilith* is an allegory of two worlds ... each revealing truths of the other not even dreamed of so long as only one is frequented.... It both binds in one and unfolds the world of concrete Beauty and the realm of abstract Truth. Necessarily also it treats of their condition in dimensions — of which there be seven in all, three concrete ... and four abstract interblending but more positively vital. The four compose an inseparable unity commonly spoken of as the much debated *fourth dimension* — that concept of existence which, being spiritual, is not indeed independent of the concrete, but contains and controls the concrete three dimensions in creative manifestation [549].

Precisely. All meanings in the imagery of *Lilith* beyond the literal level are closely intertwined, forming an "inseparable unity," which may be simply referred to as a fourth dimension. In separating them, MacDonald was highlighting his basic conviction that arriving at the true meaning and purpose of life requires appreciably more than simply understanding the "spiritual" or anagogic level. A moral component is indispensable. The end of the process is a transformed soul that has radically altered attitudes.

Dante had set a very helpful precedent. In his famous letter to his patron, Can Grande della Scala, explaining his purposes in constructing *The Divine Comedy*, he set forth very explicitly the four levels of meaning in terms of which he wanted his work to be read:

> The meaning of this work is not simple ... for we obtain one meaning from the letter of it, and another from that which the letter signifies; and the first is called *literal*, but the other *allegorical* or *mystical*. And to make this matter of treatment clearer, it may be studied in the verse: "When Israel came out of Egypt and the House of Jacob from among a strange people, Judah was his sanctuary and Israel his dominion." For if we regard the *letter alone*, what is set before us is the exodus of the Children of Israel from Egypt in the days of Moses; if the *allegory*, our redemption wrought by Christ; if the *moral* sense, we are shown the conversion of the soul from the grief and wretchedness of sin to the state of grace; if the *anagogical*, we are shown the departure of the holy soul from the thraldom of his corruption to the liberty of eternal glory. And although these mystical meanings are called by various names, they may all be called in general *allegorical*, since they differ from the literal and the historical [14–15].

These four levels of meaning function as dimensions to the text in a manner very like they may be detected to do in *Lilith*. It seems safe to conjecture that MacDonald added Dante's four "dimensions" to the familiar three, hence his seven.

MacDonald, however, entertained one large exception to Dante's theology and voiced it with vehemence. It is, as one would expect, his quarrel with Dante's view of the inexorable nature of hell. He faces the issue foursquare in his sermon "Justice," contained in *Unspoken Sermons, Third Series*:

> Take any of those wicked people in Dante's hell, and ask wherein is justice served by their punishment. Mind, I am not saying it is not right to punish them; I am saying that justice is not, never can be, satisfied by suffering — nay, cannot have any satisfaction in or from suffering. Human resentment, human revenge, human hate may. Such justice as Dante's keeps wickedness alive in its most terrible forms [125–26].

Dante's hell not only cannot satisfy God's justice; its very nature defeats God's purposes.

MacDonald undertook in *Lilith* to explore imaginatively an alternate way of dealing with the problem of evil, one that seemed to him more just and more in harmony with the character of God. In his view, the soul faces steady emaciation towards annihilation unless it chooses to repent, submit to be transformed, and undertake to right all wrongs it has committed. But this large difference with Dante aside, his respect for the rest of Dante's thought and the achievement of his art ran very deep. Investing his text with the same four levels of meaning that Dante did enabled him to communicate his vision thoroughly, with harmonious artistic complexity. MacDonald's efforts to make them all work harmoniously help account for his elaborate reworkings of the text through its various manuscripts.

Neither author, of course, intended that every image and episode in their respective works would function on all four levels in a mechanical fashion, so that separate meanings could be readily distinguished one from the other; however, some images do. For instance, at the very beginning of *The Divine Comedy*, the "way" that Dante the character has lost is, literally, a path through a forest; allegorically, it is the journey of life; morally, it is the path of right conduct from which to stray is to err; and anagogically, it is the path that leads to divine redemption.

Likewise, many of the main images of *Lilith* carry these same multiple levels of significance. Lilith herself may serve as an example. On the literal level she is a temptress; on the allegorical, Vane's soul in its unredeemed state; on the moral, his soul possessed by its lower "selves," the self-centered passions that threaten to steadily diminish it (note the leech imagery); and on the anagogical, his soul surrendered to be transformed (sleeping in Eve's house), a process that ends in its fully redeemed state.

Further parallels between Dante's work and MacDonald's are striking. First, just as Dante in the text of *The Divine Comedy* recounts his own personal experience of being made aware — by way of his journey — of the nature of sin, its consequences, the means of its purgation, and the glory of being set free from it, so does Vane in *Lilith*. And just as Dante put a version of himself in his text, so that it had certain autobiographical implications, so does MacDonald's text adumbrate several aspects of his life. We have not room in this paper to develop these. The main point for our present purpose is to suggest how the final scene should be considered in terms of these layered meanings.

Both authors focus attention upon the anagogical level by taking the reader into the inner life of each protagonist. Just as Dante the character gains much good from having lost his spiritual compass and then finding it again by coming into an understanding of the realities of the afterlife, so Vane, as a typical young Britisher in the 1890s who has lost contact with higher reality, gains much good by achieving the orientation that the tale relates. Vane begins his story by recounting how he, as a young student, was preoccupied with the natural sciences and wanted to see all of life's mysteries in terms of material reality. His error was that he had embraced a strongly empirical, materialist, and rationalist approach to life. Although he occasionally had "metaphysical dreams," he was totally ignorant of the supernatural world with which his ancestors were familiar.

MacDonald made much point in the text that Vane's ancestors had had the orientation to this higher reality of which he stood in need. Chapter VIII, entitled "My Father's Manuscript," makes this clear. Dismayed that the nineteenth century was experiencing a steady falling away from a traditional acceptance of a Christian view of reality, replacing it with an agnostic outlook shaped by a rising materialism and scientific realism, MacDonald was telling his age it should return to the faith of its fathers.

Vane stumbles into The Region of Seven Dimensions unexpectedly. He reveals his need by being unable to answer the Raven's question, "Who are you, if you happen to know?" (14). He does not know, because he has not yet become a true self. In the material, workaday world that he has left behind, "nobody is himself, and himself is nobody" (15). The Region of the Seven Dimensions is the one in which the true self is discovered and developed.

The Raven's first task is to make Vane aware of the relation of The Region of Seven Dimensions to Vane's everyday world. He shows him how the two realms are coincident and interpenetrating. They are integrally related in that actions and attitudes in our world are transformed into either beautiful or ugly realities in the higher world. Sweet piano music here becomes wild hyacinths there, a prayer here a beautiful snow white pigeon spiraling upwards there, and so forth. The anagogical reality of human acts is so radically different from their empirical reality that they compose a different world. The soul that becomes aware of this higher realm must either submit to its demands or suffer dire consequences.

Dante in his day did not have to labor to impress his readers with the nature of anagogical reality, but MacDonald in his day did. MacDonald's text conveys more vividly than Dante's the radical differences between empirical and anagogic reality and the necessity of allowing one's inner life to be transformed. He followed Dante's lead in giving his readers an account of an *inner* journey, but MacDonald emphasized that it is within the human consciousness that the higher world is encountered. The most distinct statement to this effect occurs in the A manuscript. After Vane has refused to sleep in Eve's house and thereby has taken himself out of the Raven's hands, he wanders alone into the Bad Burrow. There an earth-tiger frighteningly bursts out of the ground; then a serpent huge as a polar bear appears and, after winding Vane round and round, retreats back into the ground. We read:

> When in some after time, I speculated on what, vision or reality, the thing might mean, I thought I knew that the ground of that moor outside the house of death was but the out-issue of my own soul, the under soil of the vineyard of my own being, deep in which, unknown to myself, lay such nameless horrors [*First and Final* 299].

The quality of an individual's experience on this level of reality is privately and uniquely shaped by that individual's character and acts. Compare C.S. Lewis's hell in *The Great Divorce*, whose inhabitants have only to wish for a thing for it to be theirs (cf. Chapter 2). The terrain through which Vane travels is his own soul, "turned inside out."[3]

In a preface that MacDonald contributed to the 1884 edition of *Letters from Hell*, a work by an anonymous Dutch writer, he gave a succinct statement of this principle. He wrote:

> We make our fate in the unmaking of ourselves ... men, in defacing the image of God in themselves, construct for themselves a world of horror and dismay; ... of the *outer darkness* our own deeds and character are the informing or inwardly creating cause ... if a man will not have God, he never can be rid of his weary and hateful self [vi].

Just as the horrors of the Bad Burrow are, allegorically, projections of Vane's inner consciousness, so indeed are *all* his adventures in the Region of Seven Dimensions.

The fact that the dramatic events of the text are subjective, an imaginative projection of Vane's attitudes and spiritual inadequacies, facilitates a smooth integration with the two other levels of meaning that Dante listed in his letter to his patron — that is, the anagogical and the moral.

MacDonald was not fond of allegory. In his essay entitled "The Fantastic Imagination" he remarked, "He must be an artist indeed who can, in any mode produce a strict allegory that is not a weariness to the spirit" (*Heart* 426). The metaphoric images in his various myths are therefore much more symbolic, that is, vague and open to interpretation, than, say, John Bunyan's. Nevertheless, most of the main characters in *Lilith* have a loose allegorical significance consistent with a set of theological conclusions he held throughout his life. Mara signifies the sorrow for wrongdoing that precipitates repentance. Lona signifies the redeeming love that practically rescues the babies from Bulika (the fallen world) and nurses them into becoming the Little Ones. The Little Ones suggest spiritually immature converts, people who need more "water," or the Word of God, to mature. The moon is an image for Divine Providence. Lilith is herself Vane's ego, that part of himself that he must conquer and deliver to Eve's house of death. Vane's initial attraction to Lilith is gradually replaced by a purer attraction to Lona, or the redeeming love of God in its practical working. Vane's adventures throughout *Lilith* depict the successive steps by which an individual acquires the necessary orientation to anagogical reality, thus readying him to die finally into life eternal.

With his initial allusion to Dante in the final version of *Lilith*, MacDonald places an important clue to his allegorical intentions. Vane offers the following exultation when, at the beginning of Chapter VII, he first sees Eve: "It was as if the splendour of her eyes had grown too much for them to hold, and, sinking into her countenance, made it flash with a loveliness like that of Beatrice in the white rose of the redeemed. Life itself, life eternal, immortal, streamed from it, an unbroken lightning.... Her beauty was overpowering" [32]. Readers are to see in Eve the significance that Dante's Beatrice holds in *The Divine Comedy*. Both are symbols of the love of God, which demands moral purity and beckons people to receive the Real Life that alone effects it.

The other two allusions to *The Divine Comedy* in the published manuscript occur in key positions towards the close of *Lilith*, one each in the two chapters preceding the "Endless Ending." The first of these emphasizes the moral level. In Chapter XLV, after Vane and his party have slept the sanctifying sleep in Eve's house, they begin their journey to the Heavenly City. Vane expresses ecstatic joy in feeling a harmony and oneness with all nature. He exults, "A wondrous change had passed upon the world — or was it not rather that change more marvelous had taken place in us? I lived in everything, everything entered and lived in me." He notices especially the sweet sounds arising as a breeze sets the little purple heather bells to ringing, and he exclaims, "I was myself in the joy of the bells, myself in the joy of the breeze to which resounded their sweet *tintinning*, myself in the joy of the sense, and of the soul that received all the joys together" (243). A footnote attributes the coined term *tintinning* to *Del Paradiso*.

The reference at first strikes one as perplexing: why call attention to Dante's onomatopoetic coinage? A closer look, however, at the context of the quotation in *The Divine Comedy* suggests what may well have been MacDonald's subtle purpose. In Dante's journey through Paradise, he has risen to the circle of the Sun, where in the sphere of light, unimaginable in its brilliance, he beholds the spirits of the wise, twelve theologians whom Dante most esteemed. St. Thomas Aquinas is their spokesman, introducing each in turn. Last, and closest to him, is Sigier of Brabant. This is remarkable, simply because during their lifetimes on earth Sigier opposed Aquinas in several famous public debates. Aquinas saw him as epitomizing falsehood, not truth. But now, St. Thomas praises him: "That's the eternal light of Sigier, who, / Lecturing down in Straw Street, hammered home / Invidious truths, as logic taught him to" (10.136–38). In other words, these two fierce questors for truth were, while on earth, avowed opponents, but now, like Eliot's boarhound and boar in "Burnt Norton," they are "reconciled among the stars." As the celestial sphere containing them begins to move, Dante describes the heavenly music he hears with the coined term. He was confronting the problem of conflicting theological stances among earnest scholars and suggesting that, as they stand glorified in the full light of heavenly truth, their differences are forgotten, and they stand in full harmony and love each to the other. MacDonald stands in relation to Dante not unlike Sigier in relation to Aquinas. Although MacDonald was at loggerheads with Dante on the issue of the eternality of the consequences of temporal sins, he signaled that morally he held no disdain for Dante himself. He viewed the great Florentine poet as an earnest Christian brother and looked forward to full fellowship with him in eternity.

MacDonald's third and final allusion, which emphasizes the anagogic, occurs as Vane and his party near the gates to the Eternal City. They are met by an angel who welcomes them "home." In a footnote, MacDonald credits Dante as the source for the image of angels as heavenly officers. It directs our attention to one of Dante's most splendid descriptive passages, which occurs in the second canto of *Del Purgatorio*. Dante and Virgil, having just emerged from the Inferno, are filled with joy and awe at the enthralling blend of light and color that surrounds them. The contrast to the gloomy darkness, stench, and terrible horrors they have just left behind is dramatic and exhilarating. Vane, feeling similar exhilaration, remarks, "Thought cannot form itself to tell what I felt, thus received by the officers of heaven. All I wanted and knew not, must be on its way to me!" (249).

This brief glimpse of heavenly glory helps explain Vane's quiet anticipation of the full realization of his eternal destiny in the "Endless Ending" chapter. His attitudes now stand in sharp contrast to those he entertained at the beginning of the fantasy. He has become transformed from a young materialist to a mature soul quietly awaiting his demise, now ready to enter eternity.

Returning, then, to Professor Collins's concern, the periodic revisiting of Vane to his library serves to strengthen the imagery of interpenetrating realities and to mark the steps in Vane's spiritual transformation. In the return related near the middle of the fantasy, Chapters XXVIII through XXX, he is more open to the Raven's instructions than formerly, but the necessity of his sleeping, or dying into true life, still seems to him irrelevant. The urgency he feels to help the Little Ones will not allow it. His problem is that of relying on his own judgment and resources rather than first receiving the requisite life that alone would invest his actions with eternal worth.

In the garden of his estate, Vane receives from the Raven instruction as to Lilith's nature that, allegorically, applies as well to his unredeemed self. Much of the instruction comes from his overhearing an extended poem that the Raven reads to a cat, an emanation of Lilith. The final stanza enrages her because it succinctly expresses how she went wrong during her earthly life. It provides a crucial statement as to the relation of the everyday and the anagogical levels of experience:

> Ah, the two worlds! So strangely are they one,
>   And yet so measurelessly wide apart!
> Oh, had I lived the bodiless alone
>   And from defiling sense held safe my heart,
>   Then had I scaped the canker and the smart,
> Scaped life-in-death, scaped misery's endless moan! [147].

Lilith — here allegorically the unredeemed self— is enraged by being reminded that it was her own freely willed decisions that precipitated her life-in-death experiences. She indulged, by her rebellion and self-centeredness, the world of "defiling sense" and thus rejected the "bodiless" realm of spiritual worth.

The last we hear of Lilith in the text, she is still sleeping in Eve's house. Vane in the "Endless Ending" chapter finds himself in a higher spiritual state than he was in Chapter I, yet, being still in his earthly life, is not fully transformed within. His is the condition of the mature Christian saint still in this world. The aged MacDonald was identifying with his character and, in describing Vane, was depicting his own spiritual state as he wrote, "As yet I have not found Lona, but Mara is much with me" (250). Although not yet completely transformed (Mara, or suffering, is "much" with him), his soul is fully weaned away from its former materialism and is filled with longing for its complete union with divine redeeming love (Lona).

Lilith is MacDonald's vision of the meaning and purpose of life, a final composite and definitive expression of a dream that had been his throughout his own. He had expressed it, at least in part, in each of his earlier works. The question that had always teased him was, "Is the entirety of my vision but an empty hope?" MacDonald's resolution is suggested by the voice from within Vane that inquires why God had invested him with such intense longings if the dream did not come from Him. If God had given the dream, he was content to allow God to fulfill it in His own time. Hence, the quotation taken from the archetypal sufferer, Job: "All the days of my appointed time will I wait till my change come" (251).[4]

Vane refuses to tempt God by again seeking the mirror, that is, by continually trying to revisit the dream in order to pamper curiosity. To indulge a mere intellectual probing would be tantamount to committing again the error he made in Chapter X. Upon entering the Bad Burrow, he had tried to possess a beautiful bird-butterfly, only to discover that to conquer it was to kill it. To have an intellectual understanding of spiritual reality without a commensurate experiential participation in it is deleterious to the soul's well-being. Participation begins with a complete submission to sleeping — utter death to the self — and issues in a transformed self. Vane, having submitted, is transformed, and now waits upon the divine timing: "When a man dreams his own dream, he is the sport of his dream; when Another gives it him, that Other is able to fulfil it" (251). Waiting in patience for whatever may come next was, for the aged MacDonald, the mark of spiritual maturity. He was completely convinced that Divine Providence so controls events and circumstances that all that befalls a person is precisely appropriate to that one's anagogic needs: "That which is within a man, not that which lies beyond his vision, is the main factor in what is about to befall him: the operation upon him is the event" (81).

To say, therefore, that Vane in the "Endless Ending" chapter is in a state in which the past is "momentarily negated, suspended or abrogated, and the future is not yet begun" (Turner 44), is not wide of the mark. Vane's quest for the meaning and purpose of life has ended, and he waits in hope for the "endlessness" for which it has prepared him. I question, however, that his state is "ontologically indeterminate." By having received real life, Vane has achieved an altered perception of the same world he has always inhabited: the world of all of us. Like Dante, who returns to his place "beneath the stars" at the conclusion of each cantica of *The Divine Comedy,* Vane periodically returns to his library. And like Dante, who states at the beginning of his narrative that he has received "such good" from the experiences he is about to relate, so Vane, now having told his story, patiently waits for his demise. Both visions, that of *The Divine Comedy* and that of *Lilith,* seem suspended in time. They offer their authors' respective paradigms for an individual's achieving the necessary orientation to reality, that orientation which fulfills the basic quest of life. The good of the quest is not a message to be intellectually communicated, but a vision to be experienced.

Notes

1. The lines quoted concern Virgil's explaining to Dante that "in the inheritance of the saints, that which each has goes to increase the possession of the rest," and when Dante inquires how this can be, Virgil explains that the very nature of love is sharing, thus multiplying its effects. In applying the principle to the future life of the redeemed, MacDonald wrote, "In his inheritance then a man may desire and endeavour to obtain his share without selfish prejudice to others; nay, to fail of our share in it would be to deprive others of a portion of theirs" (*Unspoken Sermons* 247–49). Dante's thought provides the kernel idea for the entire sermon.
2. See *First and Final* and Hein, *Variorum.*
3. A phrase MacDonald often used to describe a person's perceptions of the world. Cf., for instance, "The Imagination: Its Function and Its Culture," *Orts,* 9.
4. Job 14:14.

Works Cited

Dante. *The Comedy of Dante Alighieri.* Trans. Dorothy L. Sayers and Barbara Reynolds. Baltimore, Md.: Penguin, 1949.
Hein, Rolland. *George MacDonald: Victorian Mythmaker.* 1993. Whitethorn, Calif.: Johannesen, 1999.
_____, ed. *The Heart of George MacDonald.* 1994. Vancouver, B.C.: Regent, 2004.
_____, ed. *Lilith: A Variorum Edition.* 2 vols. Whitethorn, Calif.: Johannesen, 1997.
Lewis, C.S. *The Great Divorce.* New York: MacMillan, 1946.
MacDonald, George. *At the Back of the North Wind.* Whitethorn, Calif.: Johannesen, 1992.
_____. *Lilith: First and Final.* 1895. Whitethorn, Calif.: Johannesen, 1994.

_____. *Orts*. London: Sampson Low, et al., 1882.
_____. Preface to *Letters from Hell*. Trans. Julie Sutter. London: Macmillan, 1911.
_____. *Unspoken Sermons: Third Series*. 1891. South Pasadena, Calif.: J. Joseph Flynn, 1987.
MacDonald, Ronald. *From a Northern Window*. 1911. Eureka, Calif.. Sunrise, 1989.
MacDonald, Greville. *George MacDonald and His Wife*. 1924. Whitethorn, Calif.: Johannesen, 1998.
_____, ed., *Lilith: A Romance* by George MacDonald. London: George Allen and Unwin, 1924.
Turner, Victor. *From Ritual to Theatre: The Human Seriousness of Play*. New York: Performing Arts Journal Press, 1982.

Chapter 8

Collins Agonistes; Or, Why Did I Bother To?
Roger C. Schlobin

After decades of reading through the kingdom of Professordom, there are those works that had to be read, were pronounced valuable, and didn't seem worthwhile at the time. For me, the worst was John Dryden's *The Hind and the Panther* (1667). In 1966, I read a couplet, closed my eyes, and tried to recall the meaning ... *nothing*! Years later, with the wisdom of experience and with gathered knowledge, I tried again ... still *nothing*!

George MacDonald's *Lilith* is another on my short list of Why Did I Bother. The luminous (if, at times, purple) prose tells of his great skill and effort. Its crescendos and sweeps signal great significance, but what promises does that stylistic *tour de force* satisfy? One promise it rejects is any reader expectation of resolution or confirmation.

The revolving portals of its library, which Robert A. Collins (see chapter 1) refers to as "*limen*," seem more like a deranged, madly revolving door spitting and sucking the untethered Vane in and out through the interconnected, alternate worlds filled with polymorphs (e.g., Lilith, Raven). Certainly, by the end of the novel, the spitting and sucking are empty of meaning. Bob's dismissal of Campbell's monomyth is appropriate, especially since the heroic protagonist can never rest. The passive heroic is an oxymoron; heroes and heroines at rest in gardens or ensnared by the voluptuous are dead. When Vane comes to rest in the library at the end of the novel, the monomyth is gone if it ever existed in the first place.

Also, Bob's reference to Vane's loss of "customary orientation" when he first blunders into Raven's multidimensional world is equally applicable to the end of the novel, indicating that no epiphany has occurred. At both the beginning and the end, if not throughout, Vane is constantly in transition — not being, not becoming, and not been. He never achieves a state of being or a stasis.

Perhaps *Lilith* is an example of classical nihilism, or an early prototype of the literature of exhaustion, existentialism, or deconstruction? Certainly, the era had such qualities. Both George Eliot's and Thomas Hardy's darker views of the world, among others', were popular. Charles Darwin's *Origin of the Species* (1859) and *Descent of Man* (1871) had rocked cosmology, fueling the attack of empiricism on spirituality, although it's more likely that any influence on MacDonald would be philosophical, not biological. In fact, as Bob indicates, Raven thwarts Vane's claim on materialism.

To find any pattern or sense in *Lilith* would seem to require delving the invisible, not the visible, world and seeking non-linear structure. Certainly, Samuel Taylor Coleridge's *Kubla Khan* (1816) with its modeling of the mind and imagination provided an antecedent for an excursion into the realms of thought and consciousness. Also, Lewis Carroll's *Alice's Adventures in Wonderland* (1865) had set a conspicuous precedent for allusion and symbolism. The last chapter of *Lilith* specifically encourages an emphasis on the unseen. Vane, having lost Lona (or having had her taken from him), rests in the library in Hope's company with his grief, but also with his non-heroic passivity, as he ponders the Eastern conundrum of what is awake and what is dream: "Maybe Zhuangzi was the butterfly, and maybe the butterfly was Zhuangzi? This is what is meant by the 'transformation of things'" (4th century B.C.E.). The "transformation of things" and beings is a good description of *Lilith*. It isolates change, not being, as the prime motive and supports Raven's refusal (or inability) to explicate or stabilize. As Bob points out, Mr. Raven says that everyone has many selves and language is polysemous amid the "world of seven dimensions." Not even "dead" is definitive. Thus, Vane realizes that he cannot tell when he is awake and when he is dreaming. He knows language is unstable. Raven even scoffs at Vane's idea that two objects cannot exist in the same place at the same time. Thus, *Lilith* presents a variation on René Descartes's "*Cogito ergo sum*" (1637) because, while Vane is obviously sentient, he is cognitively impotent. Vane's condition is "I am awake *or* dreaming; therefore, I am."

There may very well be much more specific spiritual, bibliophilic, imaginative, didactic, and/or allegorical underpinnings to *Lilith*. However, if there are, their discovery requires astonishing perseverance and knowledge. In contrast, Dante's *Commedia* is enjoyable and meaningful without any arcane awareness of the Guelfs and Ghibellines. As a result, I think few would chime *Belles-Lettres* for *Lilith* in the annals of intellectual thought or artistic achievement.

CHAPTER 9

The Revelatory Potential of *Lilith*'s Immanent Eternity
Lucas H. Harriman

With his discussion of liminality in *Lilith* (chapter 1), Robert A. Collins has drawn our attention to what is arguably the most critical aspect of George MacDonald's fantasy masterpiece. While the other world into which Mr. Vane repeatedly travels certainly holds much that warrants consideration by the careful reader — the multiple layers of symbolism, the appropriation of ancient myth, the delightfully toyed-with intricacies of seven-dimensional existence — it is in considering the relationship between that world and the one containing Mr. Vane's library that the reader will discover *Lilith*'s most crucial contribution to the genre of fantasy literature. For in the cyclic oscillation between these two worlds, we see an idealized depiction of reading fantasy itself. MacDonald's sustained interpenetration of the two worlds suggests that, although fantasy obviously does not attempt to hold up a realistic mirror to mundane, time-bound existence, neither should it merely provide an extra-temporal realm into which the reader can escape from that same mundane temporality. Vane's repeated excursions into the fantastic serve to develop in him first an intense longing for that other reality, and second an awareness of the immanence of that reality within his own. Although such a reading may go a bit beyond the author's conscious intent, the concept of immanence offers insight as we attempt to grapple with some of the story's profound and often incongruous elements.

Obviously, if *Lilith* presents on some level the role of the fantastic in the life of the responsible reader, any attempt to classify it simply as mythopoeia, a quest story, or a "portal fantasy" will ultimately come to nought. Professor Collins has effectively demonstrated the inconsistencies in such attempts, and they need not be repeated here. However, it is perhaps helpful to take a second look at C.S. Lewis's comments on myth in his introduction to *Lilith*. When dealing with such an elusive term, one must take into account the wide disparity in definition and connotation the word has elicited throughout its history. Sometimes it proves beneficial to ignore the word itself, focusing instead on an author's intended focus. For Lewis, the key aspect of *mythopoeia* seems to be its eye-opening quality:

> It goes beyond the expression of things we have already felt. It arouses in us sensations we have never had before, never anticipated having, as though we had broken out of our normal mode of consciousness and "possessed joys not promised to our birth." It gets under our skin, hits us at a level deeper than our thoughts or even our passions, troubles oldest certainties till all questions are reopened, and in general shocks us more fully awake than we are for most of our lives [x–xi].

It is crucial to note in this description that we are not dealing with the simple conceptualization of myth as being equated to "that which is untrue." On the contrary, Lewis sees revealed in myth "the quality of the *real* universe, the divine, magical, terrifying and ecstatic *reality in which we all live*" (xii; emphasis added). Where the former definition presumes in its reader a complete withdrawal from his own historical existence, the latter sees myth as deepening one's experience of temporal reality. For Lewis, it is "our normal mode of consciousness" that is broken out of when we come in contact with mythic content, not our time-bound existence. The reader reaches a state of mind that is "more fully awake," as opposed to the ethereal somnolence often supposed to result from an immersion in fantasy.

Lewis claims that MacDonald's forte is writing "fantasy that hovers between the allegorical and the mythopoeic" (ix), and this hovering is evidenced most completely in *Lilith*. While a work like Tolkien's *Lord of the Rings* trilogy is obviously mythopoeia—or, myth-making—there is an element of *Lilith* that resists such a classification. Given Lewis's statement, one could see the book as some combination of the two, but how might that work? The story is not an allegory of myth-making, for we never become acquainted in the story with the world's creator. Instead, Vane's journey could be read as an allegory of myth-*receiving*—a depiction of a process Lewis describes as being shocked more fully awake. If this is so, then understanding the relationship *between* the two worlds—the one comprising Vane's ancestors, his inherited estate, and his library, on the one hand, and the world of Mr. Raven, Lilith, and the Little Ones, on the other—is pushed to the fore as we attempt to locate the role of the fantastic authentically within the sphere of our own temporally conscious existence.

In "The Demon Lover: Lilith and the Hero in Modern Fantasy," Karen Schaafsma describes Vane's cyclic returns as being progressive in nature: "The circular course of his adventures actually involves a gradual stripping away of his illusions, the deflation of his vanity, and the reduction of his rational consciousness and self-will" (54). The fact that his experiences in this alternate reality shape the personality with which he will ultimately return to his own reality creates a powerful ligature between the two. The narrative circle from library to library is seen as indicating resolution, not unproductive futility: "In the conclusion of MacDonald's novel, all oppositions are dissolved in a transcendent unity, and Vane has come full circle in his quest for selfhood"; and the treasure that is won by the hero is represented in the release of the river, "baptizing and sanctifying all life" (58). For Schaafsma, the message of balance in *Lilith* is vital for our current society, where the spiritual is either reductively denied through a secularized view of temporal existence or else "relegated to a heavenly other-world that never intersects with this one." She goes on to say that "in both cases, contact is lost with the sacred, numinous presence immanent in the world" (61). It is often this loss of immanence that initially draws many readers to fantastic literature. However, if the writer merely creates a fascinating world and populates it with memorable creatures, any positive effect on readers will be lost the moment they close the book and "re-enter" their own reality. Great works of fantasy, like the "myths" that Lewis describes, will alter readers' perceptions of their own historical moment, awakening in them the knowledge that they live in a filled present. This is the process so dramatically rendered in *Lilith*.

The notion of a "filled present" can be traced back to Augustine's *Confessions*. In Book XI of that work, the contemplative saint wrestles with the various aporias of experiencing time. Augustine's moment of revelation occurs as he suggests that the extension of time can be explained as a "*distentio animi*," a distension of the mind in which it "performs three functions, those of expectation, attention, and memory" (quoted in Ricoeur 19). Of course, as Paul Ricoeur points out in *Time and Narrative*, even though this revelation is highly significant for the history of Western thought, it is far from a joyous one for Augustine. His contemplation on the nature of time appears within a meditation on eternity that casts a shadow of sorrow on the constant "passing away" of time. According to Ricoeur, the thought of eternity becomes a "limiting idea against the horizon of which the experience of the *distentio animi* receives, on the ontological level, the negative mark of a lack or a defect in being," and eventually, "the experience of distension is raised to the level of a lamentation" (26). This sense of "a lack" effectively describes Vane's attitude toward his own brief excursions back into "time and sense" (except, perhaps, the final one). Indeed, as Professor Collins points out, "Mr. Vane perceives all of his more or less involuntary returns to his 'dreary old house' as misfortunes, interrupting his quest for divine perfection." When seen against the backdrop of eternity, the beauty of Lona, or the ecstasy of expectation, Vane's empty library provokes a lamentation that echoes that of the contemplative Augustine.

Paradoxically, Ricoeur sees within this apparently negative conceptualization of the temporality of human existence not a pious desire to passively await the swallowing up of time by eternity, but instead a positive impetus toward "extracting from the very experience of time the resources of an internal hierarchization, one whose advantage lies not in abolishing time but in deepening it." (30). In sentiments that echo those with which Augustine concludes Book XI, Ricoeur proceeds in his study to characterize narrative as a potentially "deepening" and intensifying response to the somewhat lamentable "within-time-ness" of the human being. There is no room here for a full explication of Ricoeur's use of Augustine's *Confessions*, nor would there be any point in providing one for our present discussion of *Lilith*. However, the proposed movement toward a deeper sense of time could be seen as the driving force behind the novel's cyclic structure. Rather than presenting a fantasy world as an extra-temporal realm into which the protagonist can arbitrarily escape, MacDonald maintains an oscillation between the two worlds, depicting an attempt to navigate between the attenuating withdrawal into the "timeless" and the distressing linearity of successive time.

We can see that MacDonald's particular presentation of temporal existence as containing within it another quasi-eternal reality reveals an artistic sensibility similar to that of Augustine. The contemplative saint closes his comments on temporality with an expression of longing for an experience of time that would be nearer to the "changelessness" of eternity—an experience, according to Ricoeur, in which "the advantage lies not in abolishing time but in deepening it." That the longing for the eternal present, when he "shall be cast and set firm in the mould of your truth," occurs within time testifies to the redemptive potential of such longing. Existence within time becomes hierarchized based on "how close or how far a given experience approaches or moves away from the pole of eternity" (30); thus, the sensitive artist will attempt to press toward that pole within his own time-bound restraints.

Christopher Fry is another artist that strains against the bonds of time while resisting the urge to locate meaning in some "heavenly other-world." Though MacDonald's struggle results in fantasy and Fry works with drama, both reveal a pressing motivation to alert their audiences to the immanence of divinity within temporal experience. In the brief essay "A Playwright

Speaks" that bears the weighty subtitle "How Lost, How Amazed, How Miraculous We Are," Fry attempts to describe his ontological stance: "Reality is incredible, reality is a whirlwind. What we call reality is a false god, the dull eye of custom" (27). The goal of the artist should be to shock the reader/audience out of complacent perception: "Our difficulty is to be alive to the newness, to see through the windows which are so steamed over with our daily breath, to be able to be old and new at one and the same time. And the theatre we should always be trying to achieve is one where the persons and events have the recognizable ring of an old truth, and yet seem to occur in a lightning spasm of discovery" (96). When reading this passage, the devotee of MacDonald will immediately think of the lightning spasms in *Lilith*'s penultimate chapter, and again we are reminded of the density of the novel's symbolism. Fry's artistic goal is more of a desire to disclose than a desire to present; not to show the audience something they have never seen before, but to show them something they have seen many times — have in fact grown quite accustomed to — and urge them to see it in a different way. Although MacDonald's Vane may repeatedly return to the same point physically, each time his paradigm has been transformed. At the end of the story, he has been altered to the point that he says, "Now and then, when I look round on my books, they seem to waver as if a wind rippled their solid mass, and another world were about to break through" (251). He perceives his world as being veritably filled with another world — one which his heart longs for.

One element of interpretation that seems fairly ubiquitous in critical commentary on *Lilith* is the attribution of some degree of failure to the story's end. The tendency of readers to attach a sense of unalloyed negativity to the climax of the novel certainly adds to the general confusion, serving to conceal the theme of immanence with which I am claiming MacDonald is occupied. The impression is that Vane is shoved back from the throne, utterly rejected in his attempt to climb the rocky ascent. As Professor Collins indicates, such a view presents the reader with a dilemma when considering the (otherwise) ostensibly progressive nature of Vane's experiences:

> Why, as the novel comes to a close, do we have such a negative pattern of reversal twice repeated within relatively few pages? And why do the negative patterns enwrap his joyful account of "resurrection morning"? We have assumed in the course of the novel, that by trial and error, several times refusing the Raven's advice, going off on his own for silly, selfish, egotistical reasons, all of which end in disastrous returns, Vane has indeed learned, made spiritual progress, as all souls are supposed to do. Does the ending reflect a pilgrim's progress, or perhaps a pilgrim's regress? Or is it presciently postmodern, reflecting an apparently meaningless circuit, a cynical return to square one which negates the idea of progress altogether? [12].

Indeed, these questions all serve to trouble the careful reader, and, in light of the proposed allegorical status of the novel, an utter rejection seems to necessitate discarding any notion of positive effect from fantasy that has been assumed up to this point. But fortunately this is not the only way of reading the book's second to last chapter.

If we consider the entire passage, ignoring the response of the narrator, the tone hardly suggests a rejection. It may seem unwise to disregard Vane's own sentiments at this point, but we must admit that his emotions have consistently proven unreliable for accurately assessing the significance of his circumstances. There is no doubt that the climactic climb up the rocky slope is a joyous one. Even as he sees the Little Ones welcomed into the cloudy heights, Vane anticipates a similar welcome. And he in fact receives it. "A hand, warm and strong, laid hold of mine, and drew me to a little door with a golden lock," and the push through the door is a gentle one (250). This is not the language of rejection or disapproval—although we have seen several times in the course of the novel where Vane has faced coldness and open disdain due to his haughty and insubordinate decisions. For example, he is left alone when he refuses to sleep during the first visit to Adam's house. The warmness of hospitality ceases, and the host tells Vane to return to his own world:

> "Then know," he returned, and his voice was stern, "that thou who callest thyself alive, hast brought into this chamber the odours of death, and its air will not be wholesome for the sleepers until thou art gone from it!"
> They went farther into the great chamber, and I was left alone in the moonlight with the dead [36–37].

Here we find the tone of rejection, as we do later in Chapter XXVIII, "I am Silenced" (139–42), where Vane is reprimanded by Mr. Raven for his string of foolish, rebellious decisions. His course has often run contrary to the divine will in this alternate world.

On the other hand, the last few chapters of the novel read much differently than do either of these two instances. As Vane makes "The Journey Home," there is nothing negative laid to his account. His conscience is clear, and he is welcomed on all sides. It would be rash of us to view the end of the story as an arbitrary thrust back to the humdrum library, dashing Vane's dreams of a "happily ever after" ending with Lona in some ethereal, undefined sphere. It appears that MacDonald requires more of his reader.

It is no accident that, as Vane is welcomed into the presence of the Ancient of Days—the source of the "unceasingly new-born" river of the water of life—he finds himself back in his library. It is no mere narrative trick utilized to close the discursive frame. Instead, it is meant to alert the reader to the immanence of glory within the mundane, the very "filledness" of our present existence. As he hears the words above him, "Welcome home," Vane describes his state as one of ecstatic anticipation: "Thought cannot form itself to tell what I felt, thus received by the officers of heaven. All I wanted and knew not, must be on its way to me!" (249). He in fact does receive all he wants but knows not. While he may have certain preconceived notions of what awaits him, the true reward of his spiritual journey is one of widened perception. We find hints of this heightened perception earlier, as he makes his joyous journey to the celestial city.

In the description of his surroundings, Vane is fairly bursting with the topic of renewal: "It was a summer-day more like itself, that is, more ideal, than ever man that had not died found summer-day in any world. I walked on the new earth, under the new heaven, and found them the same as the old, save that now they opened their minds to me, and I saw into them" (245). The only difference between "the new earth" and the old is revealed to be a subjective difference of deep perception. The power of the "fantasy" in Vane's life is ultimately shown to be revelatory, opening his perception and revealing an "unceasingly new-born" quality that he can then discern in his own temporal existence. The goal is not to reach a certain place, but instead to open to a new way of seeing that will infuse his self-centered, mundane world with significance and transcendent value. When Vane had earlier contemplated the prospect of fellowship, as he nursed the dying Lilith back to health, he had called himself a "possible man" (103). With the renewed perception born on resurrection day morning, we can see that he has become actual, and his brush with this quasi-eternal reality has served its purpose. The acme of his hopes and dreams turns out to be his own library viewed through re-born eyes.

While MacDonald does not give us an extensive depiction of Vane's further experiences in the world of time and sense, the shimmering reality that he sees around him speaks of the change that has occurred within him. If we consider the experiences in the alternate world to be speaking allegorically of the role of the fantastic in the authentic life, we find that the author has not only provided us with a densely-layered world of fantasy that will captivate our imagination again and again. He has directed our attention toward a way of reading fantasy that will prove valid in the extensively time-conscious milieu of the twenty-first century. Cultivating the fantastic in our lives need not preclude meaningful commitment to our own historical moment. On the contrary, it could in truth develop in us a far sager perception that will enable us to make responsible decisions in an age of cynical complacence.

Works Cited

Fry, Christopher. "A Playwright Speaks: How Lost, How Amazed, How Miraculous We Are." *Theatre Arts* 36 (1952): 27 and following.

Lewis, C.S. Introduction to *Lilith*. By George MacDonald. Grand Rapids: Eerdmans, 1988. v–xii.

Ricoeur, Paul. *Time and Narrative*. 3 Vols. Trans. Kathleen McLaughlin and David Pellauer. Chicago: University of Chicago, 1984.

Schaafsma, Karen. "The Demon Lover: Lilith and the Hero in Modern Fantasy." *Extrapolation: A Journal of Science Fiction and Fantasy* 28 (1987): 52–61.

CHAPTER 10

Frustrated Interpretation in *Lilith*

John Pennington

Chapter I of George MacDonald's *Lilith* is aptly titled "The Library." In this library, Mr. Vane, "alone in the world," bemoans the fact that he has "made little acquaintance with the history of [his] ancestors" (5). For Vane, the library becomes a space for investigating his family identity, and it is a space filled with books and manuscripts that seemingly have such answers. In the library Vane discovers a book that appears to be residing in two worlds:

> Beginnings of lines were visible on the left-hand page, and ends of lines on the other; but I could not, of course, get at the beginning and end of a single line, and was unable, in what I could read, to make any guess at the sense. The mere words, however, woke in me feelings which to describe was, from their strangeness, impossible. Some dreams, some poems, some musical phrases, some pictures, wake feelings such as one never had before, new in colour and form — spiritual sensations some of the phrases, some of the senseless half-lines, some even of the individual words affected me in similar fashion — as with the aroma of an idea, rousing in me a great longing to know what the poem or poems might, even yet in their multilation, hold or suggest [17].

In effect, the opening of *Lilith* is centered on reading and interpreting, around the "great longing to know."

Robert A. Collins, in "Liminality in *Lilith*" (see chapter 1), also has this great longing to know. He admits of *Lilith*, "For at least a dozen years now, I have been attempting to explicate it for my seminar in fantastic literature, but with decreasing confidence." Collins increasingly struggles with "the anticlimatic 'return' of the ending [which] demands explanation." By engaging the idea of liminality—"the moment of 'pure potentiality, when everything

..." trembles in the balance'" and where "protagonists lose their customary orientation, because the past is 'momentarily negated, suspended or abrogated, and the future is not yet begun'"—Collins hopes to interpret *Lilith* in a way that resolves an apparently flawed ending. He concludes, however, that the "endless ending" of the fantasy "communicates an air of didactic failure on some level, though the failure is perhaps as likely to be that of its readers as of its author."

Failure and *fault*. These are not two words that one should want to apply to *Lilith*. Perhaps the fault is not with MacDonald or the reader primarily but with the interpretive approaches that critics apply to the fantasy; more specifically, the problem may be that we try to make *Lilith* conform to a particular interpretation that the novel ultimately defies. "Liminal worlds are indeterminate ontological landscapes located in between alternative worlds," writes Mihai Spariosu (as quoted by Collins), and I find the notion of these indeterminate ontological landscapes an appropriate metaphor for my discussion. Both Mr. Vane and Mr. Collins find themselves in such indeterminate spaces because interpretation resides in the liminal — that is, reading and interpreting are worlds of potentiality that hover between the known and the unknown. Early in *Lilith*, Vane tells us, "I found myself in a region almost unknown to me" (10), and when he walks in the cemetery from an alternative world, he states, "I was lost in a space larger than imagination" (35). The question becomes, "How can we interpret these regions that are beyond conventional comprehension?" Collins's frustration with MacDonald's ending is actually the response the fantasy must evoke, for the endless ending reflects truncated or frustrated desire in both characters and readers of *Lilith*. The fantasy's lack of adequate closure reinforces the frustrated desire for certitude in an indeterminate landscape.

When Vane first encounters Lilith, he attempts to read her: "She was beautiful, but with such a pride at once and misery on her countenance that I could hardly believe what yet I saw.... But she began to writhe in such a torture that I stood aghast. A moment more and her legs, hurrying from her body, sped away serpents." Vane flees and hears "a waste and sickening cry, as of frustrate desire" (50). Rosemary Jackson reminds us that fantasy "is a literature of desire, which seeks that which is experienced as absence and loss" (3). According to Jackson, a fantasy can either "*tell of*, manifest or show desire ... or *expel* desire, when this desire is a disturbing element which threatens cultural order and continuity" (3–4). *Lilith* confounds readers, in part, because it does both: it shows the desire for erotic longing and expels that desire by denying closure and transforming sensual desire into a religious desire, what Georges Bataille calls "religious eroticism."

Lilith's closure mirrors this frustrated desire. In fact, the "endless ending" is consistent with the picaresque quest that Vane encounters once he enters the realm of the seven dimensions and returns to the supposed real world. Rolland Hein believes the ending is correct because it lends itself to "narrative plausibility"; I agree, but I want to push Hein's idea further into the realm of narratology. In *S/Z*, Rolland Barthes defines texts as *readerly* or *writerly*. The readerly text is "a classic text," argues Barthes, "characterized by the pitiless divorce which the literary institution maintains between the producer of the text and its user…. This reader is thereby plunged into a kind of idleness... he is left with no more than the poor freedom either to accept or reject the text" (4). The writerly text, on the other hand, is open, "gaining access to the magic of the signifier, to the pleasure of writing" (4); the writerly text allows the reader to be part of the reading process because such a text does not determine *for* the reader how to read and how to interpret a text. *Lilith* is certainly a writerly text that invites readers to enter that liminal space of interpretation and recognize that the novel is one of process more than product. As a writerly text, consequently, *Lilith* must circumvent traditional closure and remain open for the reader to "write" his or her interpretation of the endless ending. D.A. Miller contends that "what discontents the traditional novel is its own condition of possibility. For the production of narrative—what we called the narratable—is possible only within a logic of insufficiency, disequilibrium, and deferral" (265). Traditional novelists (those writing readerly texts primarily), continues Miller, "typically desire worlds of greater stability and wholeness than such a logic can intrinsically provide" (xiii). Miller suggests that the traditional novelist creates a form of tyranny over the reader by constructing "a narrative so thoroughly predestined that it does nothing but produce spurious problems for a solution already in place" (xiii). In "Balzac's Illusions Lost and Found," Miller concludes that a "failure of closure" becomes "a text's most powerful and seductive effect" (164): "Suppose we take that coming-to-fail not as a negative phenomenon, but as a positive strategy, not disruptive but constitutive of a text's social implications and usefulness" (165).

I think it useful to view *Lilith*'s problematic ending in light of Miller's argument. *Lilith*'s ambiguous ending, then, can be analyzed for its powerful and seductive effect, not for its perceived faults. MacDonald is a rare Victorian writer who wrote in multiple genres — sermons, poetry, realistic triple-decker novels, and fantasy and fairy tale to name a few. In *The Allegory of Love*, C.S. Lewis remarks that MacDonald, "a mystic and natural symbolist is seduced into writing novels" (232). Lewis suggests, consequently, that MacDonald's strength resides not in the classic, traditional narrative of the novel but with something unique and original, which most critics would label the fantastic, whether for adults or for children. One of my major concerns about

Lilith is that it is pegged as a mythopoeic fantasy. Collins seems to accept this label and concludes his essay with the statement that the ending "fails to solve ultimately the mythopoeic problem: what is the mythic significance of the 'endless ending'?" Earlier in the essay he also suggests that *Lilith* does not adequately follow Joseph Campbell's monomyth of "Departure," "Initiation," and "Return," a circular structure that he famously diagrams in *The Hero with a Thousand Faces,* in the chapter entitled "The Keys" (245). *Lilith* seems to create, though, a hero with a thousand-and-one faces. In other words, Campbell's monomyth engages a traditional sense of closure, which makes the myth a readerly text, one that controls the characters and readers. The same, I argue, is true of the mythopoeic. Lewis's claim that MacDonald is a mythopoeic writer has done much to confine MacDonald to a particular kind of fantasy. While Lewis famously tells us that his imagination was baptized by MacDonald, he has unwittingly marginalized MacDonald, ironically, by defining him as a mythopoeic writer. Lewis admits that "if we define literature as an art whose medium is words, then certainly MacDonald has no place in its first rank—perhaps not even in its second" (viii). Not generous praise by any means. Lewis continues: "What really delights and nourishes me is a particular pattern of events, which would equally delight and nourish if it had reached me by some medium which involved no words at all" (ix). To Lewis, finally, MacDonald is a great mythopoeic writer, who operates beyond words to create myth. But Lewis's notion of pattern suggests, similar to Campbell, that closure will bring the myth into focus, into meaning. In other words, Lewis posits that myth is a self-contained, closed system where plot is resolved by the mythic pattern. I would argue that Collins struggles with the Campbellian and mythopoeic elements of MacDonald's fantasy because its closure does not bring that sense of an ending (to paraphrase Frank Kermode). However, if we view *Lilith* as a writerly text that flaunts its lack of closure, then we can better understand why MacDonald resisted the tendency to bring unity to the text.

The question, consequently, remains: Why does MacDonald problematize his ending? One answer could be that the fantasy is flawed, that it is not a sustained, unified work. I do not think, however, such an interpretation takes us very far in our understanding of the work. By viewing *Lilith* as a writerly fantasy of desire, we may at least speculate more generously about its closure. A key concern that complicates the fantasy is that *Lilith* must provide closure for two characters—Vane and Lilith. Collins's essay presupposes that the book is about Vane, yet the fantasy is titled *Lilith.* And Vane's adventures seem driven by Lilith, who appears to be the main concern of Mr. Raven (Adam) and Eve. The desires of Vane and Lilith are complementary but also diametrically opposed, giving the novel a sustained tension as when two opposing magnets force each other away. That magnetic zone becomes a liminal space of interpretative potentiality. In an article for *North Wind*, I argue that Lilith has frustrated desire for erotic longing of Self and immortality. She tells Vane, "Men and women live but to die; we, that is such as I — we are but a few — live to live on. Old age is to you a horror; to me it is a dear desire: the older we grow, the nearer we are to our perfection" (129). Lilith finds herself in the throes of self-postponement, unable to fulfill her full potential. Her frustrated desire leads to what Leo Bersani calls "ontological slipperiness" (198), where being is always somewhere else: "Desire makes being problematic; the notion of a coherent unified self is threatened by the discontinuous, logically incompatible images of a desiring imagination" (84). This slipperiness of character can lead to narrative fragmentation, argues Bersani, which is a form of narrative subversion: "Desire can subvert social order; it can also disrupt novelistic order. The nineteenth-century novel is haunted by the possibility of these subversive movements, and it suppresses them with a brutality both shocking and eminently logical" (66). If MacDonald were writing a traditional, realistic novel, then we should be concerned with an ending that violates genre expectations. MacDonald, however, is writing something new and does not completely suppress Lilith in the fantasy.

MacDonald attempts to control Lilith by having her transform — she is silenced and made to sleep and rise again, converted by God into Christian goodness. But there is a problem with this approach, and MacDonald seems to be aware of the potential danger. MacDonald reinterprets the Lilith myth, which by its very nature does not have closure: Lilith, created as an equal, flees Adam to become independent and free, a succubus who tempts and destroys. Eventually, Eve replaces Lilith as the docile creature made from Adam's rib, and Adam and Eve become a powerful force of conversion in *Lilith*. MacDonald simultaneously evokes the Genesis story of the Bible and a subversive element of that story. Lilith's story is one of outcast, of apocrypha, that has no ending. Lilith literally exists in a mythic story that has an endless ending. MacDonald attempts to transform her, which violates the myth, and he is aware of the limits of such a metamorphosis. Lilith's story in *Lilith* ends in process: her hand is cut off and she falls asleep waiting to be reborn. But the novel does not end here. The fantasy continues on for seven more chapters, as the narrative now traces Vane's quest for fulfillment. Lilith tends to dissolve into the narrative, haunting the fringes of the fantasy. While MacDonald appears to silence Lilith so she can become a whole, unified self that represents God's goodness, the reader never sees this transformation — Lilith's change is delayed, is frustrated, not only for herself but also for the reader. And this delay creates tension in interpretation. Robert Lee Wolff states bluntly: "As we near the end, the imagery of *Lilith* breaks down completely. On the one hand MacDonald paints the picture of triumphant resurrection. On the other, evil is all about, even on the 'frontiers' of heaven itself" (369). Wolff's complaint is accurate, but one could argue that this complaint is not a weakness of the fantasy but a strength, for as Roderick McGillis argues, "The book resists systematization; it delights in paradox, in synecdoche, in riddle, in metaphor, in pleonasm, in oxymoron, in change" (53–54).

On the one hand, *Lilith* is about Lilith and her process; on the other, the fantasy is about Vane's process, which Collins focuses on in his essay. Of course, Lilith (the tempter of Vane) and Vane (the one forcing Lilith into change) are symbiotic, doubles of each other. As Vane states, "Her words were terrible with temptation" (223). Like Lilith, Vane finds himself frustrated at the end of the novel: as he awaits, with his "heart beating with hope and desire" (250), to be reunited with Lona in paradise (Heaven), a god-like hand pushes him through a door, and he returns to his library. The novel ends with Vane waiting—"I wait; asleep or awake, I wait"—unable to determine whether he is asleep in the death chamber dreaming or fully awake in his library. Vane finds himself in that liminal space of potentiality. MacDonald concludes *Lilith* with a quotation from Novalis—"Our life is no dream, but it should and will perhaps become one" (252)—a sentiment he also evokes at the opening of *Phantastes* at the end, as Anodos waits for "a great good [that] is coming" (185). MacDonald returns Vane to the beginning of the narrative in *Lilith* and to the beginning of his career as a fantasy writer in *Phantastes*. This circular structure, then, appears more complex than a matter of closure particular to *Lilith*. It suggests that MacDonald is concerned with potentiality, with a perpetual process of transformation that by its nature can never be fulfilled.

That Vane returns to the library is quite fitting, for it also returns him and the reader to a space of reading and interpreting. The ending beckons us to decipher the text, which resists conventional interpretation, as Collins posits. Vane returns to the library to find himself once again in a liminal space of "pure potentiality, when everything trembles in the balance." As Lilith lies on the death-couch waiting to be reborn, Vane waits in a world in flux: as he looks "round on [his] books, they seem to waver as if a wind rippled their solid mass, and another world were about to break through" (251). That world is not the realm of the seven dimensions (Vane has been there and back); the new world is beyond that one, a world we assume is that of death, a world at the back of the North Wind. In death, in this new world of potentiality, Vane will find eternal life and be reunited with Lona. That world, ultimately, is a world of fulfilled desire for immortality. Vane and Lilith remain, however, in "indeterminate ontological landscapes" at the end of the narrative. Collins is unable to resolve the endless ending, I would argue, because there can be no satisfactory ending to a work that is in such process. The ending of *Lilith* is consistent with the fantasy's attempt to create a language for the desire of Lilith and Vane who desire to live, Lilith in the supposed temporal world of the Self, Vane in the immortal world of the Eternal. Both desires, however, cannot be fulfilled because they are states of process and transformation. A Lacanian approach would suggest that Lilith and Vane search for that *objet a*, which is temporarily found and then lost (similar to Vane's rescuing of Lilith and her subsequent fleeing). In other words, *Lilith* cannot have traditional closure and be true to its narrative world and overall theme.

Georges Bataille in *Death and Sensuality* can help us better understand *Lilith*'s conundrum. Bataille argues that humans are fragmented because they cannot find wholeness in life: "Discontinuous beings that we are, death means continuity of being," for we "yearn for our lost continuity" (16). That continuity is found in death. And that continuity becomes, according to Bataille, a fulfillment of desire where death is "concerned with the fusion of beings in a world beyond everyday reality." Bataille labels that continuity, simply, a form of "religious eroticism" (16). MacDonald certainly is obsessed with such religious eroticism in *Phantastes* and *Lilith*, as well as in his all-ages fantasies, particularly *At the Back of the North Wind* and "The Golden Key," maybe the finest example of such desire. If my application of Bataille is accurate, then what MacDonald desires is more life via death, with Lilith forced against her will into a Christian typology of death as a means of more life, and Vane passively waiting for a death that is withheld from him at the end. Such a lack of closure becomes a strength rather than a weakness. Structurally, too, the "endless ending" is logical, for there is no end to narrative when characters live on to the eternal. Vane's waiting symbolizes that eternal life, that eternal plot that would be a plot of the infinite.

I want to end with one final issue: the desire of the reader. Collins's essay is also one of desire — he desires to understand and resolve the paradox that is *Lilith*'s endless ending. As he himself states of the fantasy's "air of didactic failure," it "is perhaps as likely to be that of its readers as of its author." Earlier, I suggested that *Lilith* is a writerly text, and I would further this claim by arguing that the reader is, finally, asked to write the end to the fantasy. How does the reader write closure in *Lilith*? Miller's notion that a failure of closure is a "text's most powerful and seductive effect" (164) is significant when analyzing the role of MacDonald's reader, for part of the book's seduction resides in that liminal realm of interpretation. In a way, the reader becomes Lilith and Vane, hoping for fulfillment of desire; in the reader's case, this desire is a longing for closure or completeness of the narrative. Another way of putting this is that the fantasy requires the reader to do something to the text, to write a meaning onto an ending, which frustrates that kind of writing. Closure is denied. Peter Brooks argues that "the sense of beginning, then, is determined by the sense of an ending" (1035). Thus Hein's contention that the ending completes the narrative by having Vane, as the narrator of the story, return to his library so that he can finish his narrative as he awaits death makes structural sense. But this analysis does not necessarily appease readers who long for a better explanation that takes into account a complex narrative evoking multiple interpretations. If Brooks is correct, then endings control an entire narrative from the start, forcing texts, to a degree, to be readerly texts rather than writerly ones. But Brooks is not one-dimensional in his theory; he also argues that "if the end is recognition which retrospectively illuminates beginning and middle, it is not the exclusive truth of the text, which must include the processes along the way — the processes of 'transformation'— in their metonymical complexity." Reading, then, is process and transformation, akin to the experience Lilith and Vane find themselves in. Brooks contends that endings, in appropriate Freudian fashion, are concerned with "the human end, with death" (1035)—"the narrative must tend toward its end, seek illumination in its own death" (1039)—constituting what Brooks labels Freud's masterplot.

When Vane laments at the end, "I wait; asleep or awake, I wait" (252), he experiences what the reader experiences — that endless ending. Brooks further supports the notion that fantasy is a literature of desire: "Desire is the wish for the end, for fulfillment, but fulfillment delayed so that we can understand it in relation to origin, and to desire itself" (1043). Scheherazade's stories are the prototype — her stories are endless as they perpetuate her life. The end of her stories will be the end of her existence. Only after 1001 nights does Scheherazade escape the infinity of story, gaining her life back, which becomes a new story that lives on. There's a metaphor here working. What Brooks brings to the interpretative table is that "Freud's masterplot speaks of the temporality of desire, and speaks to our very desire for fictional plots" (1044). Lewis's mythopoesis provides such a plot, where plot even supersedes words — story is all. But Collins recognizes the problem with the Lewis reading too. And, I think, we find ourselves back at that liminal space. Brooks concludes, "It may finally be in the logic of our argument that repetition speaks in the text of a return which ultimately subverts the very notion of beginning and end, suggesting that the idea of beginning presupposes the end, that the end is a time before the beginning, and hence that the interminable never can be finally bound in a plot" (1042). The reader finds him- or herself caught in the liminal space of interpretation, desiring closure to an endless ending, frustrated by the inability to adequately find closure to a narrative whose writerly world defies such closure. This frustration seems to be at the heart of *Lilith* itself.

My response to Robert Collins may be frustrating to many readers, for I find in *Lilith*'s perceived problematic ending a strength that returns us to Collins's initial concern — that of the seemingly inadequate endless ending of the fantasy. My argument is not necessarily a contradiction; rather, it is descriptive of the narrative's inability to limit closure to Lilith, Vane, and the reader. *Lilith* is an endless ending; it is a limitless text that seduces us to place limits on it. We become as frustrated as Vane, and we often align ourselves with Lilith, who cannot abide by any limits. MacDonald's story becomes oxymoronic: it forces limits on Lilith as it opens up the possibility of the limitless. Lilith's sleeping and Vane's waiting are metaphors for our reading experience. Early in *Lilith*, Vane questions Mr. Raven about the impossibility of multiple dimensions: "Two objects," Vane says, "cannot exist in the same place at the same time." "Can they not?" questions Mr. Raven, "I did not know!" (23). That exchange takes place in Chapter IV, "Somewhere or Nowhere?" Later in the novel, Vane becomes frustrated with Mr. Raven's play on words: "'Enigma treading on enigma!' I exclaimed. 'I did not come here to be asked riddles.'" Mr. Raven, in a moment of compassion, provides Vane with a more solid response: "Indeed you are yourself the only riddle. What you call riddles are truths, and seem riddles because you are not true. And you *must* answer the riddles! They will go on asking themselves until you understand yourself. The universe is a riddle trying to get out, and you are holding your door hard against it" (45). The narrative riddle of *Lilith* is not solved because it cannot be solved in Vane's life or in the reader's time. *Lilith* delays answers to the riddles because a riddle has closure, its ending controlling the beginning. As much as MacDonald wants to solve the great riddle, he is genius enough to know that a delayed answer is more frustrating *and* fitting for such an enigmatic fantasy world.

Works Cited

Barthes, Roland. *S/Z*. Trans. Richard Miller. New York: Hill and Wang, 1974.
Bataille, Georges. *Death and Sensuality: A Study of Eroticism and the Taboo*. New York: Walker, 1962.
Bersani, Leo. *A Future for Astyanax: Character and Desire in Literature*. New York: Columbia University Press, 1984.
Brooks, Peter. "Freud's Masterplot" in *The Critical Tradition: Classic Texts and Contemporary Trends*. Ed. David H. Richter. 2nd ed. Boston: Bedford, 1998. 1033–44.
Campbell, Joseph. *The Hero with a Thousand Faces*. Princeton: Princeton University Press, 1968.
Jackson, Rosemary. *Fantasy: The Literature of Subversion*. New York: Methuen, 1981.
Lewis, C.S. *The Allegory of Love*. New York: Oxford University Press, 1958.
_____. Introduction to *Lilith*. By George MacDonald. Grand Rapids: Eerdmans, 1981. v–xii.

MacDonald, George. *Phantastes*. Grand Rapids: Eerdmans, 1981.
McGillis, Roderick. "*Phantastes* and *Lilith*: Femininity and Freedom" in *The Gold Thread: Essays on George MacDonald*, 31–55. Ed. William Raeper. Edinburgh: Edinburgh University Press, 1990.
Miller, D.A. *Narrative and its Discontents: Problems of Closure in the Traditional Novel*. Princeton: Princeton University Press, 1981.
———. "Balzac's Illusions Lost and Found." *Yale French Studies* 67 (1984): 164–81.
Pennington, John. "Of 'Frustrate Desire': Feminist Self-Postponement in George MacDonald's *Lilith*." *North Wind* 21 (2002): 26–70.
Wolff, Robert Lee. *The Golden Key: A Study of the Fiction of George MacDonald*. New Haven: Yale University Press, 1961.

CHAPTER 11

Liminality as Psychic Stage in *Lilith*

Roderick McGillis

"we breathed homeward our longing desires" [245].

    Robert A. Collins begins his exploration (chapter 1) of liminality in *Lilith* by examining a passage from the book's penultimate chapter. I'll begin my exploration in the book's second chapter, "The Mirror." In this chapter, Vane follows a shadowy figure to regions of his house he had never before known, and in a small chamber in the expansive garret he comes across "a tall mirror with a dusty face, old fashioned and rather narrow — in appearance an ordinary glass" (11). The glass, however, proves to be anything but "ordinary." Like mirrors in many of MacDonald's books, this one proves to be a portal, a threshold, a doorway, an entrance to another world from the one in which the protagonist lives in what we might, loosely, think of as normal reality. The reality beyond the portal, inside or on the other side of the mirror, differs from the reality we experience in the here and now. And so we have at least two realities, one on either side of the mirror. What are these realities? Or more precisely, what function does the mirror serve in the negotiation between these realities? If liminality is relevant to MacDonald's vision, then the mirror itself is a liminal zone, a place where one passes between realities; the mirror activates a rite of passage. In this function of passageway, the mirror is similar to the many doors that Collins cites in *Lilith*: coffin lids, a masked door, a closet door, books, graves, and even a fountain. Each of these portals indicates the intensely inward movement of this book. The rite of passage enacts a psychic change, usually the change from immaturity to maturity. In Freudian terms, what we have is the individual's encounter with forces (usually manifested in the father) demanding repression, demanding the individual turn from libidinal obsessions to socially sanctioned actions. MacDonald's emphasis on the library as the location for Vane's experiences (he begins and ends in the library of his house), and Vane's description of his own "mental peculiarities" (5) cue the reader to the psychological interest the story takes in its protagonist. *Lilith* is the story of Vane's passage from one state of psychic development to another. His story is the story of the transition from adolescence to adulthood, that transition that MacDonald chronicles many times in his works, perhaps most directly in his essay, "A Sketch of Individual Development" (1882).

The mirror has a rich history as a trope, both as a dark glass hiding from us the vision of truth and spiritual finality and as a luminous surface that reflects truth and wonderment (see LaBossiere and Schell). The mirror has also served as a metaphor for the book itself when writers spoke of holding a mirror up to nature (see Abrams). The mirror has been the soul, the conscience, and the window to all things essential. The mirror has also had its narcissistic implications. For Jacques Lacan, the mirror usefully images the transition from an oceanic jouissance into desire, and I think Lacan's insight might be helpful for our understanding of *Lilith*. If Vane carries any message back to us at the end of the book when he fails to find fulfillment and a place in the "city among the blue clouds" (247), then this message has something to do with patience. Collins, like a number of readers, finds the ending of *Lilith* disconcertingly abstruse or at least not completely satisfying (see Wolff 365–371 and Robb 107, for example). He senses an "air of didactic failure" at the end, although he suggests that the failure "is perhaps as likely to be that of [the book's] readers as of its author." I like this. I think we are wise to defer to an author, even in these heady days of perplexity at the notion of authorship itself. MacDonald found inspiration for *Lilith* in several places, not least in the work of William Blake, and like Blake, he had a vision that contemplated both the possibility of completeness and the acceptance of incompleteness. Things will be complete, but not in our knowing this side the grave. *Lilith* is, as Manlove says, eschatology (92), but eschatology only contemplates an end; it cannot accomplish it. MacDonald returns again and again to the notion of "endless ending"; things do end, but we can only speculate and imagine an ending. We cannot experience ending, that is an apocalyptic ending, not yet, not until, perhaps, our life becomes that dream that both Vane and Novalis mention. While we exist this side of perfection, we can only see what the eye/I offers, what Vane identifies, when he looks at Eve for the first time, as "continuous creation" (26).

Myths, of course, imagine both beginnings and endings. They are ways we have of speculating on the why of things, and in speculating, myths offer not explanations in any absolute sense, but rather comfort, what Tolkien called "consolation" (60). The consolation is for the condition in which we find ourselves, a condition that is perpetually between, perpetually longing for completion, perpetually aware of completion's inevitability, and also of completion's unknowability. We know and yet we do not know. We see by glimpses only. The dream continues, even while we wait for the dream to become reality. MacDonald's prose delivers paradox as one of its most insistent rhetorical devices, and it does so precisely to communicate this condition of knowing and not knowing. Perhaps this is the condition of myth itself. Certainly, we might argue that this is the condition of human material existence as it tries to understand itself in non-material ways. Myth is one attempt we make to understand that which exceeds material knowing, but myth itself derives not from some metaphysical zone, but from the very materiality we sense is only part of our experience.

Another way of articulating this sense of our being "in between" is, for me, to contemplate the conception of "home." As Collins points out, *Lilith* offers speculation on home as "the only place where you can go out and into.... The one place, if you do but find it, where you may go out and in both, is home" (*Lilith* 15). The Raven tells Vane: "Home is ever so far away in the palm of your hand, and how to get there it is of no use to tell you" (45). Home is, in other words, reality, that condition in which we are at one with things. In Lacanian terms, home is that amorphous and chaotic state of being in which subject and object are one. Home is where we come from and where we hope to return. It is the Imperial Palace from which we come and the Celestial City to which we hope to go. To be home is to be prior to birth. To be home is to be dead. Reality lies prior to being in the world and it lies beyond the grave. From a psychoanalytic perspective, home is where desire finds completion, and when we reflect that desire can (by definition) not find completion in consciousness, we realize just how elusive home is. From a spiritual perspective, home is in the ether, in the Celestial City, the city in the clouds from which Vane is turned away. *Lilith* emphasizes the attractions and the elusiveness of home partly through MacDonald's language that is necessarily paradoxical. Our life is no dream, and yet it ought to become one; our life in the mundane world is a dream from which we will awake to find ourselves in reality. As Stephen Prickett puts it, at the end of *Lilith*, "It is not clear if [Vane] has at last 'awoken' from death in that other world, only to be returned to this, or if he has merely dreamed that he has awoken — so that his existence in this world is only part of the dream until he finally 'awakes'" (192). The point is that humans, like Mr. Vane, yearn for home, but fear it at the same time because home contains death as well as life. When Eve enters the cemetery, Vane finds her as lovely as "Beatrice in the white rose of the redeemed" (32), but when Adam invites him to sleep in the cemetery, Vane refuses. He is not yet ready to "come alive and die" (35).

Vane's experience nicely corresponds to Lacan's Mirror Stage (*Ecrits* 1–7). Clearly, Vane is at a transitional stage in his life, having recently completed his studies at Oxford. His parents are no longer living, and he will shortly assume "the management of the estate" (5). Commentators on *Lilith* sometimes see the plot as chronicling Vane's search for his father, and to a certain extent, this is the case (see Wolff 331; Hein 404, although Hein's "the Father and the Son" differ from Wolff's father). His reading of his father's manuscript starts him on his journey in earnest. But we can, I think, assume that both parents are important for Vane, the mother representing that home Vane desires and the father representing duty and labor associated with what Lacan terms the symbolic. I might as well come clean and state that I am using Lacan's three "stages" (the Real, the Imaginary, and the Symbolic) to structure my thinking about *Lilith* here. The Real I am considering as home. We might think of the Real in a Platonic sense as an ideal, and this would not be completely askew; however, Lacan's Real is a psychic phenomenon rather than an ideational or spiritual one. It exists at all times as the "place" and the "time" we yearn to return to, and as in Freud it has connections with the mother. Vane's desire for a variety of female figures—Eve, Mara, Lilith, and Lona—expresses his desire for the lost mother. These women have no existence outside of Vane's desire; they are symptoms of his desire. In other words, the entire story constitutes Vane's fantasy. We may remember Lacan's infamous assertion that woman does not exist (Mitchell and Rose 145). The non-existence of woman is especially clear in the case of Lilith herself. Vane brings her to life when he cares for her beside the stream in Chapters XVIII and XIX, and later in Chapter XXIX Adam reads a poem in which we learn that in the earlier incident Lilith took shape from Vane's own desire. The poem's speaker is Lilith:

> For by his side, I lay, a bodiless thing;
>   I breathed not, saw not, felt not, only thought,
> And made him love me—with a hungering
>   After he knew not what—if it was aught
>   Or but a nameless something that was wrought
> By him out of himself ... [144–45].

Lilith clothes herself, she says, "in the likeness true / Of that idea where his soul did cleave" (144). Before Vane gives Lilith life, she is "bodiless," a negation, virtually a nothingness. Clearly, from one perspective Lilith represents the ontological certainty of evil, but from another perspective, she represents only possibility and desire, nothing more and nothing less. We might remember that she has little or no power of agency in herself; she needs Vane and we can assume that she also needs the Great Shadow that appears to control her. In other words, Lilith is a creature of male desire. She exists as evidence of the male fantasy of fullness. She is, strangely, Vane's *objet a*, that thing that activates and focuses his desire for the Real. Insofar as she is unattainable, she is the Real. She represents indulgence, hedonism, algolagnia, chaos, darkness drawing down, and ecstasy. We can assume that she will be waiting for him, along with Lona and the others, when he eventually dies into life.

Vane comes to Lilith after looking in and passing through a mirror. The mirror stage in Lacan is the moment of separation, the moment in which the subject (in this case Vane) becomes aware of otherness. What the infant sees in the mirror is a reflection of himself; Vane does not see himself when he looks in the mirror, but what he does see is an aspect of himself, his psychic geography, as it were. Manlove comments that "all the figures in *Lilith* are, as it were, parts of one huge imagination" (90). Indeed, everything in *Lilith* is part of Vane's (and by extension, MacDonald's) imagination. Once on the other side of the mirror, Vane discovers that he has an identity problem; he understands that "I did not know myself" (14). Later, when he succors Lilith, he learns for the first time "what solitude meant." He tell us: "I saw now that a man alone is but a being that may become a man — that he is but a need, and therefore a possibility." The perfection of man depends upon otherness. Vane asserts, "A man to be perfect — complete, that is, in having reached the spiritual condition of persistent and universal growth, which is the mode wherein he inherits the infinitude of his Father — must have the education of a world of fellow-men" (102–03). He uses the word "gaze" to indicate his specular relationship to the woman he is nurturing, and this fits with the Lacanian notion of the gaze as the subject's construction of the Imaginary "other" that derives from the reflected self first perceived in the mirror. To put this bluntly, when Vane brings Lilith back to life, he is creating his Imaginary, that ideal self he would like to enjoy. The creation or even the awareness of the Imaginary precipitates the subject into the Symbolic, the world most of us inhabit, the world of language and quotidian reality, what Lacan refers to as the "law of the Father." This is the world that Lilith also inhabits, a world of getting and spending, in which possession is the most prized condition. This is the world in which self and "other" meet and communicate with language, in some sense at least.

Collins notes that in the world behind the mirror, Vane encounters difficulty with language. He puts it this way: "the most critical incompatibility Vane discovers concerns Language." In Lacan's view, language and the unconscious share a structure. Like aspects of the unconscious, language is arbitrary. Lacan here picks up on Saussurian linguistics, the notion that the relationship between a word and that which it signifies is agreed upon uneasily in that word and signification are more often than not elusive, and they are certainly arbitrary. Words are "live things" that scurry from person to person and from meaning to meaning. Vane tells us more than once that he has difficulty matching word and meaning, and the reason for this is simply that words are incompetent to say anything with finality or complete accuracy. At one point, he interrupts the narrative to explain that he is engaged in a "constant struggle to say what cannot be said with even an approach to precision." He notes that where he is, a "single thing would sometimes seem to be and mean many things" (46). MacDonald is here echoing the Romantic idea of what Wordsworth refers to as the "sad incompetence of human speech." But this idea has relevance for the Lacanian notion of language as itself an *objet a*, that which focuses our longing, that which attempts to fill in for the absent home. Language is symbolic precisely because it is always just a cover for that which cannot be said or that which is missing. In other words, language reminds us that we lack the completeness of the Real. Once we re-enter the Real, subject and object, word and meaning will coalesce. We have a glimpse of this in Chapter XLV, "The Journey Home." Vane tells us that the "world and my being, its life and mine, were one" (243). He, Lona, and the Little Ones are on their way "home to the Father!" (244). We know what he means, but perhaps I can take the liberty of inserting a psychoanalytic observation here and point out that the "father" inevitably represents the world separate from the mother, and therefore we can know that Vane must find not completion, but in-completion in his journey. The law of the father dictates that the world this side of death is incomplete; it is as much a vale of longing as it is a vale of tears. Until he is truly dead, Vane can only wait, asleep or awake, wait for the end that we cannot know beyond imaginative projection.

And so we return to the end, to that point in the book when the narrative closes. Collins, like readers before him, finds the end of *Lilith* teasingly difficult. Why, he asks, does the close of the fantasy have a "negative pattern of reversal twice repeated within a few pages"? Isn't the protagonist supposed to learn something during the course of his experiences, and is not the learning process supposed to fit into a mythopoeic pattern? His sense of mythopoesis derives from C.S. Lewis's influential argument that MacDonald excels not as a literary writer, but as a myth-maker. For Lewis, myth appears to communicate "the quality of the real universe, the divine, magical, terrifying and ecstatic reality in which we all live." Myth has a spiritual significance; without myth, life is dark and mechanical. I am not sure, however, that we need to think of myth precisely in this way. Obviously, we do have myths that contain spiritual significance, that give us glimpses of our origin and perhaps glimpses of our destination. Such myths purport to organize and even explain deep truths, to put into words that which lies deeper than words. The origins of such myths are obscure, perhaps even beyond human knowing. On the other hand, myths derive from the human imagination, and when we think of myths as having their origin in human materiality, we can think of them as deliberately concerned with the stubborn facts of human interaction that involve such things as desire and relationships. If the end of *Lilith* poses a problem, then the problem may have something to do with how we interpret "myth."

One possible answer to what Collins perceives to be a problem at the book's closing lies in the notion of liminality. Perhaps the book chronicles a space between one condition and the other, between material reality and spiritual reality. But we know that MacDonald thought of these realities as "mingling" and therefore as really one reality. And Collins closes his own suggestive exploration of *Lilith* by asking "what is the significance of the 'endless ending'?" The ending of the book, he asserts, "does not seem to most serious readers to mirror what they already know of MacDonald's religious beliefs." Frankly, I don't know whether I count as one of MacDonald's "serious readers," but I have never found the end of this book either a failure or negative. On the contrary, I have always found the book, ending and all, as a visionary experience that confidently speaks of human possibility even while it speaks from within an incomplete world. The myth MacDonald delivers is the myth of human possibility that includes the possibility both of victory and of failure. Victory must confront us as a possibility, as it does Vane when he approaches the City in the blue clouds, but failure is our necessary ground. Failure is necessary because without it we would have nowhere to go. Without contraries there is no progression. Opposition is true friendship. Such aphorisms contain the myth I sense in *Lilith*. Vane's rite of passage takes him from a condition of relative infancy into the Symbolic. His triumph is that in passing into the Symbolic, he has learned something. He has learned of loss and its relation to desire, and he has learned patience, the patience to know that desire can only find fulfillment elsewhere, in the Real from which we are barred, "until death do us bring together."

The end returns us to the mother, as if Vane understands that the Real entails a necessary return of the world to the mother. He writes, "But when I wake at last into that life which, as a mother her child, carries this life in its bosom, I shall know that I wake, and shall doubt no more" (252). The symptom of Vane's longing is the series of women he meets beyond the mirror, and each of these women is, in one way or another, a mother. Child mother (Lona), demon mother (Lilith), sorrowful mother (Mara), first mother (Eve)— Vane finds each of these women attractive and compelling. And none of them can he have, at least not yet, not in the here and now of this mundane world of just three dimensions. Even seven dimensions are insufficient for *jouissance*.

For now, he has the knowledge of desire's reach. Just as Lilith herself learns to relinquish false desire, the paternal desire for ownership, control, and power, so too does Vane learn the vanity of such desire. His name offers a clue. The vanity he learns to set aside is only one aspect of his name's signification; "vane" also is that which changes as the wind blows. Persistent growth is necessary to all creatures, as we see in the story of Lord and Lady Cokayne. These two grotesque and comic figures remind us of the necessary continuation of growth. "Vane" is also a variant of the older word "fane," which is a temple or church. The body as a temple dates back a long way. The bodies of Lord and Lady Cokayne are ruined temples, but reconstruction will take place, in time. My point is that Mr. Vane is changeable, he is vain, and he is also holy. He is, in short, a walking contradiction. Mr. Vane is just like the rest of us. This is why he ends up back in the library. We leave him surrounded by ghosts of possible relationship and love. The books in the library, like the book *Lilith*, are necessary reminders of the ongoing work of understanding and connectedness.

Works Cited

Abrams, Myer H. *The Mirror and the Lamp*. New York: W.W. Norton, 1953.

Hein, Rolland. *George MacDonald: Victorian Mythmaker*. Nashville, Tenn.: Star Song, 1993.

La Bossiere, Camille and Richard Schell. "Glass, Mirror." *A Dictionary of Biblical Tradition in English Literature*. Ed. David Lyle Jeffrey, et al. Grand Rapids, Mich.: Eerdmans, 1992. 308–10.

Lacan, Jacques. *Ecrits: A Selection*. Trans. Alan Sheridan. New York: W.W. Norton, 1977.

Lewis, C.S. *George MacDonald: An Anthology*. London: Geoffrey Bles, 1946.

MacDonald, George. "A Sketch of Individual Development" in *A Dish of Orts*. 43–76. London: Sampson Low, Marston, 1895 (1882).

Manlove, Colin. *The Impulse of Fantasy Literature*. Kent, Ohio: Kent State University Press, 1983.

Mitchell, Juliet and Jacqueline Rose, eds. *Feminine Sexuality: Jacques Lacan and the ecole freudienne*. Trans. Jacqueline Rose. New York: W.W. Norton, 1985.

Prickett, Stephen. *Victorian Fantasy*. Bloomington and London: Indiana University Press, 1979.

Robb. David. *George MacDonald*. Edinburgh: Scottish Academic Press, 1987.

Tolkien, J.R.R. *Tree and Leaf*. London: Unwin, 1964.

Wolff, Robert Lee. *The Golden Key: A Study of the Fiction of George MacDonald*. New Haven: Yale University Press, 1961.

CHAPTER 12

Cosmic and Psychological Redemption in *Lilith**

Bonnie Gaarden

George MacDonald, Scottish Victorian author, wrote the first fantasy novels for adults in English. He dedicated himself to literature after failing as a Congregational minister, ultimately producing over 50 books — novels, fairy tales for children, poetry, sermons, literary criticism. His current literary reputation rests largely on his fairy tales and fantasies. C.S. Lewis considered him a mythopoetic genius pressured by financial need into abandoning the fantastic in favor of the novels preferred by the public (*George MacDonald* xxix). Whatever the reason, MacDonald produced only two book-length fantasies for adults. These works bracketed his long career: *Phantastes*, in 1858, was his third publication, while *Lilith*, in 1895, was almost his last.

The concerns MacDonald expresses in his writing are largely religious. He was devout but heterodox, having been ejected from his first and only pulpit after suggesting that animals had souls and a share in the afterlife and that the heathen might, after death, be given a chance at salvation (Greville MacDonald 180–83). He eventually found a mentor in F. D. Maurice, whose church in Vere Street, London, the MacDonalds attended and who shared MacDonald's Universalist convictions (Greville MacDonald 397–99). MacDonald was convinced that all humankind, not just Christians, would eventually enjoy reconciliation and unity with God because God loved all people

---

* This essay first appeared in *Studies in the Novel*, v. 37 no. 1, Spring 2005, copyright © 2005 by University of North Texas. Reprinted by permission of the publisher.

so much that he would send them deeper and deeper into the Hell of their miserable, isolate natures until — before or after physical death — they finally became desperate enough to repent, turn toward him, and undergo a spiritual education and/or purgation that might take millennia. In *Lilith* he goes so far as to join Origen (third century) and John Scottus Eriugena (ninth century) in suggesting that even Satan himself (388) will eventually be saved and brought into the Divine being so that, as St. Paul put it, "God might be all in all" (1 Cor. 15.28). MacDonald's wife found *Lilith* disturbing and protested its publication (Raeper 364), while his eldest son Greville hailed it as the best statement yet of "the Revelation of St. George the Divine" (321). The bulk of contemporary reviewers sided with Louisa, but Greville too was correct. As Jeanne Walker has pointed out, *Lilith* contains its author's strongest affirmation of his doctrine of universal redemption. If, as the story has it, even a Lilith can be saved, who then shall be eternally condemned?

Anyone familiar with Jungian psychology who reads MacDonald (particularly his sermons and criticism) must be struck by the classically Jungian character of MacDonald's views of the soul and its development. Although separated by nationality, professional disciplines, and two generations (MacDonald was 51 years old in 1875, when Jung was born), both Jung and MacDonald rejected the rigid Protestant traditions of their upbringing to produce Neo-Platonic, Hegelian models for human spiritual growth. Both were widely read in, and show the strong influences of, the German Romantics, Christian mystics, and medieval hermetic philosophy (in MacDonald's case the hermetic influence probably came through Jacob Boehme). Jung theorized that the psychic and the material are but two sides of the same reality, while MacDonald believed that the material world of nature is God's direct self-expression. Both believed that God dwells in, and speaks from, the unconscious. Both believed that spiritual growth is achieved through a union of opposites in the soul. Both were marginalized by the religious establishments of their times but stubbornly adhered to the Christian tradition. MacDonald all his life considered himself a Christian teacher, while Jung, according to Aniela Jaffe, "explicitly declared his allegiance to Christianity" and was "grieved" that his religious ideas were "not properly understood" (Jung, *Memories* x–xi).

MacDonald's theology modifies mainstream Christian orthodoxy in the direction of the influences he shares with Jung. For instance, in mainstream orthodoxy, the agent of spiritual maturation is the indwelling Holy Spirit, which brings Christ's life (new birth) to the Christian soul in baptism (or, in some Protestant denominations, at conversion). Thus God indwells Christians only, and only Christians are able to "be transformed ... by the renewing of your minds" (Rom. 12.2) to achieve a spiritual maturity "measured by nothing less than the full stature of Christ" (Eph. 4.14). MacDonald believed, however, that each individual at his or her deepest core was indissolubly united to deity. He held that God "sits in that chamber of our being in which the candle of our consciousness goes out in darkness" (*Orts* 25). MacDonald distinguishes between the "bastard self" of our consciousness, subject to sin and error, and the true self, or "Christ-self" (*Diary* 17), the true God-made individuality of which God is root and ground (*Sermons* 3: 80). The "Christ-self" is the agent of spiritual development in all people, and destines all for union with God. MacDonald's "Christ-self" thus has obvious similarities to Jung's concept of the "self." Jung distinguishes the self from the conscious ego as being the totality of the personality, conscious and unconscious, and the origin of the drive toward psychological development, or individuation.[1] Individuation, though productive of a "larger" and more complete personality, is painful because it requires people to withdraw their projections and acquire self-knowledge they find repellent. People dread becoming more conscious, and every advance toward individuation entails suffering.[2] The suffering caused by unwanted self-knowledge is also an inextricable part of spiritual growth for MacDonald. Before one can repent of sin and thrust it from him, he must see the sin in himself, in all its ugliness. This is a major component of the purgatorial agony and is graphically pictured in *Lilith*.

Besides the similarities in their models of the human personality, there is also a theoretical connection between the psychology of Carl Jung and the literary works of George MacDonald. Edmund Cusick's article, "George MacDonald and Jung," lays out the case that much of MacDonald's work, particularly his fantasies, falls into Jung's category of "visionary" art. As contrasted with what Jung calls "psychological" art, which is based upon the materials of conscious life, visionary art presents material from the collective unconscious, and therefore teems with archetypal images and characters, and depicts archetypal processes. Jung cites Dante's *Divine Comedy*, Part II of Goethe's *Faust*, and Blake's poetry as examples of visionary literature. Cusick contends, I think rightly, that MacDonald's fantasies fit Jung's descriptions of visionary literature in their dreamlike quality and their employment of the mythological, the monstrous, the grotesque, and the archetypal (63–66). His exploration of MacDonald's use of anima figures (67–75) pays particular attention to *Lilith*.

Jung says that visionary works "flow more or less complete and perfect from the author's pen.... Here the artist is not identical with the process of creation; he is aware that he is subordinate to his work or stands outside it, as though he were a second person (15: 72–73). MacDonald felt a divine mandate to write *Lilith*, and he completed the first draft seamlessly and nearly without correction, which method Greville MacDonald reports was "unlike anything else he ever did" (548). Greville MacDonald also reports that even fans of his father's other work disliked the book (547). Jung says that visionary literature is usually "repudiated" by a public "astonished, confused, bewildered, put on ... guard or even repelled; we [readers] demand commentaries and explanations" (15: 91). I wish to suggest that the most illuminating commentary and explanation of *Lilith* is produced by consideration of MacDonald's Neo-Platonist Christianity and the archetypal psychology of Jung himself. Like the *Divine Comedy* to which MacDonald alludes (243, 249) *Lilith* can be read on an individual, psychological level as well as a universal one. On one hand it retells the story of humanity's fall and foresees its redemption, following a Universalist model of Christian history and eschatology. On the other, it sketches a process of individual redemption much resembling the progress toward psychic wholeness described in Jungian psychology.

The Lilith of legend is a figure as shadowy, and with as many antecedents, as King Arthur. In Kabalistic tradition she was Adam's first wife, created like Adam out of earth, who rebelled against the inferior position in intercourse and the subservience it implied, and left him. When a hundred of her demon children were killed as punishment, in revenge she became a slayer of infants and seducer of sleeping men. She seems to be a Jewish adaptation of the Babylonian incubi and succubae, and in the fourth century she was identified with the Greek Lamiae, who were vampires.[3]

MacDonald's *Lilith* is structured around two groups of characters: the stable "little family" of Adam, Eve, and Mara and the dynamically evolving triad of Vane, Lona, and Lilith. Adam, Eve, and Mara form a trinity of archetypes of the collective unconscious that represent a glorified humanity, outside of time in the Divine mind. One of the leading characteristics of archetypes is wholeness, meaning that they unite opposites, having a light and a dark side.[4] This quality of wholeness or paradox is one of the most prominent features of these three characters.

Adam, for instance, first appears to Vane as the ghost of an ancient librarian who later claims to have read all the books in Vane's enormous library; thus he is a repository of human culture through the ages. He next appears as a raven—a bird that has negative as well as positive associations; it is the devil's bird, cursed for not returning to Noah's ark, the bird of the underworld, but also the bird sacred to Apollo and the God-sent bringer of food to Elijah the Tishbite. Adam's appearance as a raven demonstrates his protean quality, later confirmed by his observation that everyone has "a beast-self—and a bird-self, and a stupid fish-self, ay, and a creeping serpent-self ... he has also a tree-self and a crystal-self, and I don't know how many selves more—all to get into harmony" (30). Adam, in other words, is the true microcosmic man, who has balanced and can manifest the whole human and sub-human creation. He unites and contains culture and nature, spirit and body. His raven-self is a corrective opposite to his librarian-self; as a raven he exhumes worms and flings them into the air where they become glorious winged creatures. This, he says, represents his role as sexton, in which he watches "for the hour to ring the resurrection-bell, and wake those that are still asleep" (35). The true role of a sexton, imaged in the raven, is to raise the dead, and, "except you are a true sexton, books are but dead bodies to you, and a library nothing but a catacomb!" (30). Truth which is but intellectually perceived, MacDonald believed, is dead; a live truth is a lived truth. A librarian who is a true sexton, therefore, must not simply know, but he must realize — resurrect and embody — all truth expressed in human culture. MacDonald's Adam is indeed Man, with a capital M. Vane calls him "the old and new man"— biblically, that is to say, humanity both fallen and redeemed, corrupted and incorrupt. In Vane's final vision of him, he appears as a kingly man "in the prime of strength, beautiful ... large and grand, clothed in a white robe, with the moon in his hair" (233). Notice that the kingly man, who in traditional symbolism we would expect to be accompanied by the sun (sun = man and king) is instead lighted and crowned by the traditionally feminine moon — another paradox, or indication of completeness. This final appearance of Adam is not Man as the male half of a male/female polarity, but Man as incorporating the feminine, and therefore Man as whole.

We find in Eve the same archetypal quality of paradox. Biblically Eve is "the mother of all living." MacDonald says her "still face might be a primeval perfection; the live eyes were a continuous creation"; they have "life in them for a nation" (28). Yet this vision of life comes to Vane through a door that looks like an upended coffin, in a dark cottage room illuminated by a candle and invaded by a wild-looking black cat, and she ushers him into a deathly cold room filled with the dead. When these sleepers mature — grow young enough, in the text's terms — they will awaken, rise and go. As with Gimbutas's Neolithic goddess, this cavernous tomb is Eve's womb (cf. Schaafsma 54). The House of Death belongs specifically to her; Adam calls it "my wife's house" (27). Even her sleepers are described with opposing metaphors. Adam says the dead out on the moor "lie thick as the leaves of a forest after the first blast of your winter" (35) and later makes the reference to Dante even more explicit with a direct quote: "Thick as autumnal leaves that strow the brooks / In Vallombrosa" (36). Yet in the same breath he adds another description: "... thick, let me say rather, as if the great white rose of heaven had shed its petals over it" (35). Eve's dead are likened, therefore, both to the damned and to the redeemed in the *Divine Comedy*, and she is a Beatrice surrounded by the traditional paraphernalia of witchery (cottage, candle, coffin, cat [28–31]). We remember that witches, in folktale and rumor, eat children — even, and sometimes especially, their own (Russell 239–40). Eve is thus the great all-Mother: all-birthing, all-nurturing, yet all-devouring.

Mara, daughter of Adam and Eve, is also a paradoxical, ambiguous figure. Her face is beautiful, yet she muffles it as if it were ugly; she is graciously hospitable yet entertains her guests with dry bread and water, a cold attic, and a hard cot. The Little Ones fear her as they fear the giant-princess, yet she seems benign and honest enough with Vane. She tells Vane that "Cat-woman" is "not my name" (73), yet she sends cats, large and small, on her errands. For instance, on Vane's second trip to the Little Ones' orchard valley, when his horse dies under him, Mara sends a horde of cats which first save Vane from a menacing pack of wolves, then turn on him and drive him all night, relentlessly scratching and biting when he stops, on the smoothest and shortest way to the Little Ones. This incident expresses Mara's essential paradox: she takes Vane where he needs to go by hurting him until he goes there. Mara is a savior, but her name means *bitter* (Ruth 1.20) and she incarnates MacDonald's notion of life (and, if necessary, an afterlife) as purgatory: human suffering as the necessary instrument of sanctification. In Jungian terms, this parallels the individuation process, in which the attainment of salvation (psychic wholeness) is preceded by the ego's crucifixion, an agonizing suspension between irreconcilable opposites.[5] It is neatly appropriate that Mara is the daughter of Eve, for when Eve plunged herself and Adam into despair, she brought Sorrow into the world. This child is blessed indeed, however, for she is the redemptrix of her parents and all their other progeny, her brothers and sisters (225). Vane calls her the "shepherd whose wolves hunt the wandering sheep home ere the shadow rise and the night grow dark" (239).

In contrast to this archetypal trinity whose leading characteristic is wholeness, we have a mirroring trinity of incomplete or fragmented humanity: Vane, Lona, and Lilith, who end up sharing adjoining couches in the House of Death. Lona, the only child of Lilith and Adam, is an underdeveloped Eve. Innocent and maternal, she rules over the Little Ones as Eve rules her dead. The name "Little Ones" is almost certainly an allusion to the passage in Matthew 18 which, with its cognates, MacDonald utilized heavily in developing his notions about the divine nature. Jesus here tells his disciples, "Unless ye be converted and become as little children, ye shall not enter into the kingdom of heaven ... But whoso shall offend one of these little ones which believe in me, it were better for him that ... he were drowned in the depths of the sea" (Matt. 18.3,6). The Little Ones might represent actual children, whom MacDonald saw as fresh from God and therefore generally morally superior to adults, or the adults who, during their lives on earth, have become as little children and so entered the kingdom of heaven — or both. As the Little Ones correspond to Eve's sleepers, the bad giants and the inhabitants of Lilith's city Bulika are an equivalent, on earth and in time, of the dead being purged in the Evil Wood and the Dance of Skulls. There clearly seems to be a relationship between the giants and the Bulikans. While the Little Ones presumably come from Bulika, brought to the orchard valley by the white leopardess Astarte or by their own mothers to save them from Lilith's program of infanticide, some of them grow into bad giants — possibly Bulikans without the cultural advantages of civilization! Lona, upon entering Bulika, describes its citizens as "just bad giants" (179). The situation of the Little Ones at the beginning of the novel, then, though they seem happy enough, is hardly satisfactory by most standards. They either remain children or grow into bad giants. Without water to cry with, Adam says, they cannot grow into a true maturity (141).

Lona is thus the immature counterpart to Eve the eternal Mother. Though she cannot stop some of her children from growing into bad giants, she takes as good care of them as she can. She is described as a sort of Holy Innocent on the verge of womanhood. The distinguished MacDonald scholar Roderick McGillis finds her insipid compared to her dynamic mother ("Femininity" 51),[6] and the characterization is hard to dispute. At least to modern taste, Lona *is* insipid, but there is good reason for this. Lona, too, is a Little One, though the tallest of the lot. She has never cried, never developed any depth or complexity of character. She is the "heart's wife" of Vane, who according to Adam is "but beginning to become an individual" (21). She is simply, blandly, good.

Opposing Lona's one-sided goodness in this trinity of fragments is her mother, Lilith. MacDonald's Lilith is Evil incarnate; the ultimate negative goddess. As the consort of the great Shadow, she represents cosmic evil; as the princess of Bulika who taught avarice and brutality to an innocent agrarian people, she represents evil as institutionalized in society;[7] as a vampire who lives on the blood of others, she represents exploitative evil in human relationships; as the enforcer of sterility, enemy of children (who in MacDonald almost always evoke Christ or the Christ-self) and eventual slayer of her own daughter, she represents the self-destructive evil in the human psyche.

Vane, the third figure in the trinity of incomplete humanity, is described as a young man so isolated among his books that he has hardly developed a personality. His loneliness in the world of seven dimensions makes him realize that he is, in fact, "but a consciousness with an outlook" (82). He has "preferred the company of book or pen to that of man or woman," and "if the author of a tale I was enjoying appeared, would wish him away that I might return to his story. I had chosen the dead rather than the living, the thing thought rather than the thing thinking!" (83). These preferences of Vane's are dramatized when he grasps after the Raven's bird-butterfly only to have it become a dead book in his hand, thus acting the part of those whom Wordsworth described as murdering to dissect. But from this psychologically embryonic state, Vane in the tale retraces the developmental steps of the archetypal Adam from bookworm to butterfly.

Symbolically, Vane too first espouses Lilith, then Lona (Eve). Vane, like Adam, has loved Lilith, been rejected by her as an equal partner in a love relationship, and finally suspected her evil nature. As Lilith attempted to use Adam to establish her own dominance, so she used Vane, tricking him back into his own world so that she could follow, using his world as an avenue through which to invade the orchard valley and kill the Little Ones. In his second visit to the orchard valley, Vane re-enacts the second phase of Adam's prehistory. He falls in love with Lona and is received as king by the children, who have made friends with the animals of the forest and taken to sleeping in trees. This is a sweet, sexless Eden, complete with serpent — a woman from Bulika, who fled from Lilith with her baby, and now wishes to return. She has started the children on the project of invading and liberating Bulika and taught them to use stones as weapons.

To determine MacDonald's attitude toward this military project, we may consult his sermon on the wilderness temptations of Christ. Christ did well to reject Satan's offer of the world's kingdoms, MacDonald argues, because true good must be rooted in people's hearts, and therefore lasting good cannot be achieved by conquest and rule, even if it were the conquest and rule of Jesus (*Sermons* 1: 154–60). The mission to Bulika is, then, doomed to futility, but Lona in her innocence supports the plan, and Vane lacks both wisdom and will to do anything but agree — thus, in leading the venture, he eats the apple himself.[8]

This interesting re-rendering of Eve's temptation and fall in terms of the wilderness temptations of Christ is reinforced in Bulika, where Lona quickly discovers her mistake ("Let us leave the horrible place ... This people is not worth delivering") and her mother. She flings herself into Lilith's arms, Lilith dashes Lona to the floor and kills her, and Lilith is immediately withered back into the skeletal form in which she first appeared to Vane. Lona's death, like Christ's, has disabled Evil. The equivalent in religious imagery is found in the early *Christus Victor* theological tradition, which sees Christ crucified as the bait God dangles before the ever-greedy Devil who, by swallowing Christ into death and taking him to hell, imported his own ruin as surely as did the Trojans.[9] Lilith, the slayer and consumer, wishes to absorb Lona's life back into her own, but in thus swallowing her daughter and opposite she finds herself immobilized rather than rejuvenated. In Lona's destruction, Lilith seeks to stop up the open channel through which she conceives her own immortal life might leak away (169). But in thus consuming her daughter she cannot, in fact, gain new life — energy and strength — for her evil purposes. Just as, in life, Lona's adoption of the Little Ones foiled Lilith's efforts to kill the children of Bulika, in death, too, Lona's goodness counteracts rather than potentiates her mother's wickedness.

There are a couple of noteworthy points about this re-telling of the Eden myth. First, though Lona gives heed to the temptress, whatever fault is involved is shifted to Vane, who, if he'd slept in the House of Death as he promised, presumably would have known better than to endorse the Bulikan scheme. Second, this Eden, though charming, is not conceived of even by its inhabitants as perfect. It is, in fact, a state of arrested development. The children need to grow, and they badly want mothers; in fact, hope of finding their mothers largely motivates their interest in invading Bulika. Static, sexless innocence may be preferable to evil, but is not MacDonald's idea of a terminal Paradise. Third, it presents a highly condensed version of the Christian history of creation, fall, and crucifixion/redemption.

Vane's situation now is like Adam's after the fall; his two Eves have plunged him into despair. Like Adam, his natural innocence (symbolized by Lona) has been slain by his capacity for evil (Lilith)[10] and now he must eat his bread in sorrow (Gen. 3.17). Appropriately enough, his next stop is at the House of Bitterness, where Mara brings Lilith to repentance. The conversion of Lilith says much about MacDonald's definition of evil and its cure. Lilith's essential sin is her insistence upon sovereignty over her own being: "I am content to be to myself what I would be. What I choose to seem to myself makes me what I am.... My own thought of myself is me. Another shall not make me!" (200). In Jungian terms, she insists upon her ego's right to define and control her self, the right of her consciousness to dictate to her unconscious. The "Law of Liberty" to which Mara refers (213; cf. James 1.24–25) is a simple reality of MacDonald's universe: "freedom" is the liberty to obey the God within, or in other words, to live out our true selves. To disobey the inner God is not liberty; it is slavery to the false ego-self. Or, as Mara puts it, it is to "do as the Shadow, overshadowing your Self inclines you" (199).

The human capacity for evil, therefore, in MacDonald's terms, is simply the human capacity for perverting our true natures, for refusing to be the selves God made. Evil is *essentially* an individual phenomenon (though its outworkings are corporate and pervasive) and the cure must be administered to people as individuals: that cure being a long hard look (enforced, if necessary) at reality. When Vane brings Lilith to Mara's house, Mara sends an inchworm-like creature into the fire until it glows with heat, and allows it to crawl into the dark spot on Lilith's side, whereupon Lilith begins to writhe and sweat in horror. Yet this torturing worm (or serpent) is nothing but self-knowledge — knowledge of herself as she is, not as she prefers to think herself. Vane says the worm "was piercing through the joints and marrow to the thoughts and intents of the heart" (201). This phraseology echoes Hebrews 4.12: "For the word of God is ... sharper than any two-edged sword, piercing even to the dividing asunder of soul and spirit, and of the joints and marrow, and is a discerner of the thoughts and intents of the heart." The torture pictured here is clearly a physical representation of the psychological suffering entailed by, first, a clear vision of the distorted self of one's own making; second, an experience of one's powerlessness over the nature of one's own being; and third, an experience of what a person becomes who insists on killing her true Self to feed the self of her fancy: "one who [knows] existence but not love ... nor life, nor joy, nor good ... a live death" (206). Both the word of God (which, in John's gospel, is Christ himself) and the serpent are associated with wisdom. The agony Lilith finds so excruciating is nothing more than the truth.[11] Similarly, the psychic suffering involved in Jung's individuation process is caused by the painful and relentless alteration of one's own self-image: withdrawal of projections, integration of one's contra-sexual characteristics (anima or animus), and acknowledgement of one's shadow, characteristics repressed because they are socially or morally unacceptable.

Her resistance blasted by these unremitting doses of reality, Lilith abandons her defiance. But the process of purification requires more than passive yielding. The only way for Lilith to complete the process is for her to open her closed hand; that is, to restore that which she has taken. The hand is clenched so that the fingers have grown into the palm; Lilith cannot open it, so Mara, Vane and the children take her to Adam and Eve for help. As Adam and Eve escort Lilith to the chamber of death, the Shadow shakes the house. Lilith, terrified, asks if the children are inside, and "at the word the heart of Eve began to love her." When Lilith cannot rise to her feet, "the Mother lifted, and carried her inward" (215). Thus Lilith's arrival upon her couch of death and regeneration has proceeded through transforming encounters with each of the three positive feminine principles. In absorbing her daughter and opposite she paralyzed her own evil nature; in the House of Bitterness she was led to turn from that evil and share Mara's tears; in the House of the Mother she speaks as a mother herself. Yet even having attained that couch, Lilith is told she will not be able to sleep until she opens her hand.

In Jungian terms, Lilith's development is blocked. She cannot make the required gesture by force of conscious will. She needs the intervention of the unconscious, or God Within, and that is what happens: at her request, Adam cuts off the hand with the sword of the angel who used to guard the gate to Paradise. Biblically, as noted above, the sword symbolizes the word of God, or Christ, who in Revelation is described as having a two edged-sword coming out of his mouth. Jung, quoting Simon Magus, associates the flaming sword of the angel at the gate with the divine *pneuma* (spirit) and says Simon's description of the *pneuma* corresponds to alchemical descriptions of the uroboros — the serpent![12] The sword, therefore, has the same associations as the "worm" that tortured Lilith with self-knowledge: It is God's spirit, holy wisdom, which transforms the natural being into the divine.

The symbolism of the clenched hand is rich, but its basic significance is clear enough that we need not explore its many possible correspondences. Though this is never explicitly stated in the text, Schaafsma, reasonably enough, infers that in that clenched hand Lilith holds the egg containing the land's waters (75), for Vane must bury the hand in the desert to restore the river that once ran in the orchard valley and the lake that will drown the monsters in the Bad Burrow — or, as MacDonald explicates the image in his text, the inhabitants of the unwholesome mind (244). But the process resembles surgery far more than mutilation. The wound does not even need to be dressed, for it is "healing and not hurt"; in place of the dead deformity, "the true, lovely hand is already growing" (219). The image is certainly violent, but the violence is not of MacDonald's making; rather, he has provided some mitigation (the new hand) for Jesus's uncompromising direction: "If thy right hand offend thee, cut it off, and cast it from thee: for it is profitable for thee that one of thy members should perish, and not that thy whole body should be cast into hell" (Matt. 5.30).

Lilith, her offending member purged from her, sleeps. The agent of cosmic, social, interpersonal and psychic destruction has given herself up heartily to the Divine transformation. Reading the text on its universal level, Lilith's reclamation sets the stage for the folding up of the two trinities: the incorporation of the immature, fragmented humanity represented by the Vane/Lona/Lilith trinity into the glorified humanity symbolized by the "little family" of Adam/Eve/Mara. The body of the white leopard Astarte, who died in crossing the Bad Burrow, is brought in and laid at the feet of Lilith, who was the spotted leopard. As McGillis has observed, Astarte is Lilith's "inmost soul" which will wake when she does ("Lilith Legend" 8). Astarte is Mara's agent, and to say she is Lilith's inmost soul is to say that, at the end of time, Lilith the Slayer will be raised as Mara the Savior. In other words, humanity's capacity for evil and the suffering it has caused will be truly perceived to have been midwife to human sanctification and bliss. In his book *The Great Divorce*, MacDonald's best-known disciple, C.S. Lewis, puts these words into the mouth of a dead and glorified George MacDonald:

> The good man's past begins to change so that his forgiven sins and remembered sorrows take on the quality of Heaven ... at the end of things,... the Blessed will say, "We have never lived anywhere except in Heaven.... What seemed, when they entered it, to be the vale of misery turns out, when they look back,

to have been a well; and where present experience saw only salt deserts memory truthfully records that the pools were full of water [68].

Not only will Lilith become Mara, but Vane and Lona will become (or, in the language of St. Paul, become incorporate in) Adam and Eve. After burying Lilith's hand and restoring the country to fertility, his own act of atonement for "both [his] cowardice and [his] self-confidence" (220; cf. Mendelson 211), Vane lies down beside Lona in the House of Death and begins to dream. His last and most climactic vision is that of the eschaton, when the golden cock crows and he, Lona, the Little Ones and their animals, representing the world family (Mendelson 313) and animal creation, cross the new earth, are welcomed into the new heaven, and begin to ascend the throne of God. On the new earth, Vane says,

> The microcosm and macrocosm were at length atoned, at length in harmony! I lived in everything; everything entered and lived in me. To be aware of a thing, was to know its life at once and mine, to know whence we came, and where we were at home — was to know that we are all what we are, because Another is what he is! [243].

Humanity again communes freely with nature and finds that they "mean the same" (245). This is the flower and fulfillment, the fertile maturity, of that perfection of which the Eden of the Orchard Valley was but the seed. Vane's two espousals, the Bulikan invasion, and Lona's death retold the stories of the creation, fall, and redemption; Lilith's repentance ushers in the last judgment. Vane is the Adam, and Lona the Eve, of the new Creation.

In the symbolic tradition of Christian orthodoxy, this trinitarian imagery works perfectly. To be orthodox Jungians, though, we must ask ourselves, Where is the fourth? Wholeness is symbolized by quaternios: we have here instead, at the end of space and time, an Adam/Eve pair (which incorporates Vane/Lona), plus Mara their daughter (who incorporates Lilith). Who or what might be Mara's missing male complement?

For answer, we must look to figures on the fringe of the text, but hardly on the fringe of the Christian tradition out of which MacDonald operates. Mara incorporates Lilith, and Lilith's male complement is the great Shadow. The Shadow's significance is demonstrated when he attacks the army of Little Ones invading Bulika. He possesses the children upon whom he falls: "He did me quite different. I felt like bad. I was not Odu any more — not the Odu I knew. I wanted to tear Sozo to pieces" (188). Mendelson identifies the Shadow as "Satan and Death" (206) and certainly the Shadow performs the functions of those traditional concepts in estranging people from their true selves and so spiritually murdering them. He is the agent of spiritual devolution. Mara casts him in the role of the false or ego-self, for to do evil is to do "as the Shadow, overshadowing your Self inclines you." Interestingly, when Vane sees the Shadow in Bulika, he (the Shadow) is closely followed by Astarte. The black void of death, therefore, possesses a "white shadow" (199) named for a goddess of fertility—suggesting that the principle of Evil is itself shadowed by a divine agent ready to redeem the harm it does. Where the Shadow falls, Mara will be near to save.

Who, then, is Mara's male complement—the male figure who throws the Shadow into space/time as Mara, the Lady of Sorrows, throws Lilith? The Man of Sorrows, of course—the agent of spiritual evolution that MacDonald terms the Christ-self and the true self. He, like Mara, is the child of Adam and Eve as well as their redeemer. He appears in the text only as the "beautifullest man" (247) who comes to claim the Little Ones as they approach the heavenly city. Jung saw the Satan of Western culture as the split-off shadow of its Christ, and here we see that image working more than psychologically. Jung made no metaphysical truth-claims for his reading of Western mythology as psychological projection, but such a metaphysical truth-claim is necessary for MacDonald. If it is true that "only good where evil was, is evil dead" (153), then all evil must be transformed, not conquered, subdued, or even annihilated. In terms of the text, the Shadow, too, will come to the House of Death to "lie down and sleep also" (218). In leaving, essentially, a textual hole where the figure of Christ belongs and working out the incorporation motif through the goddess-figures of Lilith and Mara, MacDonald proposes as metaphysical truth a linkage that, more clearly stated, might have disturbed his Victorian Christian audience far more than the book actually did. The male counterpart of Mara, who does/will incorporate Lilith, is a Christ who does/will incorporate the great Shadow, or Satan.

So much for the tale as an eschatological prediction. Obviously there is another level that strikes us closer to home. We can also read it as imaging an individual's struggle after psychic wholeness. On this level, the characters become personifications of psychic entities and potentials within Vane himself. The Adam/Eve pair become a representation of psychic wholeness in the tradition of the prince/princess marriage in fairy tales or the hermaphrodite in alchemy; Adam representing the conscious of a male personality, Eve the unconscious. Note the night imagery MacDonald uses to describe Eve in her first appearance in the novel: "A whole night-heaven lay condensed in each pupil; all the stars were in its blackness, and flashed; while round it for a horizon lay coiled an iris of the eternal twilight" (28). The night, of course, is a classic symbol of the unconscious in Jungian thought. And, as mentioned above, in Vane's last encounter with the Eternal Trinity he does not see Adam and Eve but a kingly man with the moon in his hair.

The inner fragmentation that reflects Vane's immaturity is represented by the division of his anima into Lona/Lilith, who between them constitute his Eve. Their mutually disabling encounter represents, in Jungian terms, that suspension between irreconcilable opposites that immobilizes the psyche. At the novel's end, when he brings Lona and Lilith to Eve's house and lies down beside them, he is, in the world of seven dimensions, on his way to the healing transformation that will unite them. Mara, Bitterness, is here the agent of the transformation; as Sorrow led Adam and Eve to repentance, so she is the one who takes Vane and his Eves to the House of Death.

Therefore Vane's eschatological vision at the novel's end, in which he is united not only with Lona, but also with the Little Ones and the beasts in approaching the heavenly city, represents his own future as a whole human being — a microcosmic Adam — as well as the redemption of the universe. And indeed this is a true vision of Vane's *telos*, but he has not realized it yet. Although in the world of seven dimensions Vane has, through the crucible of guilt, self-knowledge, repentance, and atonement, attained sufficient spiritual maturity to yield heartily to the Divine sleep of remaking, in his own world he is still a Little One who must weep before he can grow. And to that world he must return. As he is ascending God's throne, Vane is drawn to a little door with a golden lock and pushed through to discover himself, once more, alone in his library.

This conclusion of the book is certainly an anticlimactic shock for the reader, and has been interpreted by many critics as a negation or reversal of the hope promised by the eschatological vision. However, as Mendelson observes, a return to the real world is a convention of the quest romance (214), and does not belie the visionary experience. In this case, I think the significance of the return is made clear by the final chapter. Another has given Vane this dream that he did not seek and did not willingly leave; therefore, as he says, "that Other is able to fulfill it" (251). Such an end was foretold when Vane first met Mara, and she predicted, "The time will come when you must house with me many days and many nights ... *not* willingly!" (80). This prophecy is never fulfilled in the world of seven dimensions, but the first thing Vane says to the reader about his post-visionary condition is, "I have not yet found Lona, but Mara is much with me. She has taught me many things, and is teaching me more" (250). Vane, with his dead Lona and his bound Lilith, is once more in the House of Bitterness, suffering until hard-won self-knowledge will through repentance send his capacity for evil into a transforming sleep, until he by faithful obedience restores that which it has taken, and until his primal innocence, which has died as the virginal Kore, is resurrected as Eve, the goddess who, through her bearing of ancient sorrow (33), has become the true and fertile mother of our Father's children (148).

In the final chapter, Vane is uncertain whether he is still sleeping in the House of Death and dreaming his return to his "own" world, or whether the whole other world experience itself was a dream. The deliberate blurring of the distinction between dream and waking makes what was for MacDonald an essential point about the nature of human life, which he asserts both here and in *Phantastes* in the quotation from Novalis: "Our life is no dream, but it should and will perhaps become one." When, in this life or the next, Vane "wakes" as his true self, the reality he perceives with his cleared vision (or, in Blakean terms, through his cleansed doors of perception) will make everything he experienced while his self was overshadowed seem a cloudy dream that has passed. Then, as he says, "I shall know that I wake, and shall doubt no more" (252). And then, in and as the eternal Adam, he will indeed walk on the new earth, under the new heaven, and ascend the throne of God.

In this essay I have emphasized the commonality of MacDonald's thought with Jung's, but I do not wish to overstate the similarity. Both men criticized Western Christianity's tendency toward dualism in setting up an opposing principle as the implicit or practical (if not the technical, theological) equal of God, and anticipating an eternity divided into two camps: the Good God and his adherents forever separated from and triumphant over the Bad God (Satan) and his. Jung resolved the difficulty by approaching the problem from the psychological angle, dealing with the "God-image" in the human psyche rather than God as a metaphysical concept. Evil, he insisted, has real psychological existence; that is, the Self, the whole of the psyche, contains evil as well as good. The end of the individuation process is not goodness but *wholeness*, which means recognizing in ourselves both good and its opposite. Christ, the Perfect Man, is only an adequate symbol of the Self if we include an opposite — Satan or Antichrist — to complement Christ's goodness.[13] Following the logic of prioritizing the psychological, Jung in one of his most famous works, *Answer to Job* (*Collected Works*, vol. 11), analyzed the biblical God as a rather undifferentiated consciousness in which benevolence and tyranny were uncritically mixed, who was seeking to complete his own individualization process through union with humanity. Thus, Jung avoids dualism by seeing evil as part of God.

MacDonald takes a more traditional approach, affirming God as *Summum Bonum* and denying, as do the Church fathers, that evil has actual existence, being rather a lack or perversion of goodness. MacDonald's Christ-self, unlike Jung's Self, does not include evil. MacDonald is only more self-consistent than mainstream Christian tradition in his insistence that because evil is no thing, it will be eradicated from God's creation as soon as God's creatures — slowly and painfully — cease to prefer phantoms of their own manufacture to the selves that God made, and that much of what people call "evil" (sorrow, pain, and death, for instance) is actually the Shadow of the Good — or, if one prefers, the refining fire of purgatory. Thus our text's last word on Lilith, the primal carrier of evil, is given in answer to Lona's question, "Who were her parents?"

"'My father,' answered Adam, 'is her father also'" (240).

NOTES

1. See Chapters 1–3 of *Aion* (*Collected Works*, vol. 9).

2. See "Transformation Symbolism in the Mass" in *Psychology and Religion: East and West* (*Collected Works*, vol. 11).

3. See McGillis ("Lilith Legend") and Walker for a more complete history of both the Lilith legend and the characteristics MacDonald assigned to his Lilith, including her roles as a princess and as a consort of Satan, and her association with cats.

4. See "The Phenomenology of the Spirit in Fairytales" in *The Archetypes and the Collective Unconscious* (*Collected Works*, vol. 9).

5. See "Christ, a Symbol of the Self" in *Aion* (*Collected Works*, vol. 9).

6. In "*Phantastes* and *Lilith*: Femininity and Freedom," McGillis argues that in writing *Lilith* MacDonald "was of the Devil's party without knowing it" (53) and subverted the conscious message of his text by making Lilith its most fascinating and sympathetic figure. While I understand this position, I attribute much of Lilith's attraction less to MacDonald's double-mindedness than to the partial failure of his art, and to the tendency of the romance genre to distance its readers from horror even while, by using archetypes, it sharpens horror's portrait. For example, vampires are more overtly horrible than a Ted Bundy, but the vampire possesses a romantic *cachet* that a Bundy lacks. Similarly, the child-murderess Lilith, *because* she is a demoness, can be attractive in a way that a human child-murderess cannot. And regarding MacDonald's art: If the Little Ones displayed more childlike vulnerability, or if their insisted-upon charm were dramatized by something other than badly rendered baby talk, perhaps Lilith's attempts to slaughter them would affect more deeply our emotional reactions to her.

7. As McGillis ("Lilith Legend" 8) notes, in the nineteenth century, paradoxically, the figure of Lilith was often used either to represent opposition to patriarchal values or to symbolize the patriarchy itself. He observes that MacDonald's Lilith is clearly of the second sort. Karen Schaafsma argues that the figure of Lilith is a psychological creation of patriarchal societies whose values and consciousness have, in effect, murdered the mother, and that therefore project the "the murdering female, who is both the enemy of masculine consciousness and, paradoxically, its shadow" (54).

8. Mendelson notes that the Bulika campaign "amounts to a repetition of Adam's original failure to obey a divine command" (209).

9. For a more in-depth explication of this tradition, see Aulen.

10. Lilith's poem, read by Adam to Vane, and the details of Vane's discovery and healing of Lilith, have been thoroughly discussed by other critics as supporting the interpretation that Lilith, as well as being a universal force, is derived psychologically from Vane. See Mendelson 205 and McGillis ("Lilith Legend") 6–7. Though Walker sees Vane's resuscitation of Lilith as an act at least symbolically guilty, Adam denies that Vane was blameworthy in this (331).

11. For an exposition of this theory of redemption through tortuous self-knowledge, see MacDonald's sermon, "The Consuming Fire" (*Sermons* 1: 27–49).
12. See "Transformation Symbolism in the Mass" (*Collected Works*, vol. 11).
13. See "Christ, a Symbol of the Self" (*Collected Works*, vol. 9).

WORKS CITED

Aulen, Gustaf. *Christus Victor: An Historical Study of the Three Main Types of the Idea of Atonement.* Trans. A. G. Herbert. New York: Macmillan, 1961.
Cusick, Edmund. "George MacDonald and Jung" in *The Gold Thread: Essays on George MacDonald*, 56–86. William Raeper ed. Edinburgh: Edinburgh University Press, 1990.
Gimbutas, Marija. *The Civilization of the Goddess: The World of Old Europe.* New York: Harper Collins, 1991.
Jung, Carl G. *The Collected Works of Carl G. Jung.* 2nd ed. 21 vols. Trans. R.F.C. Hull. Bollingen Series. Princeton: Princeton University Press, 1970.
_____. *Memories, Dreams, Reflections.* 1973. Ed. Aniela Jaffe. Trans. Richard and Clara Winston. New York: Vintage, 1989.
Lewis, C.S. *George MacDonald: An Anthology.* New York: Macmillan, 1947.
_____. *The Great Divorce.* New York, Macmillan, 1946.
MacDonald, George. *Diary of an Old Soul.* 1880. Minneapolis: Augsburg, 1975.
_____. *A Dish of Orts: Chiefly Papers on the Imagination and on Shakespeare.* 1893. London: Dalton, 1908.
_____. *Unspoken Sermons.* 3 vols. 1866, 1885, 1889. Eureka, Calif.: Sunrise, 1989.
MacDonald, Greville. *George MacDonald and His Wife.* 1924. Whitethorn, Calif.: Johannesen, 1998.
McGillis, Roderick. "George MacDonald and the Lilith Legend in the XIX Century." *Mythlore* 6 (1979): 3–11.
_____. "*Phantastes* and *Lilith*: Femininity and Freedom" in *The Gold Thread: Essays on George MacDonald*, 31–55. William Raeper ed. Edinburgh: Edinburgh University Press, 1990.
Mendelson, Michael. "George MacDonald's *Lilith* and the Conventions of Ascent." *Studies in Scottish Literature* 20 (1985): 197–218.
Raeper, William. *George MacDonald.* Tring, England: Lion, 1988.
_____, ed. *The Gold Thread: Essays on George MacDonald.* Edinburgh: Edinburgh University Press, 1990.
Russell, Jeffrey Burton. *Witchcraft in the Middle Ages.* Ithaca: Cornell University Press, 1972.
Schaafsma, Karen. "The Demon Lover: Lilith and the Hero in Modern Fantasy." *Extrapolation* 28 (1987): 52–61.
Walker, Jeanne Murray. "The Demoness and the Grail: Deciphering MacDonald's *Lilith*" in *The Scope of the Fantastic—Culture, Biography, Themes, Children's Literature: Selected Essays from the First International Conference on the Fantastic in Literature and Film.* Ed. Robert A. Collins and Howard D. Pearce. Westport, Conn.: Greenwood, 1985. 179–90.

CHAPTER 13

Lilith as the Mystic's Magnum Opus
Elizabeth Robinson

Lilith, arguably George MacDonald's greatest literary achievement, is also the mystic's visionary magnum opus which more than any other work seems to owe its existence to his mysticism. Nevertheless, close readings of the novel specifically as a mystical expression have remained undone. I intend to remedy this critical oversight as I explore how MacDonald's mysticism is expressed in *Lilith*. Greville MacDonald tells us that his father "was possessed by a feeling ... that [*Lilith*] was a mandate direct from God, for which he himself was to find some form and clothing" (548). As Richard Reis observes, "MacDonald knew that he was making his definitive statement" (94). This definitive statement was forty-five years in the making and stands in marked contrast to MacDonald's first visionary fantasy, *Phantastes* (1858), written when he was a young mystic. In this first fantasy, the young protagonist, Anodos, journeys through the early stages of the mystic life that MacDonald himself had already experienced. In a divided reality (Fairy Land vs. the material world), a spiritual state in which the "I" of self seems separate from the "Thou" of God, Anodos learns that he must act in order to become his true self. The MacDonald who writes *Lilith* has matured as a mystic, and he now sees the seeming dichotomy between the physical world and the spiritual world as an illusion; reality has become one world. In *Lilith*, MacDonald creates a unified reality in which he presents the culmination of the mystic journey as Vane accepts death in order to live, the death of the self that results in mystic union with God.

When Vane first enters the region of seven dimensions, he fears that he has entered an alternate reality: "Had I wandered into a region where both the material and psychical relations of our world had ceased to hold? Might a man at any moment step beyond the realm of order, and become the sport of the lawless?" (12). Adam, however, explains that not only has Vane not stepped "beyond the realm of order," he has not even stepped outside his own home. "Perhaps it may comfort you," he says, "to be told that you have not yet left your house, neither has your house left you. At the same time it cannot contain you, or you inhabit it" (21). Apparently, the three dimensions of the physical world are part of the seven dimensions in the region in which Vane finds himself. Adam can apprehend all seven dimensions with his senses, so he sees, hears, and smells both of the worlds Vane can only experience as distinct from each other. As part of a unified whole, though, what happens in one world influences or manifests itself in the other. The flowers in the region of seven dimensions add sweetness to the music played in Vane's world, and in a reciprocal fashion, a piece of music played in Vane's world causes a certain scent in the flowers of the region of seven dimensions. As Vane protests that two objects "cannot exist in the same place at the same time," Adam remarks, "no man of the universe" would have said such a thing (23). Clearly, Vane must somehow learn to live beyond the confines of his three-dimensional physical world.

Given that three of the dimensions contained in the region of seven dimensions are the physical ones of this world, what, one wonders, are the other four? They must be spiritual. In the region of the seven dimensions, the spiritual becomes concrete. When Vane sees what Adam tells him is a prayer pigeon, he is perfectly willing to see it as "a fit symbol or likeness for one; but a live pigeon to come out of a heart! ... A prayer is a thought, a thing spiritual!" Adam, however, argues that the bird is much more: "if you understood any world besides your own you would understand your own much better.—When a heart is really alive, then it is able to think live things" (25–26). The spiritual, MacDonald tells us, is not some sort of nebulous concept; it is as concrete as the physical world we inhabit. In fact, it is more concrete because it gives the abstract in our physical form. Furthermore, the spiritual dimensions are somehow present within individuals. Adam revealed to Vane that "there were many more than three [dimensions], some of them concerned with powers which were indeed in us, but of which as yet we knew absolutely nothing" (41). I would argue that these powers are related to the divine spark that the mystics believe is present within each person. MacDonald expresses this idea when Adam explains how a prayer can become a pigeon:

> There is one heart all whose thoughts are strong, happy creatures, and whose very dreams are lives. When some pray, they ... send up their prayers in living shapes, this or that, the nearest likeness to each. All live things were thoughts to

begin with, and are fit therefore to be used by those that think. When one says to the great Thinker: — "Here is one of my thoughts: I am thinking it now!" that is a prayer — a word to the big heart from one of its own little hearts [26].

MacDonald had earlier expressed a similar concept in his essay "The Imagination": "[As] the thoughts move in the mind of a man, so move the worlds of men and women in the mind of God ... for there they had their birth, the offspring of his imagination. Man is but a thought of God ... a man is rather *being thought* than *thinking*" (*Orts* 4). What becomes clear in these passages is that reality, along with the people that inhabit it, is the offspring, the heart-thought of God: he is the "one heart" who thought everything into being. The individual, as one of God's "own little hearts," as "the offspring of his imagination," is in essence a spiritual being because he is "being thought" by God.

For MacDonald, then, the divine spark of God that is in each individual is, in fact, the thought of God; for that matter, all creation is a thought of God, but only man can return a thought to God as a prayer. Because all people are, in a sense, a part of God, they are incomplete until they are in communion with him. When an individual returns a prayer to God, that person is entering into a relationship by which he or she becomes true; thus, Adam finds joy in the prayer-dove because the heart from which it issues is becoming true.

In the region of seven dimensions, then, MacDonald portrays reality as a "oneness," a spiritual whole that encompasses and influences the physical world that we, in our limited vision perceive as reality. More importantly, reality — whose heart is God — exists within every individual, and each person may learn to move within the region of seven dimensions. This vision of the "oneness" of reality is a marked change from the vision MacDonald presented in *Phantastes* nearly fifty years earlier. MacDonald has matured as a mystic, and he now sees the belief that reality is composed of two worlds, the physical and the spiritual, as a ridiculous illusion. He no longer merely hints (as he did in *Phantastes*) that reality is a wholeness which encompasses "this world"; he overwhelmingly affirms it.

The lesson that Vane learns through his experience with reality is that to live, he must die. This, of course, is one of the basic paradoxes of Christianity, and it is the main theme of *Lilith*. The novel is about the process through which Vane learns to desire the sleep of death in order to find true life. In this respect, Vane's journey is quite different from that of his predecessor, Anodos, yet they are two halves of the same spiritual journey. Critics have observed that together *Phantastes* and *Lilith* are two parts of the same spiritual journey to God. Glenn Sadler calls *Phantastes* "a poet's artistic diary of youthful dreams ... the record of a young man's spiritual contest with the 'false objects' which taunt his thirst for the fulfillment of 'Sweet Desire.'" *Lilith* he sees as the ending of the spiritual journey begun in *Phantastes*, and Vane, the story's hero, is "Anodos on his return journey through Fairyland" (220–26).

Colin Manlove also sees these two adult fantasies as a single story:

> Just as they circle MacDonald's literary life, so the one completes the circle begun by the other. That circle has to do ... with completing a pattern. For *Phantastes* deals with some of the [Christian] First Things; and *Lilith* with the Last. *Phantastes* has as its subject a man embarking on life, and describes a fall ... and a Christ-like act of sacrifice for others.... The narrative in *Lilith*, however, moves towards the Last Days, and describes the morning of eternity when resurrected souls make their way into heaven; the story focuses on the gradual acceptance by ... Vane of his need to lie down and sleep with the dead in Adam's house so that he may waken to eternity. In a sense *Phantastes* and *Lilith* together make up a single fantasy [74–75].

While I agree with these observations, I would argue that they are incomplete. Approaching *Phantastes* and *Lilith* from a mystical perspective sheds new light on the meaning and relationship between the journeys of the two protagonists, Anodos and Vane, a perspective that can perhaps tell us much about the mystic life of George MacDonald.

In this discussion of Vane's journey toward God, and its relationship to Anodos's journey toward his true self, I rely largely on the work of St. John of the Cross, often considered a sort of mystic's mystic.[1] While the language that John of the Cross uses to speak of mystical experience is radically different from that used by MacDonald, the model that he uses seems especially applicable to *Phantastes* and *Lilith*. Of particular interest to me is John of the Cross's concept of the two nights, the Night of the Senses and the Night of the Spirit, through which the soul passes on its way to union.[2]

John of the Cross says that the Night of the Senses pertains to beginners in the mystic way, individuals whom "God begins to bring ... into the state of contemplation" (18). Speaking of the Night of the Senses, John of the Cross writes: "[The] soul habitually enters this night of sense in two ways: the one is active; the other passive. The active way consists in that which the soul can do, and does of itself, in order to enter therein" (56). In *Phantastes*, Anodos takes the active way to enter the Night of the Senses as he seeks a way to lose the shadow of his false self. He learns "to do something worth doing," to act out of an unselfish love. When he finally loves Sir Percival with a selfless love and acts in the knight's interest at the unholy ceremony in the forest, the result is his death. This death is the Night of the Senses, the purgatory stage of the mystic life which mortifies the worldly passions of the soul.

When he becomes conscious after his death, he realizes that he is a new being, a being who knows how to love with a pure love, and he desires to share that love with the world. This death in Fairy Land, however, does not seem to end in union with God. Rather, Anodos merely experiences an awareness of love and a joy in the creation that John of the Cross identifies as one of the blessings God bestows on the one who journeys through the Night of the Senses. Harvey Egan summarizes the mystic's argument:

> [The] person may delight in remaining alone in a simple, loving awareness of God. A blind stirring of love ... [rest], quietude, sweet idleness, and a loving, peaceful attention toward God characterize [this state].... By giving the person a genuine self-knowledge, especially of his weaknesses and sinfulness, it shakes the person out of his spiritual complacency. It also fills the individual with requisite respect for the mystery of God. The person begins to do God's will for his sake, and not for the consolations received. Filled with the realization that all comes from God, the person thinks less about himself and more about his neighbors' needs [178–79].

This perfectly describes Anodos after his death in Fairy Land. His whole attitude is one of peace and rest, and MacDonald's language implies a loving awareness of God:

> My spirit rejoiced.... I felt as if a cool hand had been laid upon my heart, and had stilled it. My soul was like a summer evening, after a heavy rain.... The hot fever of life had gone by, and I had breathed the clear mountain-air of the land of Death. I had never dreamed of such blessedness. It was not that I had in any way ceased to be what I had been. The very fact that anything can die, implies the existence of something that cannot die; which ... in conscious existence, may, perhaps, continue to lead a purely spiritual life. If my passions were dead, the souls of the passions, those essential mysteries of the spirit which had embodied themselves in the passions, and had given to them all their glory and wonderment, yet lived, yet glowed, with a pure, undying fire.... I lay thus for a time, and lived as it were an unradiating existence; my soul a motionless lake, that received all things and gave nothing back; satisfied in still contemplation, and spiritual consciousness [162–63].

Reveling in this new spiritual consciousness, Anodos receives the great revelation of his life: he feels a pure love, and the result of this feeling is his desire to minister to his neighbors' needs — even the millions whom he does not know. Anodos has gone through the Night of the Senses which has mortified his shadow self, and he has moved into a state of joy in God, forever shaken out of his "spiritual complacency."

In Anodos, MacDonald, himself a young mystic, portrays the beginning of the mystic journey towards union with God. With Vane's journey in *Lilith*, MacDonald completes his portrayal of the mystic journey towards union. In the novel, Vane is brought to the place where he can accept the sleep of death, but more than this, where he desires it. From the beginning of the novel, we are aware that Vane's journey in the region of seven dimensions will be different from Anodos's journey in Fairy Land. When Adam first takes Vane into the region of seven dimensions, he takes him straight to the house of death:

> "Here is Mr. Vane, wife!" said the raven.
> "He is welcome.... Will he sleep?" she asked.
> "I fear not," he replied; "he is neither weary nor heavy laden."
> "Why then have you brought him?"
> "I have my fears it may prove precipitate."
> "I do not quite understand you," I said.... "Surely a man must do a day's work first!" ...
> "He has not yet learned that the day begins with sleep!" said the woman, turning to her husband. "Tell him he must rest before he can do anything" [28–29].

The implication of this discussion is clear: Vane has been brought (albeit precipitately) to the region of seven dimensions in order to sleep the sleep of death. Unlike Anodos, Vane is not required to act; he is required to accept the passive sleep of death. Moreover, no good action can come of him until he sleeps, and sleep, Adam tells Vane, "is a necessity," and "too fine a thing ever to be earned ... it must be given and accepted" (31). Clearly this death-sleep is a different thing from the death that Anodos receives as a result of noble and loving action.

Before I discuss the nature of the death-sleep, I must make one point. The death that Vane is asked to desire and accept must be interpreted on two levels. It is both the Night of the Spirit which leads to mystical union, a limited union with God within temporal space, and death itself, which ushers one into final, eternal union with God. For Vane, who is returned to the material world after his resurrection in the region of seven dimensions, the death-sleep is the mystical Night of the Spirit. For the other sleepers in "the burial-ground of the universe," this is death, and they await their resurrection into God's heaven. In a sense, then, mystic union is a sort of dress rehearsal for the eternal union which follows death. Christopher Nugent makes a similar argument in *Mysticism, Death and Dying*:

> But if "mystical union," as it were, a real presence to the Real Presence, a consciousness of communion, "a timeless moment," is more than a natural union — and ... this is the consensus of the spiritual masters — where or when is *full* union with God and the Blessed to be realized? *In death*. If this is the case, mystical experience is or can be a foreshadowing of death.... A foretaste of heaven is what we allude to, and it would seem that there cannot be a foretaste of heaven without a foretaste of death [13–14].

Nugent argues that mystical union is a type of death, and this, of course, is also implied in John of the Cross's night symbolism and made visual in MacDonald's house of sleep/death.

When Adam and Eve take Vane into the sleeping chamber the first time, he observes that while the sleepers there appear dead, this death is not what it seems: "I thought at first their sleep was death, but I soon saw it was something deeper still—a something I did not know" (33). Vane quickly realizes this death is not corruption. The sleepers are, paradoxically, being healed of life's sorrows and the wounds experienced at the moment of physical death:

> Here lay a man who had died—for although this was not death, I have no other name to give it ... a shadow of pain lingered about his lips, but only a shadow. On the next couch lay the form of a girl.... The sadness left on her face by parting was not yet absorbed in perfect peace, but absolute submission possessed the placid features ... if pain had been there, it was long charmed asleep, never again to awake.... The most beautiful of all was a lady.... On her stately countenance rested—not submission, but a right noble acquiescence, an assurance, firm as the foundation of the universe, that all was as it should be. On some faces lingered ... the fading shadows of sorrows that had seemed inconsolable: the aurora of the great morning had not yet quite melted them away; but those faces were few, and every one that bore such brand of pain seemed to plead, "Pardon me: I died only yesterday!" ... That some had been dead for ages I knew, not merely by their unutterable repose, but by something for which I have neither word nor symbol [33–34].

We learn later that those who sleep are growing younger, being healed of physical, emotional, and spiritual ills, and being perfected to be in union with, as Mara calls God at one point, "the Life." This death-sleep, then, is not an end of life but a beginning of perfect life, a beginning of "be-ing." As Mara leads Lilith into the house of death, she reveals the truth of death: "Death is even now on his way to lead thee to Him. Thou knowest neither Death nor the Life that dwells in Death! Both befriend thee ... wilt thou not be restored and *be*?" (214). And Adam explains to Vane that complete death is, paradoxically, life:

> None of those you see ... are in truth quite dead yet, and some have but just begun to come alive and die. Others had begun to die; that is to come alive; long before they came to us; and when such are indeed dead, that instant they will wake and leave us.... Blessed be the true life that the pauses between its throbs are not death! [35–36].

Here Adam characterizes the death-sleep as a pause between the throbs of life; the implication being, of course, that one's physical life in the world is one throb and eternal life after physical death is a second. Interestingly, though, Adam speaks of pauses—plural—between life's throbs. If I am correct in arguing that Vane's sleep in the house of death represents the Night of the Spirit — a mystical experience — Adam uses the plural because there is a pause which is not physical death, but the final death of the self which one experiences prior to moving into mystical union. Because Vane sleeps in the region of seven dimensions — because he sacrifices the self in the Night of the Spirit — when he does finally die a physical death, he will be one of those who has "begun to come alive" long before he sleeps in the house of death.

Speaking of the Night of the Spirit, John of the Cross says that souls

> begin to enter [it] when God draws them forth from the state of beginners ... and begins to set them in the state of progressives — which is that of those who are already contemplatives[3] — to the end that, after passing through it, they may arrive at the state of the perfect, which is that of the Divine union of the soul with God [330].

In the terms of *Lilith*, one may say that Vane is a progressive when (1) he understands the horror of the dead self, (2) he realizes that he is a dead self and needs sleep, and (3) he longs for the life that will result from the sleep of death.

Vane reaches this point after the battle in Bulika. After Lona's death in the battle and Vane's acknowledgement that he is at fault, he realizes, "it was not she, it was I who was lost" (184), and that he must take Lona — and himself — to Adam. Later, in Mara's house, when Vane witnesses the terrible process necessary to bring Lilith to repentance, he realizes that she has been a horror not just to the country that she has ruled, but to both God and herself as well. He is dismayed by what he witnesses in this night of repentance, and one suspects that he reacts as he does partly because he realizes he too is dead, just as Lilith is; albeit, he is not as evil as she.

This night in Mara's cottage works a change not only in Lilith but in Vane as well. Later, when he performs the task that Adam requires of him before he can sleep, Vane encounters an old man who begs him to convince Eve to let him sleep in the house of death. Vane realizes that the man desires death only as an escape from old age. When the man marvels that Vane, a young man, desires death, Vane replies:

> I may not be old enough to desire to die, but I am young enough to desire to live indeed! Therefore I go now to learn if [Eve] will at length take me in. You wish to die because you do not care to live: she will not open her door to you, for no one can die who does not long to live.... It is but too plain you have not yet learned to die, and I am heartily grieved for you. Such had I too been but for the Lady of Sorrow [Mara].... Go to the Lady of Sorrow, and "take with both hands" what she will give you.... Then ask counsel of her, for she is true, and her wisdom is great [225].

Clearly, Vane has learned much spiritual truth from Mara; he has learned to desire the death-sleep. And this young man who here "presumes to offer counsel" is much different from the one who initially fled from the house of death in terror, the young man who thought that life existed in an "honest day's work."

When Vane initially asks Eve if he may sleep in her house, his sense of his "wrongness" and his desire for death are obvious: "I know I am unworthy, but may I not sleep this night in your chamber with my dead? Will you not pardon both my cowardice and my self-confidence, and take me in? I give me up. I am sick of myself, and would fain sleep the sleep" (220). Later he returns to the house of death and finds Adam, Eve, and Mara absent. Again, his reaction indicates his new spiritual state:

> There grew in me such a sense of loneliness as never yet in my wanderings had I felt. Thousands were near me, not one was with me! True, it was I who was dead, not they; but, whether by their life or by my death, we were divided! They were alive, but I was not dead enough even to know them alive.... Never before had I known, or truly imagined desolation! [226].

Vane has now reached the state of a progressive in the metaphysical universe of *Lilith*; he is ready to progress into the Night of the Spirit, to be prepared for union with God.

John of the Cross argues that a person enters the Night of the Spirit by willingly and actively rejecting all the things of the understanding, the memory, and the will. The individual must completely empty himself *of* self in order for God to fill the void. In Harvey Egan's words, "Insofar as possible, the person must place any and all understanding, feeling, imaginings, desires, and opinions into a cloud of forgetting to walk the way of naked faith in unknowing." Then God will lead "the contemplative into a midnight experience, a total night, in which the very self must be transcended" (179). For Vane, the active and willing rejection of the things of the conscious self—understanding, memory, and will—comes when he seeks out and accepts sleep. He consciously turns the lights out, if you will. And of course, the symbol of the midnight experience into which God leads the individual is the sleep itself, for Adam had earlier said it was a gift, not something an individual can bring about himself. What more apt symbol of this experience could MacDonald have chosen than that of sleep?

According to John of the Cross, this night of total darkness is the final stage of purgation for the mystic. Through a process that may last years (as may the sleep in the house of death—many of the sleepers had been there for centuries), the dark night purifies the soul so that it may come into union with God. Harvey Egan summarizes what John of the Cross says happens during the Night of the Spirit:

> Several types of bitter experience characterize the ... dark night. The contemplative becomes acutely aware of his sinfulness.... Past and present sins stand out in their total perversity to torture the person. A powerful conviction of being unloved by God and unworthy of any love characterizes the experience. The contemplative is certain that God has legitimately rejected him, that no more blessings will come to him.... Nothing satisfies the contemplative, nor can he understand anything of what is going on. He is so full of his own misery that even the consoling words of an expert spiritual director make no impact. All creatures and every one of his friends seem to abandon him during this period. It is as if he were experiencing the very pains of hell.... [The] dark night binds the understanding, memory, and will to free them from all that is not God. This dark contemplation also illuminates and fires the spirit in love, draws the person within, and awakens in him a deep, inner alertness to the things of God [190–91].

While Vane does not experience all these things (for instance, he never feels unloved by God), his experience closely follows this description.

In *Lilith*, MacDonald symbolizes the purgation of the Night of the Spirit in the dreams that Vane has while asleep. At first, he is in a state of bliss:

> I grew aware of existence, aware also of the profound, the infinite cold. I was intensely blessed — more blessed, I know, than my heart, imagining, can now recall.... Sorrow was swallowed up in the life drawing nigh to restore every good and lovely thing a hundredfold! I lay at peace.... I grew continuously less conscious of myself, continuously more conscious of bliss, unimaginable yet felt. I had neither made it nor prayed for it: it was mine in virtue of existence; and existence was mine in virtue of a Will that dwelt in mine [230].

John of the Cross says that during the Night of the Spirit, God will from time to time relieve the individual through his consoling gifts. MacDonald incorporates periods of consolation during Vane's often troubled sleep, but he also envisions God giving the sleeper in the dark night an initial assurance of his divine love and joy. Thus Vane is aware of God's presence within himself, and he knows that he is "in the heart of God" (231).

On the heels of Vane's awareness and joy in true existence come the dreams: "Then the dreams began to arrive — and came crowding," Vane says (230). The dreams are many and at first muddled, but then they lead him into the first type of bitter experience described by John of the Cross, an acute awareness of his sins:

> Then, of a sudden ... all the wrongs I had ever done, from far beyond my earthly memory down to the present moment, were with me. Fully in every wrong lived the conscious I, confessing, abjuring, lamenting the dead, making atonement with each person I had injured, hurt, or offended. Every human soul to which I had caused a troubled thought, was now grown unspeakably dear to me, and I humbled myself before it, agonising to cast from between us the clinging offense [231].

In this painful confrontation with his sins and those he has wronged, Vane has a startling realization: "Love possessed me! Love was my life! Love was to me, as to him that made me, all in all!" (231). He has learned what MacDonald and the mystics consider the essential truth of God: He is Love. But more than this, Vane, like Anodos before him, has learned that he too can love as God loves.

After this confrontation with his sins and the concurrent revelation of love, Vane is plunged into "a solid blackness, upon which the ghost of light that dwells in the caverns of the eyes could not cast one fancied glimmer." Despite this overwhelming blackness, Vane "fear[s] nothing and hope[s] infinitely"; he is at peace (231–32). This peace, however, is shattered as Vane continues in the next dream, a dream that at the time Vane thinks is real. He thinks he awakens out of the total darkness into the house of the dead, only to find it deserted. He has, he believes, been abandoned by the sleepers as they awoke into the resurrection morning. Naturally implied in this is the fear that he has also been abandoned by God:

> My dead were gone! I was alone!—In desolation dread lay depths yet deeper than I had hitherto known! ... they were all up! they were all abroad in the new eternal day, and had forgotten me! They had left me behind, and alone! ... Now I had no friend and my lovers were far from me! A moment I sat and stared horror-stricken.... I sprang to my feet, and staggered from the fearful place [232].

Vane, like the contemplatives described by John of the Cross, feels rejected by both friends and God, and he fears being alone forever. He is not left in this state of dismay though; God provides a "consoling gift." Vane finds the lake and river which, at Adam's command, he had restored to the desert wastes before he went to sleep. The sight brings joy: "I stood a moment gazing, and my heart also began to exult: my life was not all a failure!" (233). This brings him to the realization that he has not been abandoned because he is unworthy, and Vane decides to seek the resurrected dead.

At this point, Adam finds Vane and informs him that he is not awake but dreaming a false dream. Adam fills the role of the expert spiritual director that John of the Cross advises every contemplative to have. For, according to John of the Cross, until the individual passes through the Night of the Spirit, he is still imperfect and susceptible to delusions of the self. The role of the spiritual advisor is to make the contemplative aware of what is delusion and what is God's truth. Vane has a false dream because he is not completely dead, and Adam, his spiritual director, reveals this to him:

> When you are quite dead, you will dream no false dream. The soul that is true can generate nothing that is not true, neither can the false enter it.... You *cannot* perfectly distinguish between the true and the false while you are not yet quite

dead; neither indeed will you when you are quite dead — that is, quite alive, for then the false will never present itself [234].

Vane, however, has trouble believing Adam, for the dream that he is in seems completely real; he "can neither see nor feel the truth" of what Adam says. Adam consoles Vane by explaining that he will eventually be in union with God, and then he will always know the truth of things. Adam tells him, however, that before he reaches union, he must undergo many trials:

> Trials yet await thee, heavy, of a nature thou knowest not now. Remember the things thou hast seen. Truly thou knowest not those things, but thou knowest what they have seemed, what they have meant to thee! Remember also the things thou shalt yet see. Truth is all in all; and the truth of things lies, at once hid and revealed, in their seeming [235].

One is not sure if Adam speaks here only of the trials remaining during Vane's sleep in the region of seven dimensions, or if he knows that Vane will be returned to his own world where he will face trials before he dies a physical death. One suspects that the latter is the case, and that Adam encourages Vane to remember that every truth he has learned in the region of the seven dimensions is also truth in the physical world.

Vane has one more dream that is more terrible than the others. In an effort to awaken from the false dream, Vane throws himself down a pit, hoping that the fall will wake him up. Instead, he regains consciousness in his own home. He is overwhelmed with despair because he thinks that, as a result of fleeing the dream it was his responsibility to endure, he has "left the holy sleep" behind him and is no longer worthy to sleep that sleep (236). He feels desolation, despair, and hopelessness; in short, he feels he is in his own hell.

An integral part of Vane's desolation in this last dream is his fear that he has lost Lona, the woman he loves, forever. Lona's presence in the story is an aspect that needs some explanation. William Raeper contends that the character, who was incorporated into the story after the death of MacDonald's eldest daughter, Lilia, is an embodiment of that beloved lost child (378). But she also represents an interesting aspect of MacDonald's theology. Throughout his life, MacDonald viewed the love between a man and a woman as a holy thing that was a type of God's love. He believed that when a man loved a woman with a pure love, that love could blossom and grow into a love for God. In other words, MacDonald believed that the love for God's creature can lead to love for God. Hence, in *Lilith*, when Vane loves Lona and despairs over her seeming loss, he implicitly acknowledges the same feelings for the Creator of both the beloved and love itself. Loving Lona, in other words, is part and parcel of loving God.

This particular dream is especially significant because Vane has now been returned to that which he once loved above all else, his home — the place he has spent much of his journey in the region of seven dimensions trying to reach — yet he is desperately unhappy. Vane has learned to hate all the things he had once loved; his only desire is to find his way back to the holy sleep. He has reached the point of detachment from all things, which John of the Cross says is necessary for God to fill the void left within the soul, thus perfecting the individual.

When Vane awakens from this dream, it is the dawn of the resurrection morning for him, Lona, and the Little Ones. They leave the house of death, and Vane, who is now completely alive finds that he sees the world with new eyes:

> Every growing thing showed me, by its shape and colour, its indwelling idea — the informing thought, that is, which was its being, and sent it out.... The microcosm and macrocosm were at length atoned, at length in harmony! I lived in everything; everything entered and lived in me. To be aware of a thing, was to know its life at once and mine, to know whence we came, and where we were at home — was to know that we are all what we are, because Another is what he is! [243].

One feels that this Vane would recognize a prayer pigeon for what it is! His true self is now capable of union with God. As the dawn progresses to noon, Vane and Lona make their way to the New Jerusalem and climb to the throne of the "Ancient of Days." They are climbing into the folds of the garment of God which surrounds the throne when a hand gently pushes Vane through a little door, and he finds himself in his library at home. Vane has gone through the Night of the Spirit; he has ascended the very throne of God, yet he is not allowed to remain with God. One wonders why. Concerning this rather surprising ending, Richard Reis observes,

> Perhaps the most striking attribute of *Lilith* is the fact that, at the end, its narrator has *not* attained ultimate transcendence; he only knows that there is such a thing after death, which he awaits patiently. There is no apotheosis — only an awaiting, a partial arrival at wherever Mr. Vane is destined to go.... The very incompleteness of the ending is consistent with MacDonald's view that enlightenment is never complete in this life, though we may have dreams and fleeting visions of the better world [102].

Reis's remarks imply what I believe to be true of MacDonald's experience with mystic union; either he has never achieved it in the typically understood sense, or for him, it has been a temporary state that, rather than leaving him with a sense of fulfillment, leaves him with a sense of yearning for the permanent union that lies beyond death's door. I suggest that because MacDonald himself feels a sense of incompleteness about his unitive experiences, he allows Vane only a brief experience in the lap of God; Vane must return to his normal life and await physical death and eternal union with God, just as MacDonald does.[4]

After his return, Vane sometimes wonders if his experience in the region of seven dimensions really happened at all. But a voice within his soul reminds him that even if it is a dream, it was given to him by God who "broods and wills and quickens" such dreams, and is "able to fulfill [them]." If God has given Vane the dream of the healing sleep and attainable union with God, MacDonald tells us, God will enable Vane to fulfill that dream. Hence Vane is content to say, "all the days of my appointed time will I wait till my change come" (251). One must note that Vane does not await "death" but his "change." He is indeed a changed man.

In *Lilith*, MacDonald gives us his final mystic vision: one of union with God. While only Vane experiences mystic union and awaits his final glorious union with God, all of the characters in the novel will eventually experience their own. Even Lilith, the first and most depraved of God's rebellious children, will, after she wakes, be in union with her Creator.

NOTES

1. F.C. Happold writes, "As an analyst and describer of mystical states St. John of the Cross stands in the highest rank, so much so that there has been a tendency among Catholic writers on mysticism to regard him too much as a norm for the testing of what religious experience should be labelled mystical" (325).

2. St. John of the Cross discusses three reasons that he refers to these states as night: "The first has to do with the point from which the soul goes forth, for it has gradually to deprive itself of desire for all the worldly things which it possessed, by denying them to itself, the which denial and deprivation are, as it were, night to all the senses of man. The second reason has to do with the mean, or the road along which the soul must travel to this union — that is, faith, which is likewise as dark as night to the understanding. The third has to do with the point to which it travels — namely God, Who, equally is dark night to the soul in this life [dark night because God is such an excess of divine light that the soul sees it as darkness]" (19–20).

3. Michael Cox defines contemplation as "transcendent prayer, culminating in the direct knowledge of God" (130). Evelyn Underhill calls it "a supreme manifestation of that indivisible 'power of knowing' which lies at the root of all ... spiritual satisfactions. In it, man's ... thought, love, and will become a Unity: and feeling and perception are fused ... the whole of the self ... being sharply focused, concentrated on one thing ... 'God, the one Reality'" (329–30).

4. William Raeper remarks that in MacDonald's years of silence before his death, he "became like Vane, fast asleep on the couch, awaiting the grand resurrection" (389).

WORKS CITED

Cox, Michael. *Handbook of Christian Spirituality*. San Francisco: Harper and Row, 1985.

Egan, Harvey. *Christian Mysticism: The Future of a Tradition*. New York: Pueblo, 1984.
Happold, F.C. *Mysticism: A Study and an Anthology*. Baltimore: Penguin, 1963.
John of the Cross. *The Complete Works of St. John of the Cross*. Vol. 1. Trans. E. Allison Peers. London: Burns and Oates, 1935.
MacDonald, George. "The Imagination: Its Functions and Its Culture" in *A Dish of Orts: Chiefly Papers on the Imagination, and on Shakespeare*. 1–42. 1882. London: Edwin Dalton, 1908. Reprint Norwood Editions, 1977.
_____. *Phantastes*. 1858. New York: Schocken, 1982.
MacDonald, Greville. *George MacDonald and His Wife*. London: Allen and Unwin, 1924.
Manlove, Colin N. *Impulse of Fantasy Literature*. Kent, Ohio: Kent State University Press, 1983.
Nugent, Christopher. *Mysticism, Death and Dying*. Albany: State University of New York, 1994.
Raeper, William. *George MacDonald*. Tring, England: Lion, 1987.
Reis, Richard. *George MacDonald*. Twayne's English Authors Series 119. New York: Twayne, 1972.
Sadler, Glenn. "The Fantastic Imagination in George MacDonald" in *Imagination and the Spirit: Essays in Literature and the Christian Faith Presented to Clyde S. Kilby*. 215–27. Grand Rapids: Eerdmans, 1971.
Underhill, Evelyn. *Mysticism*. 12th ed. 1930. New York: Image-Doubleday, 1990.

CHAPTER 14

Chiasmatic Christianity:
Lilith's Sense of an Ending

Kelly Searsmith

Readers of Victorian and Edwardian *Kunstmärchen*, so many of which depict journeys to Fairyland, will find no surprise in Mr. Vane's expulsion from the other dimensional side at the end of George MacDonald's *Lilith*. A protagonist's expulsion from Fairy, accompanied by a re-imposed barrier between fantasy and reality, was a generic convention: Glück returns to share the harvest of a restored but very natural golden river (Ruskin's *The King of the Golden River*); Tom leaves his water-babydom behind in the sea to work as an engineer (Kingsley's *The Water-Babies*); Alice wakes up from the dream of Wonderland to find she's still in her older sister's company (Carroll's *Alice's Adventures in Wonderland*); Jack returns home without having wed Mopsa after all to a plate of strawberries and a good night's sleep (Ingelow's *Mopsa the Fairy*).

MacDonald's first attempt at an extended fantasy, *Phantastes*, ends in this same fashion: Anodos dies ecstatically out of Fairyland and is transformed into a masculine angel, only to be returned to the mortal world to assume management of his family estate. In *Lilith*, MacDonald's last attempt, this expulsion is intensified by both its earlier repetition and final circumstances. Although Vane's earlier returns had been wanted and even self-willed, his final leave-taking occurs just as he pierces a heavenly vale to view the Throne of the Ancient of Days. He is gently pushed through a "little door with a golden lock" back into the library of his manor house. He senses a book shutting behind him, as if even the existence of the door is denied, and his whole metaphysical journey has been nothing but a story contained within its covers.

Since the popular children's genre's inception in the 1840s in England, literary fairy stories had typically introduced Fairy as a vehicle for individual moral reform and collective social commentary. That is, they made use of Fairylands and fey encounters even as *Reisfabulistik* such as *Gulliver's Travels*—not coincidentally excerpted in Andrew Lang's *The Blue Fairy Book*—made use of magical voyages to distinctive geographies. The travels provided a ready vehicle for commentary on the failings of home and the travelers' transformations a measure of their improvement, not only through tests of character, but also through an awareness of how these failings had been ingrained into them as inheritors of their civilization, historically or generationally. They echo the spiritual conversion narratives as familiar to English readers as Bunyan's *Pilgrim's Progress* and the slave narratives of Victorian abolitionists and their sympathetic wards and sources.

In English literary fairy tales, the protagonists' expulsion from Fairy helped to promote these fantasies' self-consciously reformist cultural work. In fact, I argue it is the tendency of these fairy stories to intervene in a sociohistoric discourse that defined, expressed, and governed the identity formation of a managerial class that gives shape to what Jack Zipes has identified as their "utopian impulse" (Searsmith, "News from Somewhere"). The apparent containment of fantasy refocused the protagonists on accommodating themselves to social-consensus reality and the role in it they were slotted to play. The fantastically exoticized Other was not endorsed over that of the English Self; rather, it provided a counterpoint of shame or a rallying point of inspiration, one that further impelled the protagonist's development toward the type of future colonial or domestic manager who might assume his position with renewed justification. What the protagonist does take back with him to the "real" are those operations performed on his character that only lived experience, and the moral choices that determine its course, can provide.

Of course, managerial-class identity formation was served by domestic fiction just as well as the fairy story. The domestic novel of the period—as written by Charles Dickens, George Eliot, Anthony Trollope, Elizabeth Gaskell, and many others—had its marriage plot, with an ending that meted out poetic justice to elements of disorder—the Bumbles, Heeps, and Quilps who would assert worldly power over their betters in character—and restored order through the joining of a deserving couple whose union would provide a domestic nexus for the gathering forces of social good. The marriage plot answered readers' desires through rewarding virtue with the ideal life all young Victorian men and women were supposed to want; it was, in fact, the one that would afford them the best status and most independence to which they could aspire. The domestic novel's imbrication of the *Bildungsroman* is not coincidental, nor is its drawing together the promise of a good life for its protagonists (and readers) with the enactment of domestic virtue. As a popular form, it reinforced not the social reality in which virtue often goes unrewarded and may be variously defined but the fantasy of a moral universe that punishes the wicked, rewards the good, and keeps its martyrs holy, as icons of combined domestic and spiritual virtue.

What is significant about how Victorian fairy stories like MacDonald's used encounters with Fairy to reshape developmental dramas of moral and spiritual formation was their introduction of what Vane refers to as a new "economy of conditions" (12). This new symbolic economy preempted the existing symbolic economy of social-consensus reality to reveal the "true," "right," "natural," and/or divinely determined set of relations that underwrites material existence and would underwrite social practice as well, if human self-interest had not altered such ideal forms and their Platonic relations, sometimes beyond recognition. What is particularly significant about *Phantastes* and *Lilith* is that MacDonald's use of older protagonists, young men who are just come of legal age and so into their inheritances, makes his fairy stories even more distinctively tales of moral and spiritual *re*formation, ones in which habits of thought must be put under a riddling Gnostic examination to reveal their grounding in an exploded secular epistemology. The reformist *Bildungs* through which Anodos and Vane make their ways are geared not toward expulsion, nor toward return, but toward *a desire to return*. In fact, for MacDonald, a general lack of desire among men to return to God in heaven, which he associates in his fantasies with Fairy as a sort of purgatorial preparing ground, is a special crisis in modern manhood — the signal spiritual crisis he means to address in *Lilith*. As Adam tells Vane, "Men are not coming home fast; women are coming faster" (229).

Although we may accept that this is MacDonald's thematic thrust in *Phantastes*, *Lilith*, and others of his fantasies that expel their protagonists from Fairy, as readers of contemporary fantasy we are left with a troubling reaction: our dissatisfaction over their endings. When we consider the matter, we feel that we must be missing something. Have readers' tastes so changed that we can no longer recognize why Andersen's, or MacDonald's, magic-resistant, melancholy finishes satisfied period readers (which we may suppose they did, given their sales, personal reader reports, conversions to stage, merchandising, and staying power over the period)? How might we explain the tendency of these fantasies' expulsion plots to *satisfy readers' desires*?

The very question may seem paradoxical to those of us who, after Tolkien, identify the pleasures of fantasy literature with an imaginative escape from a dissatisfying reality into a fantasy where readers may be consoled with a vision of the "old ambitions and desires" satisfied, what Tolkien refers to as fantasy's "eucatastrophic effect." Contemporary fantasy readers expect their orphaned, coming-of-age protagonist — like Tolkien's Frodo, LeGuin's Ged, Eddings's Garion, Rowling's Harry Potter — to gain through magic a special identity and a place in the world he has earned through its right use. In denying protagonists a magical reward, such as the right to remain in Fairyland or access its magics, fairy stories such as *Lilith* seem to deny readers "consolation" and to revoke their right to "escape." That *Lilith*'s narrative *telos* depends on an aesthetic, and a popular taste, historically distinctive from our own, however, requires but this example: in Andersen's "The Little Mermaid" (1836), Ariel watches her prince marry another; she is expelled from the human world (her fantasy) to become a "daughter of the air," one who must earn her way into heaven. In Disney's sentimental revision (1989), Ariel marries her prince and becomes the toast of the kingdom.

Our making sense of the historically *satisfying* nature of MacDonald's endings, and particularly *Lilith*'s, depends on understanding their relationship to the abbreviated *Bildungs* that led up to them and the ways in which such a neo-Romantic author employed those *Bildungs* to intervene in discourses of identity formation. MacDonald believed so strongly in individual revelation, because he felt that "Not only ... has each man his individual relation to God, but each man has his peculiar relation to God.... There is no massing of men with God.... Each of us is a distinct flower or tree in the spiritual garden of God, — precious, each for his own sake" (*Unspoken Sermons* 110). Elsewhere I have argued that *Phantastes* reforms Anodos from a man of the world, "a man of pride," into a Christlike man: the social type of the new gentleman ("Angel in the Cosmos"). Anodos's final transformation into a masculine angel, however, does not resolve the contradictions inherent in the new gentleman, since the romance makes clear that it is a masculine style possible only in a fantasy world. The angel in the cosmos's effect is, instead, to awaken in readers a desire for the utopian good the new gentleman can but approximate: a wholly selfless man, free from all egoism or desire. Through incorporating an ecumenical *Sehnsucht*, or spiritual longing, into the new gentleman, *Phantastes* encourages privileged men who adopt that style to yearn for an unseen divinity which might make some measure of good sustainable.[1] According to Rolland Hein, perhaps because of the otherwise Romantically inclined MacDonald's Calvinist roots, literature, and especially imaginative literature, had the potential to set individuals on a spiritually evolutionary course (xviii).[2]

Lilith's plot works on much the same principle, using Vane's journey to another, more apparently metaphysical dimension as an opportunity to teach him that he may best benefit others and earn entry into heaven thereby by reforming himself. However, the more difficult and important work for MacDonald is to give Vane a philosophical basis for and consistent desire to reform — as well as the emotional resources to maintain that reformation once he has returned to what used to be "the real" but no longer feels like "home."

Like Anodos, Vane is an orphan, a man who has not learned at his father's knee what sort of man he should become; only by sheer good fortune does he find himself an Oxford man taking a holiday before assuming the management of his family estate. As such, Vane is an exaggeration of a social type: the landed gentleman who pursues a life of leisure without fellow purpose, withdraws from the company of and concern for the welfare of others into his own "metaphysical dreams," and assumes that his station grants him these privileges and the identity upon which they are based, although he has done nothing to earn them (the squire's prodigal son, rather than the good old squire himself). Early on, the fairy story's dislocation of Vane from his "place" in the world (and who he believes it makes him) becomes the means by which its values and their hold on him are loosed. Vane's very assumption that he may trust his perceptions to guide him about the nature and relative merits of another is called into question when he apologizes for having assumed Mr. Raven a lesser creature because a bird: "We do not waste our intellects in generalising," Raven chides, "but take man or bird as we find him" (14). From Raven's perspective, Vane has not done enough to know who he is behind his *think* (16), as his dislocation from social-consensus reality and Raven's chiasmatic riddling soon bring home to him.

Carroll's *Alice's Adventures* offers a similarly existentially troubling moment when the hookah-smoking Caterpillar asks Alice the one question to which she can give no satisfying answer: "Who are you?" Alice cannot answer because she has forgotten her name, but the Caterpillar's question suggests even more, encouraging readers to question not only what is in a name, such as a family name, but also what social understandings inform it and whether these are reasonably valued and applied to self-understanding. The question leverages esoteric discourse to reveal the unstable conflation of epistemology and ontology assumed in social identifications, a conflation in which epistemology seems to prescribe ontology.

If Vane's inheritance of an estate has given him a sense of "the transitory nature of possession" (6), his entry into the Platonic realm gives him a sense of the transitory nature of himself: "The raven said I must do something: what could I do here?— And would that make me somebody, for now, alas, I was nobody!" (15). His decision to remain in that realm has everything to do with this, as he later reflects, "here I might learn to be something by doing something" (82). Later, Vane articulates this process of identity formation more fully, saying that it has to do not only with taking action, but also relating to others, for "nowhere but in other lives can he ripen his specialty, develop the idea of himself, the individuality that distinguishes him from every other" (102). Thus, Vane's challenge is to fix the identity that is yet visibly revolving on his forehead (to one with the sight, such as Mara), and in doing so, to earn a distinctive individual nature. To do so, he must learn to live consciously (what Vane describes as "awakening from a dream" [13]), rather than sleepwalking through life. He must learn to see more deeply into the multiple and *wonder*ful nature of things ("like a child" [94]), rather than accepting the habitual modes of thought and perception he has unreflectively absorbed.

For MacDonald, the key to Vane's perceptual shift is his accepting that epistemology should follow from ontology, and not the reverse, as is the case in his former "existence." Only through that formulation do we achieve a humanity that is more than what MacDonald — after Carlyle's *Sartor Resartus*—figures as mere social tailoring. Or so Vane's Adamic Virgil, Mr. Raven, teaches of the partially realized, gruesome dancers and the yet entirely skeletal Lord "of Cokayne" and his Lady: "for every grain of truthfulness adds a fibre to the show of their humanity. Nothing but truth can appear, and whatever is must seem" (94). This lesson is not lost on Vane, as he continues to associate fixing an identity with fixing a place, one more permanent and meaningful than the family estate he has left behind in what we may presume to be England: "But what mattered *where* while *everywhere* was the same as *nowhere*! I had not yet, by doing something in it, made *anywhere* into a place! I was not yet alive, only dreaming that I lived!" (82).

Vane will indeed come to make anywhere a place through his works, not all of which are good, but all of which ultimately lead to spiritual triumph: He will bring Lilith to the House of Bitterness for Mara's chastening of her soul and again to Adam for her long sleep until the end of the universe. He will himself plant her closed fist at the headwaters of the wasteland, which contains an egg brimming with the Waters of Life. The actual course of Vane's journey to these good ends matters less than the opportunities it provides for his spiritual instruction from Mara and, especially, Adam. From the start, Adam makes clear that Vane is to do something, anything, if he is to find the way back "home," by which he seems to mean the "Kansas" of his former life but later comes to suggest a heavenly rest. Vane's is to be an inward rather than an outward journey, both through his movement within an inner (and higher) dimension and his internal progress toward spiritual *in*sight.

While yet new to the other realm, Vane demonstrates his potential for spiritual growth by finding no taste for the fruit of the greedy, stupid Bags (like Swift's Yahoos); he chooses instead that of the Lovers, i.e., Little Ones

(58). He demonstrates this again by leaving the pleasures of the Lovers to give his life purpose, seeking an answer to how it may be that their "thwarted development," especially their lack of knowledge, should be essential to their good. He is rightly unable to conceive of how ignorance in the presence of wisdom and inaction in the face of evil may be as *essential* to their good as Lona believes (Lona's stunting of her charges benignly parallels her mother Lilith's refusing the Bulikans' ability to multiply). That Vane is being formed for a managerial role is clear from this moment. Neither he nor Adam perceives him as an equal to the Lovers, but as a tacit superior: a guiding, protective figure: a squire among the villagers, a man who would be, will be, "king."

In the House of Bitterness, Vane gains a clear focus for his good intentions, when he learns of the evil Bulikan queen who rules over a proud and greedy, "Bag"-like people and is destined to be usurped and overtaken by Lona and the Lovers (118). As he sets out to Bulika, to learn how he may assist in the prophecy's fruition, the narrative shifts to an Arthurian quest motif. As in *Phantastes*, our erstwhile virtuous knight is led astray from his Grail search by the phantasms put in his path. In his first temptation of the flesh, Vane restores the life of Lilith, the Bulikan queen (more often named "the Princess"). He becomes so "tempted to love a lie" (131) that he offers to be her slave (110); he nearly succumbs to becoming no more than a "tame animal for her to feed upon" (133). What saves him from this fate is not his willpower but his love of the Little Ones, whom he knows are not the "savage dwarf people, enemies to law and order" she claims them to be (130). In his limited spiritual progress, Vane has understood enough to hold to an ontological truth he has *felt* over an epistemological assertion that relies merely on a rational manipulation of perspective. Despite this progress, Lilith's "present silver seemed brighter than the gold of the absent sun" (137), continuing to give her such power over Vane that he seeks to heal her once again. For succumbing to Lilith's glamour, and choosing to ignore her palpable evil, Vane is cast out of the other realm — the first time since he chose to remain.

If Vane seems to have taken two steps back for one step forward, all is not lost. His final slip was out of pity as well as desire. This readies him for the spiritual lesson that governs the second half of the novel. Evil, Adam gives him to know, should not be suffered, nor suffering prevented. Adam illustrates this principle through assessing Vane's management of the Little Ones. Although he has gained enough wisdom to recognize his own ignorance, he has failed the Lovers in choosing to "speculate about" rather than assist them (142). Evil, Adam gives him to know, should not be suffered, but neither should suffering be prevented when it leads to spiritual growth. As Adam makes clear, for MacDonald, good managerial practice means rule by right of moral imperative and active rather than speculative philanthropy (the same that, in its telescopic and ministerial forms, Dickens attacks in *Bleak House*). He chastises Vane for remaining a slave to the Bags, and so teaching the Lovers to fear them, when he should have set them in their place. He tells Vane he might also dig the Lovers wells so that they might find their tears, tears being the necessary catalyst for further development as a race. When Vane objects, saying his object was to prevent them, Adam retorts this is "the aim of all stupid philanthropists!" It is one of the "pet falsehoods" of "his world" (141).

Given his charge to help the Lovers, Vane yet assumes his succumbing to Lilith's glamour is his greatest failing. However, Adam silences him again by asserting that his greatest failing was, rather, his refusal to find comfort in "our dead," and to take his place among them. Significantly, this statement rewrites our conventional assumptions about the course of Vane's "Arthurian" quest. It was not this Arthur's succumbing to Morgan Le Fay that seeds his harvest of sorrow, but his refusal to accept what Lilith has also rejected: "Good and not Evil," as Adam tells her, "is the Universe." So good is the Universe, so pure is God's love, that "the groaning, travailing world is the nursery of our Father's children" (148); the sorrow in it is "good" for it teaches us when we have gone against wisdom (95). To die is to come alive, although how long we sleep before that final resurrection (going "home" to God) depends on how much healing we must do, as we forget enough of the world's travails to remember more of God's love (242). When Vane doubts that the White Leopard that is Mara's shadow may defend the Lovers against the Spotted Leopard that is Lilith's, Adam asserts, "How should such eyes tell which have never slept? ... He who cannot act must make haste to sleep!" (154). It is not until Vane sleeps that he will understand the true power of Mara, who is the "voice in the wilderness before Baptist came" (239) to announce the coming of the Messiah. Sorrow is, then, that which prepares humanity for the Second Coming; it prepares us to the healing, purifying sleep that anticipates our resurrection. The theological implication is that God, through agents such as Mara, brings us suffering out of a desire for our growth. He feels a profound pity for humanity's suffering, as the traces of it on Mara's face reveal. The very moon, in its maternal aspect, watches over Vane's progress with unmistakable sympathy. As Raven's remark overtly demonstrates, this theological position on the problem of evil, and especially the reason for suffering, is meant to guide Vane as a leader in worldly affairs, both foreign and domestic.

Although a reinvigorated Vane promises Raven he will redeem himself and go to the House of the Dead before further helping the Lovers, he soon after breaks his word, now committing what Raven calls a far worse offense than his fear and heedlessness had led him to before: a "crime," one of pride in himself and desire, this time for a horse. It is Vane's second temptation of the flesh, one that now leads him to feel like a king rather than a slave (157). Again, Vane is punished through his own actions: killing the horse in his wild ride and leading the Lovers as a doomed army of innocents into Bulika, only to lose Lona and expose the Lovers to a people not fit to be redeemed, mothers not worth having. Vane is so chastened by his failure that he worries he will join the gruesome dead of the Evil Wood for his "stiffneckedness" (190). As his path takes him back through the didactic vignettes of his earlier instruction, he begins to understand the kindness the divine has shown through allowing him and the rest of humanity to suffer as a result of free will. Most instructive is the lesson of the worldly Lord of Cokayne and his Lady, whose punishment of reduced circumstance and mutual torment had so horrified him. Now, he sees how, having been deprived together, they have joined to ease one another's suffering (191). Through this, MacDonald gives readers to know that, in his love, God's focus is not on punishment, but reformation — for which punishment is sometimes necessary.

It is a lesson Lilith fails to grasp to the last, admitting that she does not "know Him" and therefore cries out "for Death — to escape Him and thee" (214). She mistakes death as an end to life, rather than as the beginning of a resurrection into eternal life. Moreover, despite Eve's reassurances, she fears her sin means she belongs to the Shadow: "I must go to the Shadow — yet I would not!" (215). Readers are under no doubt that she will be redeemed, for Eve's reassurance demonstrates Lilith's false consciousness: "You shall not go to the Shadow.... Even now is his head under my heel!" (216).

This knowledge of God's final forgiveness in no way mitigates the fairy story's developmental imperative that if a man or woman will not learn by the easy way, he or she must learn by the hard. Vane himself finally owns and articulates what for him is new wisdom to the Lovers when he returns to them in a sort of esoteric pageant, bearing Lona's body and accompanied by the captive Lilith, who is in turn trailed by Mara whom the Bags have taught them to fear as the "Cat-woman." Of Mara, Vane reassures the Lovers, "I am sure she will never be unkind to you, even if she does hurt you!" Mara is more likely to scratch Lilith than to bring her nourishment, for she is her friend, and "[a] friend is one who gives us what we need, and the princess is sorely in need of a terrible scratching" (194–95). Thus, Vane echoes Adam's sentiment that Vane's beating the Bags with a stick would, for them, have been "progress" (143). What distinguishes MacDonald's apology for suffering and advocacy for punishment from the usual Victorian law and order line is his making a sharp distinction between hating the sin and loving the sinner.

This distinction is so important to MacDonald that he makes this the final lesson before Vane may earn his couch of resurrection through one final proof of his understanding. Thus, he is present at Mara's painful intervention on Lilith's behalf in the House of Bitterness. He himself feels the chill of Life in Death's passing. He learns that even then he cannot truly understand evil — which may incomprehensibly coexist with beauty. Mara's explanation is itself a chiasmatic enigma. The Shadow may overshadow Lilith's Self, she says, but it is not herself, which can be nothing other than good because Lilith, an angel, is God's creation (199). Like all of humanity, Vane may only feel the misery evil causes those who, like Lilith, have embraced it. "None but God hates evil," Mara tells him, "and understands it" (206). Yet, to witness God's hatred of evil, and Lilith's suffering because of it, is also to witness divine forgiveness, as Mara kisses Lilith's brow, miraculously enabling her to once again listen to the land and the cleansing, life-giving rain that comes to the wasteland as a signal of her renewed potential for redemption (207). Without, all is morning and springtime, signifiers of life eternal. For MacDonald, the mere elimination of sin is not the end, as the evangelical line often held, or seemed to do. As Adam says in the case of Lilith, "Annihilation itself is not death to evil. Only good where evil was, is evil dead" (153).

Adam sets Vane one final task before he is allowed to assume his place in the House of the Dead next to his beloved Lona. He must plant the seed of life at the headwaters of the wasteland. The quest is brief. Its purpose is not to inculcate virtue or to teach new lessons, but to test that Vane has internalized the lessons already taught and readied himself to act upon them with unwavering virtue. He passes the phantasms of the proud Lilith who commands he return her hand; an army of men who would scare him off; a gentle Mara who would offer him rest; and even the Shadow itself, which would bar his way. He ignores them all, and himself, as a Son of Man, employs the Sexton's paradoxically life-bringing burial shovel.

On his return, he encounters one final test: a wandering-Jew figure who is so exhausted with life, he would rather die than live. Once again, Vane himself now teaches the chiasmatic doctrine he has been taught: "I may not be old enough to desire to die, but I am young enough to desire to live indeed! Therefore I go now to learn if she [the Mother, Eve] will at length take me in. You wish to die because you do not care to live: she will not open her door to you, for no one can die who does not long to live" (225). That Vane knows himself to be "childlike" enough to accept the Universe's good and God's loving nature is indeed final proof that he is ready to take his couch in the House of Death.[3] He has learned to act not on "knowledge" — the reasoning of his own mind based on perceived facts, which can be deceived by outward forms — but on his understanding — the guiding feelings of his heart, which respond only to truths (152).

The fantasy's end takes a spasmodic turn, as Vane enters into his deathlike sleep in which he experiences what are *genuinely* metaphysical dreams — given to him by "Another" who can "fulfill" them — rather than ones invented and frustrated by himself (251). The promise of fulfillment seems false when he wakens, only to find himself unbearably alone in his manor house. His experience of the "real world" as a dead one gives him a "heart of stone." Thankfully, he wakes once again in the House of the Dead to learn it was a troubling dream. He, Lona, and their Little Ones (all the Lovers who do not sleep by Lilith's side) experience a glorious Resurrection Day, in which they revel in creation and, finally, ascend the mount toward the New Jerusalem. It is at this point Vane is expelled back yet again to his manor house, now seemingly in fact. That he finds himself where his journey began — in the library, where he first met Raven, rather than the garret or fountain — suggests he will remain.

Lilith's ending thus gives one false expulsion from fantasy and one true; their parallel invites comparison, even as did Vane's parallel quests: the pre-empted "Arthurian" quest and the burial of the seed of the Waters of Life. As I will go on to illustrate, the effect of the false expulsion is to give readers a last profound lesson in religious consolation, one that Vane enacts in his second and apparently more lasting final return.

The course of Vane's false expulsion is this: Paradoxically, in his deathlike sleep, Vane experiences loving dreams (not a cat scratch of sorrow among them) that seem as real as waking. In fact, he believes himself to have already awakened, so vivid are his sensations of the "odors of the Earth's bosom" (the grave) and a "bliss" that is his not through prayer but "in virtue of existence." So strong is his sensation of life that he believes his vitality is itself by "virtue of a Will that dwelt in mine" (230). He is connected to creation and, through creation, to God. The scenes in which he finds himself, however, signal readers that he dreams. In one, he experiences Adam awaiting his birth, the birth of humanity, as well as the iconic manifestations of his own childhood, as a babe on his mother's white bosom, a youth on a white horse. In another, he rises into the heart of God, where he experiences for the first time the ecstatic enslavement of love, rather than that of his own pride. In yet a third, he experiences the rivers as they run across the wasteland with a "song of new born liberty," as heartening as the music of the River Jordan, "deep and wide" (231). In this, MacDonald figures for readers divine truths about the nature of creation, a creation to which Vane is now intimately tied through his understanding of and sympathy with its nature.

Finally, Vane comes to Adam, who is no longer Mr. Raven, but the biblical patriarch in his full power: youthful, beautiful, and clothed in white. Vane's trouble is that Lona is not with him. Adam assures Vane he is still dead and that as a dead man he cannot distinguish between the true and false, between the episteme (in Foucault's sense) of dreams (phantoms, forms) and a deeper, more stable ontological reality. He need have no fear, however, for

> The hour will come, and that ere long, when being true, thou shalt behold the very truth, and doubt will be for ever dead.... To him who has once seen even a shadow only of the truth, and, even but hoping he has seen it when it is present no longer, tries to obey it — to him the real vision, the Truth himself, will come, and depart no more, but abide with him for ever" [234–35].

This Vane understands, but what are readers to understand?

Here, MacDonald not only relates a spiritual principle, but also constructs the narrative so that readers may experience it, even as Vane encountered didactic vignettes and transformative experiences along his path. The implication is that readers have, along with Vane, now seen a shadow of the truth (a narrative vision — the Romantic, artistic "dream"), and, so too, may expect to know the "real" vision when it presents itself. Significantly, as Paul Riga has pointed out in "From Time to Eternity: MacDonald's Doorway Between," MacDonald often used dreams as vehicles to transport characters into the fantastic and back again, because he viewed the fantastic imagination and dreams as manifestations of the same power: modes by which individuals gain some conscious access to God and his creation's essential nature (84–85). Thus, that Vane's altered vision of the fantasy world in which he has moved is revealed in a dream conveys its deeper truth, since it comes unbidden, presumably from an agent at once both deeper within and further without. Of dreams, MacDonald writes that "man's" feeling is "that they are given to him; that from the vast unknown, where time and space are not, they suddenly appear in luminous writing upon the wall of his consciousness" ("Fantastic Imagination" 24).

Through MacDonald's fantastic revelation of a revivified gospel, readers are encouraged to begin questioning whether what we perceive to be our current lives is real, or a sort of dream out of which we ought to long to wake into death, which is eternal life. Moreover, MacDonald's attempt to quicken readers' desire for eternal life by associating it with that of being reunited with deceased loved ones is everywhere in Victorian treatments of death's consolation. The hope of being reunited with her Prince Consort was, after all, what made Tennyson's *In Memoriam* the Queen's most treasured poem. Yet, we might be sensitive too to the specifically masculine character MacDonald gives this consolation. We experience it through the longing of a man for his "heart's wife" and through the specific creation and formation of a masculine self. Although we may generalize Vane's experience humanistically, its specific masculine character also likely improves its appeal to male readers, the audience

MacDonald most hopes to reach because of what he perceives as their spiritual apathy or resistance.

Why then, by *Lilith*'s narrative logic, does Vane, along with his sympathetically identified readers, need to experience a false expulsion from these healing dreams? Vane himself has willed this expulsion, having found a grave in his dream and rolled into it. He has recalled that in the childhood of his other life, such falls often woke him and he wishes to awaken. One explanation for this impulse immediately presents itself: in doing so, perhaps he hopes he will be reunited with Lona then, rather than having to wait for God's appointed hour. However, this is not the case. His impulse, by his own account, is a perverse one, to use Poe's term, the same impulse that caused Lilith to put up one final resistance to the Lady of Sorrow. Even as she reaffirmed, "I will yet be mistress of myself" (205), Vane reaffirms that he has the ability to control his own dreams and the course of his life. When he awakens into a dead world, that of the empty manor, he realizes he has done a very foolish thing: "The dream was not of my making any more than was my life: I ought to have seen it to the end! And in fleeing from it, I had left the holy sleep itself behind me!" (236). The worst of it is, Vane experiences a crushing doubt, the very sort Adam told him he would and ought to have as an individual who is a lover of the truth, rather than one who adopts a "phantasm" of life in return for a "world of pleasant dreams" (234). The doubt is so profound that Vane questions Lona's very existence: "Was she anywhere? Had she ever been, save in the mouldering cells of my brain?" (237). He promises himself he will search for her the very moment he dies, no doubt now recalling with force Adam's promised consolation.

As before, we find Vane has walked a penitential path. His suffering and repentance lead to God's forgiveness. He awakens in the House of the Dead once more, so entirely forgiven that Mara and Eve both reassure him his devastating return to his old existence was nothing more than a (bad) dream. If it has been more of a cat-scratch than a nesting dream, he has only himself to blame. However, he need never have doubted its good outcome. Mara gives voice to the lesson, "What will be well, is even now well" (239). Vane doubts that the rest of humanity will believe that gospel should he bring it to them, but he recognizes it as a profound spiritual truth. In accepting God's infinitely good and loving nature, Vane finds himself open to all the glories of Resurrection Morning, which MacDonald mainly characterizes as a vast, organic communion. Vane lives in everything and everything finds its life in him (243); life is truth, and truth, life (244). Even the Sun itself, so long absent from Vane's skies — its absent Messianic gold once outshone by Lilith cum Judas's present silver — becomes the "coal from the altar of the Father's never-ending sacrifice to his children," with all of creation and every human neck straining toward it to see "him come" (245).

As Vane climbs the mountain toward the New Jerusalem — as reformed a metropole as one could ask to replace the fallen Gomorrah of Bulika — he expresses this religious ecstasy: "All I wanted and knew not, must be on its way to me!" (249). Thus, even to the end of Vane's travels in this metaphysical fairyland are readers encouraged to expect the fulfillment of Vane's desires. His piercing of the cloud and facing of a door with a golden lock may even mislead us, as we may expect it to be a very small, private entrance, a cottage-sized version of heaven's gate. Those of us who have read "The Golden Key" are even further prompted to view the door as an entrance to Heaven's way. On first reading, we are all no doubt as thunderstruck as Vane to find it is instead an exit back to mortal existence — one he cannot resist entering. He is pushed.

Perhaps we are meant to see this final, lasting expulsion as Vane's punishment for having wakened from the dream willingly once before. After all, Mara (the "Lady of Sorrow"), and not Lona (his "joy-fire"), he says, is much with him; she is teaching him still (250). He is tormented by the question of whether he is yet dreaming in the House of Death or whether he has awakened too soon. He longs for reassurance that his dreams are not, as his doubts suggest, born of a mothering brain and a fathering fever in the blood. If they are, his hope answers, God has made them violin and bow, and yet guides the bow across the strings of his imagination. This metaphysical reflection of Vane's, and thus MacDonald's, is not a riddling beside the point. It is the point itself.

Since the human condition is an inherently agnostic one — to dream and desire without absolute knowledge of the divine (251) — MacDonald returns Vane to that state. To allow him, and readers, to achieve the sight of God and put all doubts to rest would be to give them what they cannot hope to know in mortal life. Rather than presenting readers with a pious consolation that proves the fact of God through narrative invention alone (a phantasm), MacDonald appeals to those who would love the truth instead, urging them toward an understanding of, a feeling for, the divine within. In other words, he provides a consolation that is credible to those who must continue to struggle with belief. As "God broods and wills and quickens," Vane resolves himself to accept that it is not his time to reunite with Lona or enter the New Jerusalem (251). His last prideful desire to be self-mastered is given over to an acceptance of God's mastering. He waits for that moment when he "shall doubt no more" (252). He attempts to accept that "What will be well, is even now well" (239).

At the same time MacDonald emphasizes Vane's acceptance of God's will, he uses Vane's poignant assertion of lingering doubt and depth of desire to whet readers' appetite to believe. MacDonald is equally careful to legitimate Vane's and the reader's willingness to believe, so that those who would believe see themselves not as gullible fools but as brave adventurers: the saviors of their countries. Their reward for spiritual reform and good works, however, will not be found in the theater of their action, even as Vane's was not found in his. Rather, it will be granted through having earned their resurrection in "death" and having arrived at a depth of self-knowledge and ontological discernment that will distinguish them in "life."

In large part, the expulsion plot endings of fairy stories such as *Lilith*'s were conventionally appealing, because they portrayed their protagonists as having lost Fairyland or access to its magics in the service of a good cause; they are, effectively, martyrs. Even Alice is expelled from Wonderland because she is morally outraged at the King and Queen of Hearts's kangaroo court. In *Lilith*, Vane's service to good, and subsequent martyring, are more profound yet. By the time Vane strives to reach heaven, he has helped to save Bulika from its tyrant Princess; brought her to justice and, eventually, the couch of resurrection; set the Little Ones and Lona on a course of mental growth; and released the Waters of Life into the wasteland. He has lost his name, his way, his sense, his horse, the woman he loves, and very nearly his life, before giving it up most willingly. He has been, along the penitent's way, chastened enough to repent his pride and trust in the goodness of God, even when phantasms of desire and fright (the "loathsome" thoughts of humankind [244]) would lead him astray. By the narrative logic of any domestic fiction, this leading man ought to have his lady at the end: they have both amply demonstrated their virtue. However, the virtues Vane and Lona demonstrate are not of a social but a spiritual, order. The continued proving out of this virtue in Vane must be his patience in waiting to be reunited with Lona, from whom he is parted in body only, not in spirit.

In the case of both Anodos and Vane, we are given to understand their martyrdoms are not complete: they are men reformed but not yet redeemed. They have made it through the purifying ground of a quasi-purgatory, but heaven will not reveal its mystery. They are returned to enact their newfound virtue in the grayer, more complex mortal world, where spirit is masked over with flesh and truths are hidden beneath shifting forms. They must await their final resurrection and ascension but have been given the mental resources with which to endure: a new foundation for a faithful life. As such, Anodos's and Vane's dying back into life are not so much extensions of the beautiful child deaths so popular in spiritually minded Victorian fiction but denials to them of such deaths. They are not yet, as MacDonald would say, childlike enough; they are still good enough for this world, and thus, not yet good enough for the other. Diamond, the childish and ultimately childlike protagonist of *At the Back of the North Wind*, demonstrates the difference. His travels with the North Wind, and their spiritual influence upon him, render him "almost as clear as alabaster"; he becomes so disinterested in his love for others that he is at last permitted to go "to the back of the North Wind" (in other words, to heaven). Mossy and Tangle of "The Golden Key" are two other childlike travelers in a MacDonaldian fairyland who earn their way up the rainbow stair, out of the land of shifting shadow forms and into the country from whence the shadows fall.

Yet, even though Vane and Anodos fall short of this measure, their return to the world is not a disappointment. They are free to live a mortal span, rather than being made to die, which readers, even if they have been educated in beautiful death, may resist. They have wealth and power at their disposal and now the knowledge and imperative to do well by it. Indeed, the return of such protagonists in general from Fairyland serves as an escape from the trials they have found there. That land, with its morally redemptive dimension, is not without suffering. Although protagonists such as Anodos and Vane are driven between wonders and terrors, tasks and pleasures, we do not envy them their terrors and their tasks. Because they are not of the place and learn its laws piecemeal, they find themselves more powerless than in their originating world, more liable to falter, less sure of their path and its destination. In this sense, their return to the mundane, although it involves the loss of fantasy, does re-establish a comforting familiarity for protagonist and readers alike, one that is epistemologically empowering, all the more so in MacDonald's theological fantasies, given the epistemological shift they invite readers to make: from a socially to an ontologically (and so divinely) determined "perception."

One could argue that MacDonald's reformist narratives in *Phantastes* and *Lilith* focus merely on self-cultivation, even if that cultivation occurs in the hearts and minds of the managerial class in good, Broad Church fashion. *Lilith* does not, after all, show Vane's doing any broader good in his originating world after his return; nor can we be certain that readers will be moved to feel more than a quietist religious consolation in having sympathized with the changes he has undergone. I want to suggest, however, that we consider how Vane's journey into the "heart of lightness" may be read as having a potentially transformative effect as profound as Kurtz experiences when he voyages into the Belgian Congo's dark heart. Although Vane goes native, MacDonald is able to reinscribe the late-Victorian colonial narrative by directing his journey within rather than without, taking him into the nature of things instead of into the things of nature and the differences in men those may produce. In this way, Vane is Romantically redeemed from civilization's presence rather than defiled by its absence.

MacDonald's *Lilith*, then, can be read as employing a metaphysical liminality that, although self-consciously imaginative, destabilizes the protagonist's and readers' ideological conformity through its suggestion that the imaginative may correspond to a reality as yet unseen. In doing so, the narrative may provide a politically resistant basis for reforming the secular and (in MacDonald's view) self-interested identification of the managerial class. By unfixing Vane from one version of consensus reality, *Lilith* provides an imaginative experience of a potentially transformative ideal. To the extent that readers invest in the dream and internalize this ideal, they might be understood as no longer completely determined by their social roles; they are given some independent foundation for a more idealistic identification than their actual, immediate circumstances might otherwise encourage or allow. We may read this strategy of resistance as, ultimately, no more than a further mystification; however, as a religious and political outsider, no doubt MacDonald's hope was that it would enable relative autonomy as well as provide a much needed encouragement for those who suffered in a world not of their choosing.

Notes

1. In his elaboration of MacDonald's symbolism, Richard Reis claims MacDonald's most common mythic plot is "the search for a divine unity, an unrealized but hoped for goal," often through the journey to another world. MacDonald presents many symbolic settings, one of which is the Wasteland, indicative of the absence of maturation and growth (and, ultimately, spiritual stagnation) (122).

2. I am indebted to Stephen Prickett for the kernel of this argument about spiritual evolution and devolution in Victorian Fantasy (84–88).

3. For discussion of MacDonald's conception of the childlike, see chapter 5 of Robb: "Fiction for the Child." Of special interest is how Robb discusses Lilith as the ultimate opposite of the childlike. She is non-maternal woman whose sin is pride and whose denial of death in defiance of God is coupled with her impulse to murder her own child, Lona, and to destroy the Little Ones, who both embody the quintessential childlike. Robb writes, "It is as if MacDonald were envisaging the battle between Good and Evil — the Battle of Armageddon, as he discusses it in *Malcolm* — as meaning the conflict between the childlike vision and the adult, or parental, viewpoint" (109).

Works Cited

Foucault, Michel. *The Order of Things: An Archaeology of the Human Sciences*. 1966. Trans. Don Idhe. 1970. New York: Routledge, 2001.

Hein, Rolland. *The Harmony Within: The Spiritual Vision of George MacDonald*. Washington, D.C.: Christian University Press, 1982.

Lang, Andrew. *The Blue Fairy Book*. 1889. Dover Story Books for Children. New York: Dover, 1965.

MacDonald, George. *At the Back of the North Wind.* 1868–69. New York: William Morrow, 1989.

———. "The Fantastic Imagination" in *The Gifts of the Child Christ: Fairytales and Stories for the Childlike, Volume I.* 23–28. Ed. Glenn Edward Sadler. Grand Rapids: Eerdmans, 1973.

———. "The Golden Key" in *The Golden Key and Other Fantasy Stories.* 1–35.Grand Rapids: Eerdmans, 1980.

———. *Phantastes: A Faerie Romance.* 1858. Grand Rapids: Eerdmans, 1981.

———. *Unspoken Sermons.* New York: Routledge, 1871.

Prickett, Stephen. *Victorian Fantasy.* Bloomington: Indiana University Press, 1979.

Reis, Richard H. *George MacDonald.* New York: Twayne, 1972.

Riga, Paul. "From Time to Eternity: MacDonald's Doorway Between" in *Essays on C.S. Lewis and George MacDonald: Truth, Fiction, and the Power of Imagination.* 83–100. Ed. Cynthia Marshall. Studies in British Literature 11. Lewiston: Edwin Mellen, 1991.

Robb, David S. *George MacDonald.* Scottish Writers Series. Edinburgh: Scottish Academic, 1987.

Searsmith, Kelly. "The Angel in the Cosmos: George MacDonald's *Phantastes* and the New Gentleman." *The Journal of Pre-Raphaelite Studies* 8 (1999): 53–70.

———. "News from Somewhere: A Case for Romance-Tradition Fantasy's Reformist Poetic." *The Journal of the Fantastic in the Arts* 11.1 (2000): 62–76.

Zipes, Jack. Introduction to *Victorian Fairy Tales: The Revolt of the Fairies and Elves.* xiii–xxix. New York: Routledge, 1987.

CHAPTER 15

The (As Yet) Endless Ending of *Lilith*
David M. Miller

Robert A. Collins's chapter 1 essay, "Liminality in *Lilith*," asks of *Lilith* the question most relevant to serious art: "What do you mean?" In the postmodern world, the question is almost obscene, and I welcome it:

> If we consider Mr. Vane as hero, his sojourn in the alternate world and his epiphany there would certainly require a return to his fellows to communicate his enlightenment, but what does that enlightenment consist of and what message does the hero carry back to us? If the story is either mythopoesis or a heroic journey, it seems somehow to fail in the final phase of its mission [8].

Unfortunately, it is no longer possible to answer questions of meaning simply. Meaning and significance are no longer just "out there," no longer objective "things." On the other hand, they are not just solipsisms projected upon chaos. The reader-author contract has been nuanced but not erased. Collins's blood question is answerable, but the answer is much longer than it used to be. Critical language was born in Babel, and "diversity" has faceted our critical lens and so fragmented art's light. I saw a sign in a coffee shop that encapsulates our moment: "I've gone out to find myself. Should I return before I get back, keep me here." This essay is an attempt to keep meaning here until it gets back. I'll begin with the counter-question mandated by PC diversity, "Whose meaning?"

In the present case, there are several sites for meaning, and for significance. Vane, the protagonist, travels in the novel's meta-land of n dimensions.

George MacDonald, the author, assembles enough allusions to clog the creek at Valumbrosa. Robert Collins, the critic, deploys a dozen investigative strategies. I, and my shadow Caliban, bring additional strategies and agendas. (I have Christian proclivities. Caliban does not.) You, my reader, no doubt, can make the question even more complicated. But in the end, we all want answers. After all the chalk and essays and walks on the beach, after all the perfumes from Xanadu, what — precisely — did each of us hear the mermaids singing? Was it backed like a camel? How do we respond to the song? Inquiring minds want to know.

The pleasure of sharing in sensitive and learned investigations of genre-meaning problems has, for fifty years, kept me reading and puzzling about literature in general, and about the possible worlds of the imagination in particular. Professor Collins is a kindred spirit, and I take up his challenge with eagerness, arguing for fellowship, not victory.

Here is a critical principle, followed by a simple hypothesis. Principle: a novel's answers always precede a critic's questions. The onus, therefore, is on the critic to ask the right questions, not upon the novel to provide the right answers. Hypothesis: although Professor Collins asks his question of the *penultimate* chapter, the answer may be in the *final* chapter that he dismisses.

Clearly, Collins's question does not fit the answer MacDonald gives. One presumes that MacDonald would feel a similar dissatisfaction with the Collins question. And so there we are. As Richard Boone famously said, "Your fault. My fault. Nobody's fault." But it blows your damn head clean off.

One way out of this impasse is the old-fashioned distinction between *meaning* and *significance*. Both meaning and significance are cooperative accomplishments of the author and the reader, achieved in the stress of working out the reader-author contract. The balance of power for *meaning* resides with the author; the balance of power for *significance* lies with the reader. Here is Collins's question twice: "What is the *meaning* of Vane's forced return to his own library at the very instant he seems about to achieve paradise?" Thus stated, the question points back to the novel, to the complex structurings of MacDonald's art. "What is the *significance* of Vane's forced return to his own library at the very instant he seems about to achieve paradise?" Now the question points from the novel to the reader. The answer is to be forged among the even more complex interactions between the reader's worldview and the stimuli launched by the novel. For the twenty-first century, *interested* reader, these two processes are not discrete.

Collins is master of his *significance* question. If he finds *Lilith*'s significance perverse, puzzling, or absent, there is no arguing with him. We can, however, seek to understand the ways in which his desire and the novel's achievement are incommensurate. And our understanding of that disjunction may help us triangulate the meaning of the novel, and even enrich our own understanding of its significance.

Collins has at his disposal an impressive array of heuristics. During the fifty years we shared in the business, the age of cultural biography was followed by a brief, hyper-exuberant age of the text, which gave birth to an age of criticism, that morphed into structuralism, that ushered in an age of theory. Cut loose from its roots in art and religion, theory skidded into anthropology and was an easy mark for ideology. The rest is history (or rather new historicism and cultural critique). At the extreme, shared ideology (rather than shared aesthetics) is the source of *author*ity. The net effect of these modulations was to shift power from the author to the reader, who is now "authorized" to be resisting, recalcitrant, and, in Caliban's case, imperial. The "text" which was once the stable ground for both meaning and significance has been problematized into a one-sided de-re-constructive "project," powered by the desire of the reader and curbed, if at all, only by ideology.[1] Collins seems to know all this, but his essay is at heart "retro," a return to questions of "meaning" (and "significance") that were all but lost among the theory heads. I honor that return.

First Collins's essay; then mine (and Caliban's). Collins's essay tastes of ashes, plain old Monday morning blue blahs. In dream/reality Vane supposedly learned the key to all mythologies, and was denied the golden guerdon so that he might take a message back to those chained in the cave. Laboriously, in liminal half-sleep, he wrote down *the answer* in large block letters: GOD'S WILL. Collins, full-awake in Plato's dim cave, read the message: "GODOT." Collins's essay might have been devoted to discovering if "Godot" fits the novel's structures, but instead, it's a search for a meaning that will fit Collins's desired, but unspecified, significance. Maybe we can guess what Collins is looking for by noting where and how he looks. Understatement: the anticipation engendered in Collins by MacDonald's novel is unfulfilled.

Collins's first excursion in search of the missing boon is *biography*. If we reverse engineer the fiction, may we not surmise the epiphany that is hidden or infinitely deferred (and so effectively denied) in the text? What are the relevant formative experiences of the artist? Collins cites two symbolic *places*. As a young man, MacDonald catalogued an ancient estate library. Later he was refused a pulpit, and his failure became a life-long absent-presence. Combine the achieved library and the denied pulpit. Maybe the answer, or the reason for the lack of answer, lies in the temperament of the man: esoterically learned, didactic, and frustrated. This portrait contrasts pretty sharply with the persona of MacDonald floated by Lin Carter in the 1969 Ballantine edition of *Lilith*. No matter, Collins does not trip into the biographical fallacy.

He moves quickly from MacDonald's life-story to the furniture of MacDonald's mind: Darwin and Novalis; (proleptically) Freud and Jung. The spirit of his age. He notes in passing (but does not explore) MacDonald's theological innovations. Maybe it's the man, the moment, and the milieu? Sure. All three are pertinent and insufficient. And Collins finds them so.

Collins might have gone next to the huge portrait gallery of ancestors present in MacDonald's allusions (*The Odyssey*, *The Faery Queene*, *Paradise Lost*, e.g.). Or, he might have searched the astonishing number of descendants whose DNA can be traced back to *Lilith* (*The Lord of the Rings*, *The Last Unicorn*, *Dune*, e.g.). Or, he might have looked in MacDonald's other fantasies.

If not things literary or historical, then perhaps things timeless. Archetypes. Myths. Dreams. Initiations and quests as embroidered by Freud and Jung, and structured by Campbell and Spariosu. Jung seems to me especially useful, Spenser especially pertinent, but they all work a little, and I bet Collins's seminars on fantasy have worked them. Yet no boon of significance that satisfies Collins appears.

If not in history, or in art, or in Platonish Reality, what about in form and *genre*? Figure and ground. Frame and picture. Incremental repetition. Infinite regress. Maybe even the unmeaning of *mise en abyme*? Collins finds the structures of mythopoeic quest (and its corpse[2] celebrated so beautifully by Campbell) congenial. Collins does not seriously entertain the deconstructive boon (nothingness swallowing its own tail) that would answer his question by denying its validity. But none of the meaning structures Collins tries on *Lilith* is conclusive. According to his title, *liminality* may be the lockbox, but Collins gives the reader no key. The reader is likely to be as unsatisfied by Collins's essay as Collins is by MacDonald's novel.

Caliban, my evil twin, grows impatient. There should be a payoff. He prays for a postmodern boon:

> *Grant us, great illusionary-illusionist,*
> *some sweet sip of the reward emergent coherence yields*
> *in those quiet moments after the flashing insight pours*
> *and before the fresh-filled fragrant paradigm hardens to cliché.*

Caliban wants to transform the *illusions* of referential meaning and significance into the only truly postmodern artistic *reality*: ephemeral experiential gratification, languishing between decaying memory and abortive desire. Caliban's desire defines postmodern liminality, a between with nothing on either side.

Caliban would shift the game from ontology to epistemology. His assumption is that liminality is the defining condition of consciousness, rather than a portal to some Other Reality. Maybe the portal *to* the Other *is is*. Maybe, like the mutilated book, *between* is not defined by *here* and *there*; maybe each reader is a site of subjectivity through which play vectors of no origin and no destination. Maybe instead of standing one foot in sea and one on shore, both feet are in air. Maybe the preternatural is the proper home of us amphibians (sophistical and swarthy), at least until some sort of chance evolution grows us faces. Maybe MacDonald anticipates that in our age *ontological fantasy* will dissolve into *epistemological fantastic*. Maybe Vane has been visiting Dixie Flatliner in the v-world of cyberpunk. Maybe Caliban has been smoking those funny brown cigarettes again.

When he's really mellow, Caliban thinks that a recognition of consciousness as *the negative spin of nothingness which is always already there* is the boon offered to us in *Lilith* (and everything else). Collins does not agree, but he entertains the Escher component of Caliban's claim. "Or is [the return in the penultimate chapter] presciently postmodern, reflecting an apparently meaningless circuit, a cynical return to square one which negates the idea of progress altogether?" (12). I do not find that tap-dancing on chaos is a satisfactory substitute for learning to weep no more. Caliban does.

Let me push back at Caliban's idea of liminality, back from epistemology toward neo-ontology. In our culture, the antithetical binary habit is so strong that even scalable unities like *light* and *heat* are perceived antithetically: hot/cold; light/dark. Platonic liminality (as opposed to Caliban's postmodern liminality) can help us recognize that binaries, most especially *antithetical binaries,* though often useful and sometimes true, do not map experience adequately. Perhaps rather than constituting postmodern "reality," as Caliban desires, liminality is the anteroom to Reality.

Let's see how that goes. *Lilith* plays in the cracks between theological binaries: *good/evil, elect/damned, divine omnipotence/human free-will*. To provide a stage for that play, MacDonald creates a meta-land in which many of the binaries we habitually treat as antithetical are not even binaries: *organic/inorganic, body/mind, alive/dead, natural/supernatural, objective/subjective, dream/myth*. Such play is always going to trip the heresy button. The screaming one in *Lilith*? No creature is damned who does not wish to be. And those who wish to be (notably Lilith) are tortured with intent to save.[3] The only unforgivable sin is worshiping the autonomous ego. Grace is offered to all seventy times seven (i.e., infinitely). There is no need for Christ's atonement. MacDonald has taken *Paradise Lost*, III, 80–216, several miles further from Luther's *Bondage of the Will* than Milton left it. Perhaps this huge theological alteration has disguised the theistic core of the novel and has led Collins away from a fairly obvious meaning. For me, the register, *liminal theism,* that MacDonald implies but does not investigate, affords an arena for an accommodation between MacDonald's expressed *meaning* and the theist reader's desired significance. Collins was almost there:

> But Novalis also says, "We are near awakening when we dream that we dream." Within the symbolic structures of the book, the saying would seem hopeful. But finally, the personal nature of dream also suggests that the distress of the protagonist is MacDonald's, and thus his dream escapes the realm of myth altogether [13].

A facile, circular notion — myth is cultural dream and dream personal myth — creates an exhaustive binary that denies the reach of both dream and myth toward Other. I find Collins's heuristics congenial and potentially applicable to *Lilith*. MacDonald's meta-world is certainly theistically liminal. It includes the "now-but-not-yet" sense of "end times" that began with Pentecost and permeates most species of Christianity. This pregnant "now-but-not-yet" is a plausible description of the hero's site and state at the end of the novel. The structures of the novel certainly signal various species of the quest. I don't know how and why Collins got stuck and blamed it on MacDonald. Perhaps his significance register is incompatible with MacDonald's meaning register. Perhaps Adam speaks to each of us when he says to Vane, "The universe is a riddle trying to get out, and you are holding your door hard against it" (45).

I will begin my own contextualized search for answers by distinguishing two versions of the mythic journey, both moral:[4] the first is exemplified by Dante, the second by J.R.R. Tolkien. The workings of the two are often mutually enhancing. I distinguish them in order to show how they work together as well as how they interfere with each other. I'm pretty sure that in the interface between the two, my Christian proclivity can find a *significance* that does not quarrel with MacDonald's *meaning*. (Imperial Caliban will jeer all the way. He'll get a brief turn now and then.)

In Dante's version of the quest, a human, exemplar-self awakens in the wood of this world (meta-land), accepts a guide, journeys through hell and purgatory, and, having been purified by tutelary experiences, reaches (through grace) heaven. Dante's journey is in the broadest sense Platonic: from a lesser (*transient*) *here* to a greater (*eternal*) *there*. The medieval drama, *Everyman*, is a compressed version of Dante's journey. Spenser's *Faery Queene* makes frequent (and after Book III, confusing) use of the pattern. *Pilgrim's Progress* is a simple, coherent instance. Dante's (and Bunyan's) boon includes a museum of our sins, the assurance of a reality beyond our *here*, and applicable lessons in depravity, grace, and holiness. The validity of the quest is most powerfully affirmed by the apotheosis of the hero. Because its meaning and significance are so entwined, understanding the meaning of such a quest is difficult unless the reader shares, or at least understands, the author's register of significance. The same is true of allegory.

The beginning of Dante's journey is closely tied to our physical *here* and the conclusion is closely tied to our metaphysical *there*, so close that both author and protagonist are named Dante. Red Cross and Temperance (Spenser's knights errant) are cousins of Dante, Christian, and Vane. If these protagonists are not in some serious way you, your artful experience is unlikely to join the author's structured meaning and your constructed significance.

In Tolkien's version of the quest, the journey is there and back again, and the circle is confined to Middle-earth. The magic does not move a human being from your *here* to Frodo's *here*. Although you may feel affinity with one or more of Tolkien's creatures (as I do), they do not stand for us in quite the way Vane does. In Middle-earth you observe and *vicariously* (not representationally) participate in the dilemmas that build to a catastrophe. Frodo, Legolas, Gimli, and Gandalf are not men, and even the very human Boromir, Theoden, and Denethor are not from our here. In contrast, Vane (like Dorothy and Alice and Christian and Red Cross and Malachi Constant) is a real human in meta-land.

Something of the difference this makes is signaled by Tolkien's insistence that *applicability* grants freedom to the reader whereas *allegory* grants power to the author.[5] Perhaps the Dantean quest, like allegory, constitutes a reversible equation. If Vane is Collins, then Collins is Vane. Thus the two must share not only meaning but significance. If, despite the sub-genre signals, we read Lilith as *applicable* (Tolkien) rather than *allegorical* (Dante), we can recognize the boon gained by Vane as *meaningful* without insisting that it be personally *significant*. The fashion and passion of ideological readings has made this seemingly obvious distinction difficult. (Ideological readings depend heavily on antithetical binaries. Thus, in a curious and primitive way, ideological readings hack away at the relativism that fostered the meaning vacuum in which they flourish.)

Back to Tolkien's high fantasy quest. The disaster that occurs to the denizens of faery is re-framed as eucatastrophe. We (safe from damnation and apotheosis) weep and smile with the loser-winner. After the anticlimax, the reader *separates* from the protagonists (who may or may not sail with the elves) and returns to the earthly *here* from whence he has *temporarily* escaped. There is no suggestion that someday we too can sail from the Grey Havens. (Passing thought: perhaps those who seek to capture Middle-earth for the flower children or the tree huggers or the Luddites or the Christians are reading *The Fellowship of the Ring* as if it were the *Divine Comedy,* that is, as if the work's meaning depended on the reader's significance.)

The boon of high fantasy is defamiliarization of the reader's *here*, not identification with the protagonist's *there*. The significance of high fantasy is dependent on the difference between the reader's habitual perception of earth as more or less a-moral (random, evolutionary, and purposeless) and his perception of Middle-earth as moral (structured, created, and purposeful). Because the reader has been shown the imprint of the sub-creator in the meta-world, he can, without mistaking one for the other, seek the patterns of the creator in the created world. If he has eyes to see. *Lilith* is not a high fantasy. *Watership Down* is. *The Book of the Dun Cow* is. *The Sirens of Titan* is not. *The Last Unicorn* is. And so forth.

The *meaning* of *The Lord of the Rings* is that evil can, with grace, be defeated by great effort and at great cost. The *significance* is that the reader is renewed, in a position to see his own world as morally pregnant. (Caliban is biting at my elbow. He says he likes Tolkien because Shelob reminds him of his mama, Sycorax. He likes to see things killed so he makes Tolkien's characters into action figures for his video games. He says his favorite character is Sauron; nobody kicks butt like Sauron. Right, now go lie down.)

Vane's journey seems more like Dante's than Frodo's, but his quest is illuminated by matching it with Tolkien's pattern.[6] Chapter XXXIX, "That Night," is the catastrophe: Lilith meets her self, spiritually and psychologically naked, in a scene of brutal torture.[7] The assurance that she will eventually acknowledge that her subservience to God (or anyone else) is freedom, not slavery, is the promise that the "eu" will be added, someday, to her catastrophe.[8]

The work that must be done by the soul in MacDonald's meta-world is ordering one's many selves, not creating or destroying things and creatures: "Every one, as you ought to know, has a beast-self—and a bird-self, and a stupid fish-self, ay, and a creeping serpent-self too—which it takes a deal of crushing to kill! In truth he has also a tree-self and a crystal-self, and I don't know how many selves more—all to get into harmony" (30). That Lilith, not Vane, experiences the catastrophe is important. The novel is not called *Vane*. We observe and identify with/reject Vane. Vane observes and identifies with/rejects Lilith. Lilith is where the real action is. In one sense, Vane is merely our eye in the meta-world. But he does learn something, and if we want to read his boon, we must understand his complex relationship with Lilith. Who is Lilith? Adam tells us:

> Mr. Vane, when God created me,—not out of Nothing, as say the unwise, but out of His own endless glory—He brought me an angelic splendour to be my wife: there she lies! For her first thought was power; she counted it slavery to be one with me, and bear children for Him who gave her being. One child, indeed, she bore; then, puffed with the fancy that she had created her, would have me fall down and worship her! Finding, however, that I would but love and honour, never obey and worship her, she poured out her [own?] blood to escape me, fled to the army of the aliens [fallen angels?], and soon had so ensnared the heart of the great Shadow [Satan?], that he became her slave, wrought her will, and made her queen of Hell [147–48].

This sounds as though she is a Daughter of God, equivalent to the Sons of God who cohabited with the daughters of men (Genesis 6.3, 5–7).[9] In some ways Vane is her antithesis, in some ways her complement, in some ways her white shadow. His sentimentality makes him an easy male victim of her female power. "'What you have made me is yours!' she cried. 'I will repay you as never yet did woman! My power, my beauty, my love are your own: take them'" (131). Right. Run! She is the vampire, he the enlivening meal. (Does he really believe that bit about the white worm?)

We should notice that the novel finds Vane's air-head sentimentality a defect. Mr. Raven is quite clear:

> "In this world never trust a person who has once deceived you. Above all, never do anything such a one may ask you to do."
> "I will try to remember," I answered; "— but I may forget!"
> "Then some evil that is good for you will follow."
> "And if I remember?"
> "Some evil that is not good for you, will not follow" [95].

MacDonald's text has no sympathy for Chaucer's Troilus, Keats's wretched wight, Yeats's wandering Angus, or Faulkner's Byron Bunch. And Vane, like his brothers, is a very slow learner. He escapes from Lilith (thanks to the white leopard) and is at once infatuated with Lona. Lilith is a merciless bitch; Lona, Lilith's daughter, is an innocent child. Both distract Vane from his boon duties — if he has any. Far from finding in Lona a Beatrice to lead him to heaven, Vane finds heaven without her to be no heaven at all. His imaginings of himself as her Consort-Regent of Bulika is a wishful consummation of Lilith's sexual offer. Maybe he is a born courtly lover. (Loving your vampire's daughter as herself does not sound like the second great commandment.) His infatuation with the horse indicates that the defect runs pretty deep. At times Vane seems almost a *picaro*, blundering the margins of life. Were he not already kin to Lilith, the venom of her bite would have forged the link. One major difference between the two is that Lilith consciously chooses to worship her autonomous ego. Vane adores his own ego as if by instinct.

Burying Lilith's severed hand/sterile womb (which holds her own egg within which she has trapped half the waters of meta-land) in the desert is a successful mini-quest. (*Freud alert!*) The meta-land is restored to something like its prelapsarian state. This mini-quest provides boon-wisdom: "willfully trapping the waters of life in an empty clenched-fist womb is equivalent to emasculating the bull-king." Or something. Such a boon might be valuable, but it would not be understood by Vane and apparently not by Collins. Vane's own quest is for identity in the ultimate world, not accomplishment in the meta-world. For a "standard" quest hero, accomplishment equals identity. For example, Bilbo becomes Barrel-Rider-Cup-Stealer. Aragorn is The-King-Who-Returns, Bearer-of-the-Sword-That-Was-Broken. Vane is not a standard Campbellian hero. His ripening requires that he learn and display his true name, and his name will not be Burier-of-Evil-Hand-Holding-Water-Egg. It will be Hope, and in the chapters beyond the last chapter, maybe Child-of-God: "Your real name, indeed, is written on your forehead, but at present it whirls about so irregularly that nobody can read it [weather vane]. I will do my part to steady it. Soon it will go slower, and, I hope, settle at last" (74).

The links between Vane and Lilith (his "philanthropy" is as ego-driven as is her rapaciousness) suggest that it will be some time before the "eu" will be added to his catastrophe. But in the meta-land each failure simply creates a new reality. Vane's premature seizing of a living thought killed it into a dead book and so deprived him of a guide (47). The death of the guide opened one of the infinite alternative paths in the meta-world. Lilith's furious, "heroic," attempts to assert the ultimacy of her autonomous ego are, ironically, death blows to her dead/enlivening selves which carom in the multiply mirrored meta-world. The problem is that no act of will is ultimately consequential. MacDonald has created a mirror of hyper–Calvinism. Each of Lilith's failures opens an alternative reality, as does each of Vane's failures. Life is death is life is death. Infinitely. Readers of Frank Herbert's *Dune* series will feel right at home.

But there are likely to be many, many realities for Lilith. Removing the spots from a leopard is one of the traditional definitions of the impossible. But it is also an emblem for a miracle. The spot on Lilith is growing, not fading. There is another emblem of the impossible which also defines a miracle: washing the Ethiope white. One fits the wer-leopard, the other fits the humanoid female. Who knows?

The "progress" of the little Lovers and their diminutive animals indicates that the repetitions can be incrementally positive, at least for those born in meta-land. The harvesting of Vane's ripe parents from the house of death indicates that those from Vane's world can also grow spiritually. But there is no way to calibrate the dimensions of meta-land with the units of earth. The length of stay in death/purgatory/ruined Eden is not governed by past sins but by present character. Salvation is not event-driven or time-driven. It is character-driven. Everybody in meta-land except Lilith, Vane, and the Shadow dies to ripen to life and is grape-gathered to God. In meta-land, Vane, Lilith, and the Shadow are liminal (purgatory/limbo/*mise en abyme*) characters. Vane seems to be on the way; his salvation is now-but-not-yet. I do not know about the other two, non-human, characters.

In the penultimate chapter, Vane is thrust away from heaven not for anything he has done or failed to do, but because *he is still vain*, ignorantly self-absorbed. The relationship between vanity and pride is a clue to the relationship between Vane and Lilith. Collins is right. Vane returns to his library empty-handed. Whatever the boon, Vane does not have it. There's no flame-trembling tongue, no golden bough, no message in a bottle. He is not even Prince Hamlet.

The answer to Collins's question is the last chapter. Lilith and Lona are gone. (Although spatial/temporal calibration of spiritual growth in MacDonald is misleading, we might say that Lilith is behind Vane and Lona is ahead of him. There is also an ontological gradation: Lilith is 100 percent "angel," Lona is 50 percent "angel," and Vane is 100 percent human.) As the chapter opens, Vane's only companion is Mara (Sorrow) who has taught him many things and continues to teach. Very soon Mara (Penance) transforms into Mara (Hope). Vane's dialogue with Hope is a *psychomachia* of Doubt and Hope that frames the answer to Collins's *meaning* question. Let's read it together and watch Vane (doubt) transform to Mara (Penance) and finally to Hope:

> [Vane is speaking.] Can it be that that last waking also was in the dream? that I am still in the chamber of death, asleep and dreaming, not yet ripe enough to wake? Or can it be that I did not go to sleep outright and heartily, and so have come awake too soon? [Doubt] If that waking was itself but a dream, surely it was a dream of a better waking yet to come, and I have not been the sport of a false vision! [Hope] Such a dream must have yet lovelier truth at the heart of its dreaming! [Affirmation: Vane's time with Mara (Repentance/Penance) has made him capable of hope. Perhaps the three are one: repentance + penance = hope? Perhaps Hope is Vane's nonce name?]
>
> In moments of doubt I cry, "Could God Himself create such lovely things as I dreamed?" [Doubt]
>
> "Whence then came thy dream?" answers Hope.
>
> "Out of my dark self, into the light of my consciousness." [Ego]
>
> "But whence first into thy dark self?" rejoins Hope.
>
> "My brain was its mother, and the fever in my blood its father."
>
> "Say rather," suggests Hope, "thy brain was the violin whence it issued, and the fever in thy blood the bow that drew it forth. — But who made the violin? and who guided the bow across its strings? [Harmony] Say rather, again — who set the song birds each on its bough in the tree of life, and startled each in its order from its perch? Whence came the fantasia? and whence the life that danced thereto? [skeletons' ball, *danse macabre*/dance of life] Didst thou say, in the dark of thy own unconscious self, 'Let beauty be; let truth seem!' and straightway beauty was, and truth but seemed?" [Vane as Job-and-the-rhetorical-questions. Keats and Wordsworth. There is something, far more deeply interfused, beyond the site of subjectivity. Exit negative liminality, Darwin, and postmodern linguistics.]
>
> Man dreams and desires; God broods and wills and quickens.

When a man dreams his own dream, he is the sport of his dream; when Another gives it him, that Other is able to fulfil it. [Exit autonomous ego. Exit auto-generation. Exit "always already there." Enter Old Testament covenant. Enter (proleptically) music of Iluvatar.]

I have never again sought the mirror. The hand sent me back: I will not go out again by that door! "All the days of my appointed time will I wait till my change come."[10] [Conviction, Contrition, Confession. "I know in whom I have believed and am persuaded." Enter obedience to God.]

Now and then, when I look round on my books, they seem to waver as if a wind rippled their solid mass, and another world were about to break through. Sometimes when I am abroad, a like thing takes place; the heavens and the earth, the trees and the grass appear for a moment to shake as if about to pass away; then, lo, they have settled again into the old familiar face! At times I seem to hear whisperings around me, as if some that loved me were talking of me; but when I would distinguish the words, they cease, and all is very still. I know not whether these things rise in my brain, or enter it from without. I do not seek them; they come, and I let them go. [Vane's original world is now liminal. He is still in Plato's cave, but he senses the Reality outside. In terms of high fantasy, his original world has been defamiliarized. But it is not a matter of the meta-world contrasting with the primary world, as in high fantasy. Here, the meta-world and the primary world interfuse.]

Strange dim memories, which will not abide identification, often, through misty windows of the past, look out upon me in the broad daylight, but I never dream now. It may be, notwithstanding, that, when most awake, I am only dreaming the more! But when I wake at last into that life which, as a mother her child, carries this life in its bosom, I shall know that I wake, and shall doubt no more. [Humble-triumphant affirmation. St. Paul to the Philippians, chapter 3. Note the contrast between Vane's *psychomachia* and Lilith's spiritual monologue.]

I wait; asleep or awake, I wait.

Novalis says, "Our life is no dream, but it should and will perhaps become one" [251–52].

The answer to Professor Collins's question seems perfectly clear. At the heart of the meta-land to which he journeyed, Vane found Lilith, the vaunting, Romantic, self-generating, solipsistic, rapacious, autonomous ego. In finding Lilith, he found a dark image of himself. In MacDonald's meta-world, creatures have total free will and God has infinite power. Although salvation is offered to all, each creature must consciously and willfully accept grace or remain in death/life. At the close of the novel, our protagonist is almost there. Where's there? It is liminal. It can be anyplace. And as for schedule? "All is as ever in our great task master's eye." The theistic liminality presented in *Lilith* is timeless, spaceless, and eventless (and plenteously all three). The boon is the humble wisdom that concludes Milton's sonnet XIX: God does not *need* anything at all; "They also serve who only stand and wait." Wait for what? For the *hieros gamos* in *illo tempore* to reabsorb time and space: The Second Coming.

The marriage of Christ and his bride, the church. The inhale of the Creator. Nirvana.

Vane and Lilith have plumbed the absolute free will inherent in MacDonald's meta-world and discovered it to be encompassed in the will of an infinite God.[11] This would seem to be a register of the quest pattern that works with MacDonald's meaning and my significance. It is not reflected in Collins's search for a meaning that will consort with his desired significance.

Caliban is not defeated. Who knows what dreams are still being dreamed by Lilith, or what lessons she is refusing?[12] Lilith, presumably, is still Lilith, but the infinity of God is such that Adam-bird-librarian-sexton is confident she will eventually accept Reality. Maybe so. Patience is a matter for a temporal world. God's timeless dimension has no need of it. I haven't a clue as to what will be the Shadow's fate. Is he Satan? Adam as much as tells us that he is king of Hell. Is he Lilith's cuckold sucked dry? Has he been punished enough? Is he the reader? Is he MacDonald playing a Stephen King bit part?

Vane finally learns that *in His will is our peace*. At least three aspects of his being are in harmony: Vane-Mara-Hope. Allegorically that would be vanity, repentance, and hope. When the call comes, perhaps the mysterious hand will add love. That would be Lona. Maybe at the last Lilith will be added, if she herself has found harmony among the discordants of her self. That would be quite different from the plans Vane has for her when he finds her nearly lifeless body: "Nowhere but in other lives can [a man] ripen his specialty, develop the idea of himself, the individuality that distinguishes him from every other" (102). What he has in mind is individualism (a sort of cannibalism). Not at all the same as individuation. What she has in mind for him is cannibalism (the ultimate individualism). Still. If grace is irresistible and universal, the combination of harmonized–Vane and harmonized–Lilith would approach a syzygy of Jungian individuations in theistic liminal reality.[13]

"But," Caliban insists, "the Shadow would still be the *surd*." He's right. My extrapolation of the ending does not pretend to solve the ultimate antithetical binary. God/Satan.

Well. *That's* my answer to Professor Collins's question. My essay has bridged the gap between *meaning* (MacDonald's) and *significance* (mine). Since the two cohabit without fighting, I am likely to claim that I understand the novel, and to report, "That's a really good book." I can then go on to integrate it into my worldview. But my discovery of significance is not an answer to Collins's disappointment. From my perspective he was looking for the wrong thing in the wrong place. He may not agree.

Caliban has a mind to make *Lilith* fit *his* significance. (Caliban assumes that his *desired significance* is authorized to overpower MacDonald's *expressed meaning*.) The only metaphysical "truth" Caliban knows is that if there is a God, He is a bloody tyrant. The portals to this register are many. You can get there through the Romantics' reading of Milton's Satan, by reading Darwin, Marx, and Nietzsche. The ordinary way is to look in your heart, find only yourself, and fall in love. All those portals show us an antithetical binary: evolution/oblivion. We yearn to be reborn as a star-child, and we fear that humanity's DNA will drown in the sand-worms' gene pool. We fear the defeat of the autonomous ego even more than we fear death or oblivion.

Caliban's reading makes Lilith a Prometheus, in which case the mysterious hand has saved Vane from the digestive tract of monster Zeus. When the world's great age comes anew, Vane will free Lilith from the rock to which she has been chained by the tyrant.[14] Until then all we have is solidarity. Caliban thinks of Gollum-the-Great *making them pay*, and he smiles. He does not care that his reading of *Lilith* has the signal defect of fitting almost nothing in the novel.

Early in *Lilith,* Raven tells Vane, "You and I use the same words with different meanings. We are often unable to tell people what they *need* to know, because they *want* to know something else, and would therefore only misunderstand what we said" (45). This may be the reason Collins finds ashes instead of fruit, and why he characterizes the allegory of Vane's ending thoughts as a "hysterical dialogue with hope" (13). Humans want to reach the goal and still gain full credit for having done it "my way." Surely, a proper God is not going to get in the way of his creature's ego fulfillment?

Wrong. The title character's torment in pursuit of ego independence and the protagonist's eventual acceptance of standing-and-waiting argue against such a reading, as do the cascades of allusions to earlier (and later) meta-worlds. The core meaning of the novel is very old: *in His will is our peace.* To which MacDonald has added an optimistic, heretical codicil: *His irresistible will is that we have peace.* Our free will is complete; we can do His will the hard way (Lilith), or the easy way (Little Lovers). In MacDonald's final adult fantasy, meaning and significance are one. But the fat lady does not sing. Lilith is yet in the house of death. Many share her dreams. Maybe those dreams didn't work out, but not everybody is sorry we had them.

Perhaps I have not provided the answer Professor Collins *wants*. Perhaps it is an answer that someone *needs*. Perhaps not. Caliban gets the last words. When Vane/Mara/Hope/MacDonald quote Novalis, "Our life is no dream, but it should and will perhaps become one," Caliban hears, "Life could be a dream, Sweetheart." Here's looking at *you,* Caliban. "Sha-boom, sha-boom."

Notes

1. Fortunately, I think, this intricate ideological narcissism flowers mostly in academia. Most readers proceed as though the text in front of them were stable. The last decade of the 20th century saw lots of essays that could be described as "theory eye for the bourgeois guy."

2. Once it was possible to define myth as the record man makes of "his encounter with the divine." Freud morphed the definition into "his encounter with his own psyche." Campbell morphed the definition into "his encounter with his own culture." MacDonald does not fit with either Freud or Campbell.

3. This makes Jonah the norm rather than the exception. I wonder what Calvin might have thought of this rendering of the I in TULIP?

4. A moral quest assumes that the universe is purposeful, meaningful, and subject to metaphysical judgments. *Amoral* equals random, meaningless, and relativistic.

5. J.R.R. Tolkien, Foreword to the Second Edition, *The Lord of the Rings* (xvii).

6. Obviously, this is anachronistic. It is likely that *Lilith* suggested, if only through intermediaries, the pattern articulated as high fantasy and exemplified in *The Lord of the Rings*. But for the critic in search of meaning and significance, the historical sequence of a heuristic and a novel are almost inconsequential. Both the novel and the theory are present to the critic.

7. Caliban loved the violence, fell in love with Lilith, and quoted W.E. Henley: "It matters not how straight the gate / How charged with punishment the scroll. / I am the master of my fate, / I am the captain of my soul."

8. The implicit theology assumes universal election through universal grace (maybe not for the Shadow). MacDonald's meta-land (like Tolkien's) has no Christ, past, present, or in prospect. Yet both worlds are profoundly Christian. That's another essay.

9. Would that make Lona one of the Nephilim? In Tolkien, Luthien and Beren are such a cross-species pair. In lesser register, so are Aragorn and Arwen. Is this a typological set concluding in the Holy Spirit and Mary? On the dark side, if Lilith's stripping "That Night" is equivalent to Satan's self-torture which concludes "evil be thou my good" (*Paradise Lost*, IV, 110), we witness eternal torment, not transient purgation. If MacDonald were Milton, Lilith and the Shadow would qualify for damnation as the self-hardened hard of heart (*Paradise Lost*, III, 199–202). MacDonald is carrying on a conversation with, and possibly revising, Milton. That's another essay.

10. Who says this? The attribution of the quote will further cement this reading or call it into question. I cop out by staying inside the text and attributing it to Hope (the soul formerly known as Vane).

11. Perhaps *Lilith* refutes the notion that human freewill inevitably leads to merit theology.

12. John Hawkes, in *The Blood Oranges*, echoes *Lilith* eerily. It is a similar excursion in a different register. Cyril also waits in liminal space for the advent.

13. The desire to compress may not be a sufficient excuse for such clotted jargon. Caliban is always at my elbow. It's his fault.

14. Until the last chapter, Vane most often listens to the song of the sirens rather than to the music of Iluvatar. In Tolkien terms, Vane is more like Feanor than Frodo. And that makes Vane's experience cautionary, rather than exemplary. All that glitters is not gold. Some who wander are lost.

Works Cited

Carter, Lin. "The Land Beyond the Hidden Door." Introduction to *Lilith*. By George MacDonald. v–x. New York: Ballantine, 1969.

Milton, John. *John Milton: Complete Poems and Major Prose*. Ed. Merritt Y. Hughes. New York: Macmillan, 1957.

Tolkien, J.R.R. *The Lord of the Rings*. One Volume Edition. Houghton Mifflin, 1994.

About the Contributors

ROBERT A. COLLINS is professor emeritus of English at Florida Atlantic University. In 1979 he founded the International Conference on the Fantastic in the Arts, now in its 29th year. He edited *Fantasy Review* for eight years and *The Science Fiction and Fantasy Book Review Annual* for five. He also served for six years as managing editor for *The Journal of the Fantastic* and has published essays on Tolkien, Samuel R. Delany, Thomas Burnett Swann, and others.

VERLYN FLIEGER is a professor in the Department of English at the University of Maryland specializing in myth studies and comparative mythology. Her publications include *A Question of Time: J.R.R. Tolkien's Road to Faerie* and *Splintered Light: Logos and Language in Tolkien's World*.

BONNIE GAARDEN teaches literature of the Bible, mythology, and composition at Edinboro University of Pennsylvania. She has published articles on the work of George MacDonald and is currently at work on a book about the goddess figures in MacDonald's fairy tales and fantasies.

LUCAS H. HARRIMAN is a Ph.D. student at the University of Miami, where he is furthering his study of fantasy literature, as well as literary modernism and twentieth-century drama.

ROLLAND HEIN is an adjunct professor emeritus of English at Wheaton College and the editor of *Lilith: A Variorum Edition* (1997). His other published works include *George MacDonald: Victorian Mythmaker* (1993) and *Christian Mythmakers* (1998).

COLIN MANLOVE, reader in English literature at the University of Edinburgh, is the author of several books, including *Modern Fantasy: Five Studies* (1975) and *Christian Fantasy: From 1200 to the Present* (1992). His current project is a book on Scottish fantasy.

RODERICK MCGILLIS, professor of English at the University of Calgary, has written several articles on the fantasy literature of George MacDonald. His books include *For the Childlike: George MacDonald's Fantasies for Children* (1992) and *A Little Princess: Empire and Gender* (1996).

MICHAEL MENDELSON is a professor of English at Iowa State University. He writes about and teaches both rhetorical theory and fantastic literature. Most recently, he published an essay on prudence in *Alice's Adventures in Wonderland* and is at work on a book about rhetorical judgment.

DAVID M. MILLER is a retired professor of English from Purdue University, where for many years he taught Renaissance literature, literary theory, and fantasy and science fiction. His published work includes books on Milton, Frank Herbert, and the nature of metaphor. He is currently working on a two-volume study of the Book of John.

JOHN PENNINGTON is an associate professor of English at St. Norbert College in Wisconsin, whose publications concentrate on fantasy from its earliest forms to the present.

ELIZABETH ROBINSON is a senior lecturer at Texas A&M where she teaches children's literature, and has taught courses in technical writing and Victorian fantasy. She has published a biography of MacDonald for the *Online Literary Encyclopedia*.

ROGER C. SCHLOBIN is a professor of English at Purdue University who has published several works of reference in the field of science fiction and fantasy, including *The Literature of Fantasy: A Comprehensive, Annotated Bibliography of Modern Fantasy Fiction*.

KELLY SEARSMITH, assistant professor of English at Appalachian State University, has written on the literature of the Victorian period, with a concentration on the fantastic.

TOM SHIPPEY is the author of several publications on fantasy and medieval literature, including the often-reprinted books *J.R.R. Tolkien: Author of the Century* and *The Road to Middle-earth*. He currently holds the Walter J. Ong Chair of the Humanities at St. Louis University in Missouri and is the editor of *Studies in Medievalism*.

JEANNE MURRAY WALKER is a professor of English at the University of Delaware and was named a Pew Fellow in the Arts in 1998. Her essays and poems have appeared in *Poetry, American Poetry Review, The Chicago Tribune,* and other publications. Her latest book is *A Deed to the Light*.

Index

Abrams, M.H. 104
Adams, Richard, *Watership Down* 168
Andersen, Hans Christian 145; "The Little Mermaid" 146
Aristotle 22
Arthurian legend 114, 149–50, 153
Auden, W.H. 1, 60
Augustine 23, 87–88

Barthes, Roland 35, 95
Bataille, Georges 94, 99
Baum, L. Frank, *The Wizard of Oz* 167
Beagle, Peter S., *The Last Unicorn* 164, 168
Beckett, Samuel, *Waiting for Godot* 163
Bersani, Leo 97
Bildungsroman 145–46
Blake, William 24, 34, 104, 113, 125
Boehme, Jacob 30, 31, 36 n.6, 73, 112
Boone, Richard 162
Booth, Wayne 29–30
Brooks, Peter 100
Bunyan, John 21, 34, 77; *Pilgrim's Progress* 50, 144, 166

Cabell, James Branch 12
Calvin, John 175 n.3
Campbell, Joseph 8, 13, 40–41, 47, 96, 164, 170, 175 n.2; *The Hero with a Thousand Faces* 9
Carlyle, Thomas 148
Carroll, Lewis, *Alice's Adventures in Wonderland* 50, 84, 143, 147, 157, 167
Carter, Lin 163
Chaucer, Geoffrey 169

Christus Victor 118
Coleridge, Samuel Taylor 84, 162
Collins, Robert 15, 19, 21–22, 23, 39–40, 46–47, 71, 79, 83–84, 85–86, 88, 89, 93–101, 103–05, 107–09, 161–75
Conrad, Joseph, *Heart of Darkness* 158
Cox, Michael 141 n.3

Dante Alighieri 21, 23–24, 29, 35, 43, 49, 51, 71–81, 84, 113, 115, 166–68
Darwin, Charles 84, 164, 172, 174
Descartes, René 31, 84
Dickens, Charles 144; *Bleak House* 150
Donne, John 11
Dryden, John 83

Eddings, David 146
Egan, Harvey 132, 136–37
Eliot, George 84, 144
Eliot, T.S. 24, 78
Eriugena, John Scottus 112
Everyman 166

Faulkner, William 169
Foucault, Michel 154
Freud, Sigmund 8, 100, 103–04, 106, 164, 169, 175 n.2
Fry, Christopher 88–89
Frye, Northrop 26, 29, 69 n.2

Gaskell, Elizabeth 144
Gimbutas, Marija 115
Goethe, Johann Wolfgang von 24, 113
Grimm, Brothers 24

Happold, F.C. 141 n.1
Hardy, Thomas 84
Hawkes, John, *The Blood Oranges* 35, 175 n.12
Hein, Rolland 8, 40, 43, 52, 95, 100, 106, 146
Henley, W.E. 175 n.7
Herbert, Frank, *Dune* 164, 170
Hoffman, E.T.A. 24–25, 31
Homer, *The Odyssey* 23, 35, 164

Inge, W.R. 67–69
Ingelow, Jean 143

Jackson, Rosemary 94
Job, Book of 35, 80, 81 n.4, 171
John of the Cross, St. 131–40, 141 n.1 n.2
Jung, Carl 8, 112–14, 116–27, 164, 173

Keats, John 169, 171
Kermode, Frank 96
King, Stephen 173
Kingsley, Charles 143

Lacan, Jacques 99, 104, 105–08
Lamia 69 n.3 n.6, 113
Lang, Andrew, *The Blue Fairy Book* 144
LeGuin, Ursula 15, 16, 146
Lewis, C.S. 1, 2, 8, 19, 43, 60, 86, 87, 96, 100, 108, 111; *The Allegory of Love* 95; *Chronicles of Narnia* 18, 26, 48, 50; *The Great Divorce* 20, 51, 76, 121–22; *The Space Trilogy* 50
Lilith, in Hebrew mythology 60–61, 97, 113, 126 n.3
liminality 1, 8–13, 20, 28, 39, 41, 93–94, 97–101, 109, 159, 164–66, 170, 172–73
Lindsay, David 43
Locke, John 27
Luther, Martin, *Bondage of the Will* 165

MacDonald, George, and Christianity 7, 18–19, 30, 36, 44–45, 46, 50, 54–55, 66–68, 69 n.1, 74, 109, 112–13, 116, 119, 122, 125–26, 139, 146, 152, 158–59, 164, 170, 175 n.8; as Scot 42, 67, 111; as Universalist 111–12, 114; as Victorian 20, 59, 95, 111, 123, 143, 145–46, 151, 164; *At the Back of the North Wind* 31, 55–56, 71, 98, 99, 158; *David Elginbrod* 49, 60; *The Diary of an Old Soul* 54–55, 113; *Dish of Orts* 36, 113; "The Fantastic Imagination" 22–23, 47, 48, 77, 154; "The Golden Key" 34, 50, 73, 99, 156, 158; "The Imagination: Its Function and Culture" 34, 49, 57 n.1 n.2, 81 n.3, 130; *Life Essential: The Hope of the Gospel* 48, 49, 55, 57 n.2; "The Light Princess" 24, 29; *The Lost Princess* 56; *Malcolm* 159 n.3; *Origins of the Legend of the Holy Grail* 62; *Phantastes* 24–27, 35, 53, 55–56, 73, 98, 99, 111, 125, 128–33, 143, 145–47, 149, 157–58; preface to *Letters from Hell* 76–77; *The Princess and Curdie* 45, 47, 55–56; *The Princess and the Goblin* 24, 28–29, 45, 56; "A Sketch of Individual Development" 104; *Unspoken Sermons* 49, 55, 57 n.1 n.2, 72, 74, 81 n.1, 113, 118, 127 n.11, 146; "Within and Without" 29
MacDonald, Greville 24, 35, 36 n.2, 73, 111, 112, 113–14, 128; *MacDonald and His Wife* 28
MacDonald, Lilia 139
MacDonald, Louisa 112
MacDonald, Winifred 72
Magus, Simon 120
Manlove, Colin 104, 108, 131
Martin, Tom 11
Marx, Karl 174
Maurice, F.D. 111
Mayne, William 16
McGillis, Roderick 29, 46, 98, 117, 121, 126 n.3 n.6 n.7 n.10
Mendelson, Michael 122, 124, 126 n.8, n.10
Mendlesohn, Farah 9, 15, 40–41, 47, 50
Miller, D.A. 95, 99
Milton, John 24, 34, 72, 172; *Paradise Lost* 29, 164, 165, 174, 175 n.9

Nietzsche, Friedrich 174
Novalis 13, 18, 25, 35, 98, 104, 125, 164, 172, 175
Nugent, Christopher 133–34

Origen 67–69, 112

Pearl (Middle English poem) 17, 51
Plato 18, 30, 48, 106, 114, 145, 147, 163, 165, 172
Poe, Edgar Allan 155
Prickett, Stephen 57, 105, 159 n.2

Raeper, William 42, 43–45, 46, 139, 141 n.4
Reis, Richard 46, 128, 140, 159 n.1
Ricoeur, Paul 87–88
Riga, Paul 154
Robb, David 46, 52, 104, 159 n.3
Rowling, J.K. 146
Ruskin, John 143

Sadler, Glenn 130–31
Saussure, Ferdinand de 107–08
Schaafsma, Karen 87, 115, 121, 126 n.7

Schiller, Friedrich 25
Shakespeare, William 17, 72; *Hamlet* 171; *King Lear* 17; *The Tempest* 162
Spariosu, Mihai 1, 8, 9–11, 41, 47, 94, 164
Spenser, Edmund 24, 28; *The Faery Queene* 164, 166–67
Swift, Jonathan, *Gulliver's Travels* 144, 148
Sydney, Sir Philip 24

Tennyson, Alfred Lord, *In Memoriam* 154
Thoreau, Henry David 30, 31, 35
Tolkien, J.R.R. 36 n.2, 105, 145–46, 166, 175 n.5; *The Hobbit* 35, 170; "Leaf by Niggle" 17; *Lord of the Rings* 15–16, 18–19, 50, 86, 146, 164, 168, 170, 175 n.6 n.9, 176 n.14; "On Fairy Stories" 22–23
Trollope, Anthony 144
Troyes, Chrétien de 43
Turner, Victor 1, 8, 81

Underhill, Evelyn 141 n.3

Victoria, Queen 154
Vonnegut, Kurt, *Sirens of Titan* 168
Voyage of Bran 42–43

Walker, Jeanne Murray 112, 126 n.3 n.10
Wangerin, Walter Jr., *The Book of the Dun Cow* 168
Westall, Robert 15
Weston, Jessie 61–62, 70 n.8
Wolff, Robert Lee 46, 97–98, 104, 106
Wordsworth, William 23, 72, 108, 118, 171

Yeats, W.B. 169

Zipes, Jack 144

www.ingramcontent.com/pod-product-compliance
Ingram Content Group UK Ltd.
Pitfield, Milton Keynes, MK11 3LW, UK
UKHW042014140426
5217IPUK00015B/1162